Wilderness Basics

**Get the Most from
Your Hiking, Backpacking,
and Camping Adventures**

Fourth Edition

By the San Diego Chapter
of the Sierra Club

Edited by Kristi Anderson

MOUNTAINEERS
BOOKS

Mountaineers Books is the nonprofit publishing division of The Mountaineers, an organization founded in 1906 and dedicated to the exploration, preservation, and enjoyment of outdoor and wilderness areas.

MOUNTAINEERS BOOKS

1001 SW Klickitat Way, Suite 201 • Seattle, WA 98134
800.553.4453 • www.mountaineersbooks.org

Printed in the United States of America
Distributed in the United Kingdom by Cordee, www.cordee.co.uk
Second edition, 1993. Third edition, 2004. Fourth edition, 2013.

Copy editor: Kris Fulsaas
Design: Mountaineers Books
Layout: Shelly Garrison
Photos: See individual photos for credits.

Illustrations on pp. 59, 66, 119, 122, 123, 125, 127–131, 133–135, 137, 139, 140, 142, 143, 145, 146, 148, 155, 161, 242–243, and 271 by Marge Mueller, Gray Mouse Graphics; on pp. 73 and 83 from Stephen M. Cox and Kris Fulsaas, ed., *Mountaineering: The Freedom of the Hills,* 7th edition, Seattle: Mountaineers Books, 2003; on pp. 242–243 adapted from illustrations in an article by Ray Smutek in *Off Belay* magazine, Volume 7, February 1973; and on pp. 154, 162–165, 179, 194, 195, 198, 200, 201, 206 by Ben Pease, Robert Frost, and Bob Cram.

Cover photograph: *Backpacker eating breakfast and enjoying an amazing sunrise in the high eastern Sierra near Bishop, California* (Photo by Dan Girard)

Library of Congress Cataloging-in-Publication Data

Wilderness basics: get the most from your hiking, backpacking, and camping adventures / by the San Diego Chapter of the Sierra Club; edited by Kristi
    Anderson. — Fourth edition.   pages cm
ISBN 978-1-59485-821-5 (pbk) — ISBN 978-1-59485-822-2 (ebook)
1.Outdoor life—West (U.S.) 2. Wilderness survival—West (U.S.)
I. Anderson, Kristi. II. Sierra Club. San Diego Chapter.
GV191.42.W47W55 2013
796.50978—dc23
2013020452

ISBN (paperback): 978-1-59485-821-5
ISBN (ebook): 978-1-59485-822-2

Aubrey Wendling   *Sandy Sanders*   *Jerry Schad*

This book is dedicated to Aubrey Wendling, whose tireless efforts
resulted in the creation of the Basic Mountaineering Course in 1957,
which has evolved over the last fifty-six years into the current Wilderness
Basics Course; to Sandy Sanders, who devoted so much of his life to the
WBC as a staff member and outings leader; and to Jerry Schad, who
explored and documented all the trails and wonders of the San Diego
area. These three gentlemen represent the ideal of the Sierra Club and
the Wilderness Basics Course to explore, enjoy, and protect the
wild places of the earth. We are grateful to each of them.

Contents

Preface

John Muir, the driving force behind the creation of the national parks in 1872, went on to found the Sierra Club in San Francisco in 1892. In the late 1940s and early 1950s, the popularity of camping and hiking in the great California state parks and national parks increased dramatically. This was due, in part, to the "rediscovery" of the writings of John Muir, the thousands of young men who during the Great Depression had participated in the Civilian Conservation Corps (which helped create the facilities and trails in the national parks), and the vast number of veterans home from World War II. These people and their families wanted to discover and explore the wilderness areas of California and to find a sense of peace and adventure. Unfortunately, many people were venturing into the mountains and deserts without the knowledge to find their way, avoid dangerous animals, and survive the sudden changes in weather. After all, John Muir wrote that he would spend weeks in the Sierras with just a loaf of bread and a wool coat! How hard could it be?

Today, people still want to escape the pressures of work and society and are turning to the great outdoors in increasing numbers. Studies have shown that hiking through the wilderness is more therapeutic than prescription pharmaceuticals (for many people), and wilderness areas are some of the few places left where you can "get away from it all." With a pack on your back, the trail becomes your sanctuary and time slips away while you explore in quiet solitude.

This book, *Wilderness Basics* and the classic *Mountaineering Basics* have been revised several times over the years to reflect innovations in equipment, knowledge of nature and wildlife, and emergency procedures. One of the trends today is the popularity of lighter and more versatile gear that allows the hiker to go farther, in greater safety and comfort. This light gear is very practical, but only if the hiker is skilled and experienced. Similarly, the low cost and accuracy of Global Positioning System (GPS) units makes these devices almost irresistible, but if they fail, hikers can be left in a situation beyond their abilities, without the equipment or skill to return home.

The information contained in this book can raise that skill level considerably, but the hiker also needs practical hands-on experience. This is one of the reasons that training opportunities such as the Wilderness Basics Course have become so popular. In the Wilderness Basics Course, students are able to learn in a relaxed classroom environment and also participate with seasoned hikers in weekend outings structured to increase their hands-on knowledge in the field.

This fourth edition features a fully updated chapter on gear, including lightweight gear tips and techniques to keep backpackers happy. The navigation chapter is thoroughly revamped to discuss the adjusted declination compass, with clearer diagrams to illustrate navigation concepts. With more than sixty new photos, current updates, and completely rewritten conditioning and first-aid chapters, this edition is one that we are confident the reader will want to keep around.

Many volunteers contributed endless hours to this new edition, but if it weren't for the dedication and persistence of editor Kristi Anderson, this book would never have gone to press. We at the Wilderness Basics Course would also like to thank Diane Purkey Wilson and Skip Forsht, who spent long hours reviewing the content and helping to keep this edition on track.

As Baba Dioum, a Kenyan environmentalist, once said, "In the end we will preserve only what we love, we will love only what we understand, and we will understand only what we are taught."

I hope you enjoy this book and use its information "to explore, enjoy, and protect the wild places of the earth."

David Rousseau
Chair, 2011–12 Wilderness Basics Course

A NOTE ABOUT SAFETY

Safety is an important concern in all outdoor activities. No book can alert you to every hazard or anticipate the limitations of every reader. The descriptions of techniques and procedures in this book are intended to provide general information. This is not a complete text on wilderness travel technique. Nothing substitutes for formal instruction, routine practice, and plenty of experience. When you follow any of the procedures described here, you assume responsibility for your own safety. Use this book as a general guide to further information. Under normal conditions, excursions into the backcountry require attention to traffic, road and trail conditions, weather, terrain, the capabilities of your party, and other factors. Keeping informed on current conditions and exercising common sense are the keys to a safe, enjoyable outing.

— Mountaineers Books

Introduction: A Brief History of the Wilderness Basics Course

Robert L. Feuge and Aubrey Wendling

In 1956, on a warm Sunday morning in winter, a young couple took their children for a hike in the mountains outside San Diego. During their outing, a fast-moving storm quickly blanketed the mountains with heavy snow. It reduced the visibility of potential navigational landmarks, and it also covered the family's tracks. In their wanderings, they walked through the forest in circles, became lost, and then became fatigued. Being lightly clad and without navigation aids, the unprepared family apparently struggled for hours and then, one by one, fell and perished in the severe cold weather.

Two Sierra Club members, Henry Mandolf and Aubrey Wendling, read the shocking news in the headline of the local paper, and after some discussion, they concluded that they had the knowledge and experience to help prevent such needless tragedy. With that goal in mind, the two men developed the idea of a public service course that would teach those who attended enough skills to survive in a variety of adverse conditions.

Wendling had been an avid mountaineer in Seattle, where he had completed a course offered by The Mountaineers that was based on a book the club published entitled *Mountaineering: The Freedom of the Hills*. Thus inspired and with assistance from The Mountaineers and the Rock Climbing section of the San Diego Sierra Club, he and Mandolf hammered out a short course on mountaineering that also contained information about how to survive in diverse climates and under adverse conditions.

In the spring of 1957 the first course, entitled "Basic Mountaineering," was offered, and it attracted twelve students. The valuable course caught on as people began to increasingly explore the great outdoors in California. Word continued to spread over the following years, and hundreds signed up for the annual Basic Mountaineering Course, or BMC.

To meet the needs of large classes, Mandolf and Wendling decided to formalize their notes into a book. Under the auspices of the San Diego Chapter of the Sierra Club, their first mountaineering book, *Basic Mountaineering*, was published by Conklin Litho of San Diego and quickly became known as the "Red Book" because of its red paperback cover. It was 112 pages and covered topics such as equipment, orientation, weather, miseries and first aid, mountain travel, winter travel, rock climbing, desert travel, and rescue. It was a succinct compilation of everything a person needs to know in order to venture safely into the wilderness and cope with changing circumstances.

Through several revisions and additions, the "Red Book" stayed close to its mountaineering heritage. In 1983 the book grew to 240 pages and was renamed *Mountaineering Basics*, sporting a new red cover with a photo of Yosemite National Park's Half Dome. Important topics were added, such as how to prepare for an outing, physical conditioning for hiking, trail behavior, and camp behavior. This edition, dedicated to Mandolf, was published by Avant Books of San Diego.

From the beginning, the subject matter of the BMC was reinforced by taking participants out into the California wilderness. Those outings gave students the opportunity to experience the wilderness and practice what they had been taught in the classroom. Outings included camping in the desert, land navigation, rock climbing, and camping in the snow. To be safe and effective, the outings required qualified, skilled leadership, so training courses for BMC leaders were developed in the 1970s.

Demand soon exceeded the BMC's classroom facilities as well as its cadre of available qualified leaders, so limits had to be placed on course enrollment. By the late 1980s, the BMC was limited to the first 300 students who appeared and enrolled at the door. The news of the BMC's success spread throughout the Sierra Club, and offshoot courses were developed. A North County San Diego BMC was established, and thereafter, the Los Angeles Chapter of the Sierra Club established another BMC for the LA area. All versions of the BMC used the "Red Book," although the course content varied slightly among the different locales.

Along with adventurous outings comes risk. Consequently, the BMC, through the Sierra Club, prudently decided to carry insurance to indemnify itself against wrongful injury claims. As insurance rates increased, course organizers reconsidered using ice axes on winter outings and leading rock climbing sessions, and in the late 1980s, such riskier features were dropped from the BMC curriculum.

To recognize this more conservative response to risk management and to better serve the burgeoning demand for wilderness travel in San Diego County, the book and the course were completely rewritten and renamed under the editorship of the late Jerry Schad. In 1991 the old BMC became the Wilderness Basics Course, or simply WBC, and the book became *Wilderness Basics*, published by Mountaineers Books in Seattle. Sections were added about the western wilderness, wilderness ethics, wilderness travel with children, and travel along ocean shores, and, in later editions, animal encounters and mountain biking.

From 1961 until 1993, all editions of the book were published strictly to support the course. With assistance from Mountaineers Books, *Wilderness Basics* was greatly expanded in 1993 and republished with a view toward marketing it nationally and internationally. Proceeds from the book were used to offset the rising costs of staging and updating the course.

Today, the WBC is a thriving endeavor. It has been estimated that the course has trained well over 20,000 students in San Diego County in its fifty-six-year history. When students in the LA Chapter's course are added, that number is far higher. But has it saved lives? Has it prevented tragedy?

That question can be answered by the stories of many WBC graduates. In 2002, for example, Robert Feuge led a hike in Arizona during which a hiker collapsed and seemingly died. At first stunned, Feuge fell back on his WBC training to help organize the revival of the fallen hiker and then direct a helicopter to the site, which flew the victim out of the wilderness to safety and medical assistance. Feuge is convinced that the fallen hiker is alive today because of his WBC training.

Aubrey Wendling next to his wife and daughter in 1960

chapter
1

The North American Wilderness

Jerry Schad, Olive Wenzel, and Bob Stinton

Considerable debate exists about what defines wilderness. Some think of wilderness as land set aside so that it maintains a natural state, while to others, wilderness is a landscape virtually untouched by humans without regard to its designation. Still others may use a more novel way of defining wilderness by describing what it is not.

Wilderness is not a place dependent on human intervention—like a garden or a golf course or a city park—that will collapse into disarray without constant attention. Certainly, wilderness needs no human presence, even though humans may visit on occasion. For the purpose of this book, the definition of wilderness is a broader one: the wildlands or open spaces outside of human development.

Almost everyone feels the need sooner or later to cast aside the complexity of and links to civilization and to escape to a wild place, to reconnect with the natural world, if only for a few hours or a few days. Many people find relaxation, inspiration, fellowship, and adventure through their travels outdoors. These wild places have an uncanny way of reminding us of the important things in life, and after each adventure we return invigorated and with lifelong memories.

A hiker enjoys expansive views from a high point in Sequoia and Kings Canyon National Park. (Photo by Dan Girard)

Traveling in these vast wild spaces, we learn to observe and fit into the environment. We become more aware of the fragility of each component of the natural world and begin to recognize our responsibility as stewards of this remarkable planet.

The distinctive features of the North American wilderness inspire a long list of superlatives. Few coastlines around the world surpass the scenic grandeur of the geologically youthful Pacific, where mountains sweep dramatically down to the sea. Our continent has world-class mountain ranges and peaks in the western half, as well as gentler ranges in the East, such as the Appalachians, which are remarkable for their rich flora and fauna. North America claims the world's tallest trees, the world's most massive trees, and the world's oldest trees. It also features some of the world's lowest, hottest, and driest deserts and some of the deepest river gorges.

In the wilderness, we glimpse the world as it once was on a global scale. In the mountains, in the deserts, and along wild coastlines, our senses drink in simple pleasures: clean air scented by wildflowers, muffled silence in an old-growth forest, the blast of icy air off a glacier, the grace of a bighorn sheep moving on stone, the thunder of breakers felt as well as heard.

In the late nineteenth century, people began to look to escape their urban existence, to meet their needs for exploration, solitude, and the beauty of wild places. These outdoor enthusiasts began forming organizations such as the Appalachian Mountain Club in 1876, the Sierra Club in 1892, Oregon's Mazamas in 1894, and Seattle's The Mountaineers in 1906. These four clubs still provide wilderness adventures today because they still meet the needs for exploration, solitude, and the beauty of wild places. Their mottos and mission statements include the words *explore, enjoy, learn, conserve, fellowship,* and *protect,* which sum up the wilderness experience and the responsibility that comes with the use of wildlands.

During this same period, at the urging of individuals, the US Congress set aside the first national park, Yellowstone, in 1872, and this was followed by Banff in Canada in 1885. From this beginning, concerned citizens worked with the government to expand the park system to include many of North America's most remarkable landscapes. Many are now distinguished by their inclusion in national, state, and provincial parks.

A staggering amount of land, particularly in the western United States, including Alaska, falls within the public domain. California, even with its exploding population now approaching 38 million, contains about 35 million acres—about one-third of its total area—of parks and other lands open to public recreation. Huge swaths of public lands exist in Nevada, Utah, Arizona, and Alaska, while substantial tracts have been set aside in Canada and the eastern half of the United States. The national and state parks spread across the Appalachian Mountains from Georgia into Maine would be the envy of most other nations around the world.

Granitic boulders surround a camper enjoying his morning coffee in Anza-Borrego Desert State Park, California. (Photo by Dan Girard)

Wilderness lovers have worked for decades to improve access to remote areas without damaging them. The 2000-mile Appalachian Trail offers the dedicated walker a sizable perspective of an entire mountain range. In the West, the Pacific Crest Trail stretches 2600 miles along the roofline of California, Oregon, and Washington. The Continental Divide Trail traverses 3100 miles down the spine of the Rocky Mountains. The "New World" is spacious enough to contain large tracts of natural landscape, and stunningly beautiful lands remain relatively untouched.

It is not only the grand and remote landscapes and famous trails that are worth an explorer's attention. Plenty of wild areas lie just beyond the fringes of some of the biggest cities. Only twenty air miles from downtown Los Angeles, black bears, bighorn sheep, and mountain lions roam the canyons and crags of Angeles

The grandeur of Elowah Falls in John B. Yeon State Park, Columbia River Gorge National Scenic Area in Oregon (Photo by Jody Stell)

National Forest. A climber living in Denver, Colorado, can take on any of several alpine summits only an hour's drive away. Just over the Golden Gate Bridge from the skyscrapers of San Francisco, serene Muir Woods National Monument beckons those weary of city life. Portland, Seattle, and other cities of the Pacific Northwest have abundant opportunities for winter mountaineering on nearby glacier-draped summits such as Mount Hood and Mount Rainier. Even in America's crowded eastern seaboard, semiwild areas such as the Pine Barrens of New Jersey and the Catskill Mountains of New York lie within a one- or two-hour drive.

Wherever we find them, these wild places deserve our attention and care. This book was written to help the outdoor enthusiast prepare for wilderness outings. Enjoy the wildlands of North America, and the world, and at the same time protect both yourself and the environment from injury of any kind.

chapter 2

Leave No Trace: Outdoor Ethics

Alfred F. Hofstatter and Eugene A. Troxell

Wilderness is where you go to be closer to your roots. As T. K. Whipple wrote in *Study Out the Land,* "All America lies at the end of the wilderness road, and our past is not a dead past but still lives in us. . . . Our forebears had civilization inside themselves, the wild outside. We live in the civilization they created, but within us the wilderness still lingers. What they dreamed, we live; and what they lived, we dream."

The Wilderness Act of 1964 was the first major step of the US Congress to reserve large plots of undeveloped land as federally administered wilderness areas. Before that, certain lands were set aside as "primitive areas," but there were no officially designated and protected wilderness areas. The Wilderness Act defines wilderness as "an area where the earth and its community of life are untrammeled by man, where man himself is a visitor who does not remain. . . . It is a region which contains no permanent [human] inhabitants, no possibility for motorized travel, and is spacious enough so that a traveler crossing it by foot or horse must have the experience of sleeping out-of-doors." Wilderness, by this definition, included most of the earth's surface as recently as a hundred years ago. Today, as the global human population reaches more than 7 billion, wilderness is rapidly

A backpacker enjoys the view in Zion National Park, Utah.
(Photo by Robert Burroughs)

disappearing. Most modern Americans live their entire lives with no real experience of it.

Many, however, still distantly recognize the wilderness as home and feel comfortable there. After all, the land that "generally appears to have been affected primarily by the forces of nature, with the imprint of man's work substantially unnoticeable," as the Wilderness Act states, is the environment in which all forms of life have developed over eons.

In the wilderness, it is not uncommon to reach a clear awareness of what you have recently come from and of what you will soon return to. As John Muir wrote in his journals, "I only went out for a walk, and finally concluded to stay out till sundown, for going out, I found, was really going in."

Two hundred years ago, a person might cut brush for a campfire, remove tall grasses and saplings to make camp beside a stream, and wash up in the clear, flowing water. A few others might repeat the same actions in the same area in a year's time, with no appreciable harm done. The natural environment has sufficient regenerative power to heal the wounds inflicted by a few people each year. This does not mean there would be no evidence of people having been there. Desert environments, for example, heal even the smallest scars very slowly. But if the number of people likely to camp in the same area each year jumps to a dozen, or a hundred, or a thousand, the cumulative impact on even relatively stable areas may be well beyond the regenerative powers of the natural environment. Even John Muir, a pioneer in the realm of wilderness ethics, would need to alter his wilderness behavior were he to camp today where he camped a century ago.

As usage of parks and wilderness areas soars, managers are forced to impose regulations to minimize the cumulative impact of large numbers of people. There will be more of this as numbers increase—permit systems, trailhead quotas, and rules regulating actions as personal as toilet behavior and as sacrosanct as building campfires.

The word *ethics* comes from the Greek word *ethos,* for character. Even if there were no official rules imposed on the area you visit, you should still regulate your behavior. It is important to think of your own impact, as well as the consequences of dozens, or hundreds, or thousands of people repeating the same acts.

The staggering number of human beings, as well as advancing technology, provides good reason for rethinking and recasting traditional wilderness ethics. Wilderness ethics need to be based upon an awareness of the interconnections among all things. John Muir put it nicely in *My First Summer in the Sierra:* "When we try to pick out anything by itself, we find

Taking a moment to appreciate the sunset in Zion National Park, Utah
(Photo by Robert Burroughs)

it hitched to everything else in the universe." This ethic would enhance, not destroy, the ongoing process of evolution by supporting the web of life. If you temper your actions with concern and tread lightly upon the delicate and beautiful natural world, you can consider carrying that same ethic back into your everyday life.

Land management agencies have set in place rules and regulations to ensure safety and reduce impact. While common sense is always important, it alone is insufficient to allow you to accurately assess the cumulative effects of many seemingly inconsequential behaviors. One behavior might not seem destructive until you consider the effect of similar behavior by hundreds of other people. Therefore, it is important to be aware of the long-term cumulative effects of your presence in the outdoors, whether you visit a pristine wilderness area or a neighborhood park.

LEAVE NO TRACE

In 1964, when Congress began establishing wilderness areas, it soon became apparent that it was important to apply special rules to these untrammeled places.

Unfortunately, it also soon became obvious that rules, quotas, closures, and stricter regulations were not working. The outdoor recreation boom of the 1960s and 1970s was inflicting damage on wildland environments faster than nature could repair it. People were loving the outdoors to death, and the land could not recover. If quotas, rules, and closures were not working to protect the wilderness, what would?

Campers and hikers must take responsibility for their actions and activities in the wilderness.

By the early 1980s, several federal land management agencies were teaching and fostering "No Trace" educational programs for campers, but a standard and universally accepted program that would apply to all wilderness areas was needed. What resulted was the Leave No Trace educational program that promotes skills and ethics to support the sustainable use of wilderness and natural areas. Established in 1994, Leave No Trace, Inc., was the outgrowth of a joint effort between the US Forest Service, the National Park Service, the Bureau of Land Management, the US Fish and Wildlife Service, and the National Outdoor Leadership School. Manufacturers, outdoor retailers, user groups, educators, and individuals who shared a commitment to protect the wilderness joined in the support of Leave No Trace.

Seven core principles are the foundation of the Leave No Trace education program:

1. Plan ahead and prepare.
2. Travel and camp on durable surfaces.

3. Dispose of waste properly.
4. Leave what you find.
5. Minimize campfire impacts.
6. Respect wildlife.
7. Be considerate of other visitors.

These principles can be applied anywhere—in remote wilderness areas, parks, even your backyard—and to any recreational activity. Educate yourself and others, and adopt the habits and skills that lead to a Leave No Trace culture for your outdoor ethics.

THE PRINCIPLES OF LEAVE NO TRACE

1. Plan Ahead and Prepare

Regulations. Know the regulations and special concerns for the area you plan to visit. What are the environmental concerns? Is a permit required? What special skills are needed? Is there a group size limitation?

Popular areas. Try to schedule your trip to avoid times of high use. Consider a less-popular wilderness area nearby.

Equipment. Start with the Ten Essentials, and choose your equipment, food, and water based on the weather, terrain, and potential emergencies.

Skills. Develop your skills in navigation, first aid, and Leave No Trace practices.

Tell a friend. Leave an itinerary and map with a friend or other emergency contact, as well as a description of your intended route, the telephone number of the nearest ranger station or controlling agency, and your anticipated return date and time. Don't forget to check back in upon your return.

2. Travel and Camp on Durable Surfaces

Durable surfaces. Hike and camp on durable surfaces—trails, expanses of rock, established campsites, gravel, snow, sand, dry creek beds—that are resistant to damage. This is especially important in desert and meadow regions where recovery of damaged plants and terrain is extremely slow.

Established campsites. Concentrate your activity in established campsites and on designated trails to minimize the spread of damage to the undisturbed environment. Don't create "social trails" by bushwhacking between campsites or trails. It is best to limit the impact of your visit to established campsites that are worn rather than starting new damage in a new site. When leaving, clean the site and leave it as natural as possible.

Nonestablished (pristine) campsites. Lightly used areas that do not (or never have) seen much camping activity can be considered nonestablished campsites; however, you will encounter areas that have signs of prior camping. Let nature take its course to reclaim these sites, and seek out durable surfaces instead. Reserve the most durable surfaces for cooking

Crossing a river in Yosemite (Photo by Skip Forsht)

and eating activity and, if necessary, less durable areas for sleeping. Clear away small rocks and sticks, but do not do any trenching or grading. Move your camp daily to avoid causing lasting effects, and manage your activity to avoid harming the natural features of the site. Vary your routes to water, the "bathroom," and the sleeping area. Avoid camping in areas of animal activity (burrows, nests, game trails) or near scarce water sources.

Departing a campsite. Before leaving, replace rocks, logs, or sticks you have moved. Use a dead branch to rake away footprints. Cover bare areas with pine needles or leaf litter. Make the site less obvious as a campsite so that it can recover.

Distance to water. Establish your camp at least 200 feet (eighty adult paces) from water sources. In desert areas check the local regulations, as this distance can be as far as a quarter of a mile to protect the availability of the water to wildlife.

3. Dispose of Waste Properly

Pack it in, pack it out. Seasoned wilderness visitors are familiar with the mantra "pack it in, pack it out." This means that whatever you pack in, pack it back out: all trash, leftover food, and litter. Human food and garbage can be lethal to animals, so don't bury or burn trash or food scraps. Organic litter such as orange peels, apple cores, or banana peels take months to decompose and attract animals that may attack your (or someone else's) food supply.

Human waste. If an established outhouse or bathroom is available, use it. If not, urinate at least 200 feet from water, camps, and trails. Try not to urinate on plants, as salt-deprived animals can defoliate them to get the salt from the urine. Deposit fecal matter in a cat hole dug 6–8 inches deep and at least 200 feet from water, camps, trails, and drainages. Look for soil that contains organic matter, as the microbes found in the soil break down the feces and pathogens. Where the ground is devoid of organic matter, such as desert sand, dig a shallower cat hole in a sun-exposed but inconspicuous spot where the sand will be heated to a temperature that destroys the pathogens.

If you cannot retreat 200 feet from a water source (in a narrow canyon with high walls, for instance), pack out fecal matter; in some high-use areas, this is required, so check local regulations and equip yourself properly. Numerous kits designed for packing out human waste are commercially available, so find the product that is best suited for your trip. One product called a WAG BAG (or "waste alleviation and gelling" bag) provides a double bag system, the inner bag containing a gelling powder. The powder gels the waste, turning it to solid, and neutralizes odor. The outer bag has a secure, airtight seal, and all the components are nontoxic and biodegradable.

Whether you bury or carry out human waste, always plan ahead to pack out—not burn, because they seldom burn completely—used toilet paper, wet wipes, sanitary napkins or tampons, and soiled diapers.

Water for washing. It is best to collect water and carry it to a wash site 200 feet or more away from water sources and away from camp. Use, only if absolutely necessary, minimal amounts of biodegradable soap. Strain dishwater that contains food scraps through a sieve or cloth, put the food scraps into a garbage bag to pack out, and scatter the water (as opposed to pouring it out in one spot). Do the same for used (or gray) water from laundry.

Petroglyphs (rock carvings) loom over a canyon in the Coso Range, California.
(Photo by David M. Gottfredson)

4. Leave What You Find

Artifacts. By observing and not taking, we pass the gift of discovery on to those who follow. Historical and archaeological artifacts are protected by many state and federal laws that make it illegal to disturb or remove them. Pretty rocks, feathers, plants, and so on should be left in their natural state—not in your possession. Instead, let photos and memories be your souvenirs.

Avoid spreading nonnative plants and animals. Invasive species of plants, animals, and organisms can cause large-scale, irreversible changes in ecosystems. The following guidelines help to prevent the spread of invasive species:

- Don't transport flowers, weeds, or aquatic plants into wetlands.
- Clean dirt out of your boots or tire treads.

- Empty and clean your packs, tents, stock trailers, boats, fishing equipment, vehicles, and other gear after each trip.
- Never discard or release live bait.
- Make sure pack stock and pets are immunized and their coats are free of seeds and harmful pests (for example, ticks).
- Make sure your stock feed (hay, oats) is weed free. Feed your stock only weed-free food for three days prior to entering the backcountry.

5. Minimize Campfire Impacts

Problems of traditional campfires. The natural appearance of many recreation areas has been compromised by the careless use of fires and the demand for firewood. Campfires are beautiful at night, but rings of soot-scarred rocks overflowing with ashes and partly burned logs, garbage, and trash are unsightly. More importantly, campfires can and do ignite wildfires.

Much of the lasting damage associated with campfires in the backcountry can be avoided by using lightweight stoves, fire pans, mound fires, and other Leave No Trace techniques.

Cook on a stove. Carry a lightweight stove and sufficient fuel to cook all meals. It is much more efficient, and your pots will never have soot on the bottom.

Decide if a minimum-impact fire is possible. Ask yourself these questions to determine whether a campfire would be safe, appropriate, responsible, allowed, and desired:

- Is a fire permit required?
- What are the pertinent campfire regulations and management techniques?
- Is it really safe to build a campfire? Consider the wind, clearance from flammable vegetation, weather, location, and wood supply.
- Is there a fire ring?
- Is there a sensible alternative?
- Can it be safely put out? Have a stick or trowel and a container of water to saturate the ashes or extinguish a spreading fire.

Use an established fire ring or grate. The best choice is to use an existing site. When you are done, leave it in a cleaner condition than you found it. This encourages those that follow to use it and not construct new ones.

Use an alternate campfire method. Where there are no fire rings, use a sensible alternative, bring a fire pan, or make a mound fire:

- A buddy burner (a candle in a can—learn how to make one in Chapter 11, "The Quiet Beauty of the Desert") or a candle lantern is a sensible alternative that provides a sense of warmth and, regardless of how small it is, comfort.

- Pan fires are built on about an inch of sand placed in the bottom of a metal pan (such as an aluminum roasting pan or something similar) that you pack in. Scatter the cold ash or pack it out.
- Mound fires are built on a mound of sand, gravel, or soil with low organic content. Lay down a small ground cloth and collect enough of the mound material to build an 18- to 24-inch-diameter by 8-inch-high flat mound on the cloth. This insulates the heat of the fire from scorching the ground. When you are done with the fire, saturate the ashes and scatter them away from camp. Replace the soil to its original site.

Gather firewood properly. If gathering firewood is permitted, use only dead and downed wood. The sticks you collect should be no thicker than your wrist. These burn completely, as opposed to large logs that usually remain only half burned. Don't snap branches off trees. Many areas do not allow firewood to be transported in from other locations because of the spread of invasive insects. Before you bring wood from home, find out if it's allowed in the areas you plan to visit.

- Manage your campfire.
- Never leave a fire unattended.
- Don't put food, food waste, or trash in the fire. Trash can give off toxic fumes, and food never completely burns.
- Break up long sticks so the ash will stay in the fire pit. Unused long sticks can be returned to the habitat and will look natural.
- Burn wood completely to ash. Stop feeding the fire long before bedtime so that you can make sure the wood will burn completely to ash before you retire.
- Saturate the ash until it is cool to the touch, all the way to the bottom of the ash pile.
- In the morning, scatter the ash over a wide area away from the campsite.
- Restore the fire site to its natural appearance. Remove and scatter fire-ring rocks and replace the soil from a mound fire to its original location.

6. Respect Wildlife

Human interaction with wildlife. Encounters with wildlife inspire tall tales and long moments of wonder. Yet around the world, wildlife faces threats from loss of, fragmentation of, and encroachment into habitat, as well as invasive species, pollution, overexploration, poaching, and disease. We, not the wildlife, are the only ones who can be responsible for coexisting peacefully.

Seeing wildlife, such as this bull moose near Spiney Lake, Colorado, is memorable, but try not to disturb wildlife. (Photo by David M. Gottfredson)

Never feed wildlife. Giving human food to wildlife is unhealthy for them and alters their natural behavior. Animals are adept opportunists. When attracted by an untidy camp kitchen or a handout, they overcome their natural wariness of humans and learn to associate humans with food. This can result in your being harassed by pesky marmots or squirrels or, worse, aggressive bears. Prospects of an easy meal also lure animals into hazardous spots such as campsites, trailheads, roads, and villages where they can be attacked by dogs or hit by vehicles.

Store food securely. Check local regulations and suggestions for proper care of your food supply. In areas where there is no threat of bears, simply hanging the food bag to keep it away from rodents and small carnivores should be adequate. In bear country, use bear lockers if they are available at established campsites. Away from bear lockers, use of a bear canister is strongly recommended, and in some areas it is required. The alternative is to hang your food, which might not be an approved method in some jurisdictions (see "Food Storage in Bear Country" in Chapter 10, "Close Encounters of the Animal Kind").

Observe wildlife from a distance. Do not follow or approach wildlife. If animals react to your presence, back away and detour around the area. Large predators such as bears and mountain lions are dangerous. Check with local authorities as to the correct camping and hiking practices in the area. Always keep children in immediate sight. Remember, they are often the same size as animal prey.

Avoid sensitive seasonal times and habitats for wildlife. While mating, birthing, and guarding their young, wildlife can be overly aggressive or stressed.

Wildlife and pets don't mix. It is best to leave pets at home. If you must travel with a pet, check local restrictions. Most national parks prohibit dogs on trails, so check before you go.

7. Be Considerate of Other Visitors

Respect other visitors. Maintain a cooperative spirit in the wilderness. This protects the quality of everyone's experience. Interactions should reflect the knowledge that you can and do rely on each other in times of need.

Trail courtesies. Practice courteous behavior on the trail:

- Give a friendly greeting.
- Wear earth-toned clothing.
- When encountering horses on a trail, move well off the trail on the downhill side.
- Give right of way (the right to proceed first) to uphill traffic and heavier-laden travelers, stepping aside to let them pass.

Camping courtesies. Observe courteous behavior in camp:

- Don't disturb livestock or equipment of equestrians, ranchers, anglers, loggers, trappers, or miners.
- Leave gates as you found them.
- Place your campsite out of the sight of and sound of trails and other campers.
- Tune in to the sounds of nature. Eliminate or minimize the use of radios, cell phones, musical instruments, whistles, or loud voices.

The information in this chapter was adapted from the Leave No Trace Center for Outdoor Ethics, © 2011. For more information on Leave No Trace, see the "Resources" in the appendix. (The authors are grateful for the information and help from Leave No Trace, Inc. in writing this chapter.)

A good motto to remember: Those that follow you should not regret that you were here. (Photo by Al Hofstatter)

chapter 3

Get Up, Get Fit, and Get Out!

Nancy Jungling

There are endless opportunities to explore the outdoors, but pain, injury, or fatigue can ruin a great trip. Whether you prefer a guided nature walk or a several-hour climb up Half Dome, your best piece of gear is your personal fitness. Start early and slowly to be successful.

GETTING STARTED WITH FITNESS

You can begin outdoor exercise no matter what shape you are in. Conditioning for wilderness travel is no different than conditioning for any other fitness pursuit, and an effective training program will build physical strength as well as confidence. Novice hikers are often concerned about being able to keep up with the group, yet even experienced hikers need training for more strenuous adventures such as a Grand Canyon rim-to-rim hike or a summit of Mount Whitney. Physical and mental preparations are equally essential for a safe and enjoyable experience.

Training should be specific to your activity, and the best training for hiking and backpacking is to start hiking and backpacking! Stair climbing, elliptical training, and running are also compatible training activities because they use the same muscle groups as hiking and backpacking.

Running is a great way to combine your conditioning program with enjoyment of the outdoors. (Photo by Jerry Schad)

Running should be done at an aerobic level (jogging) versus an anaerobic level (sprinting). Cross-training with several different activities is a great way to prevent boredom, and it allows you to stay active and advance your conditioning without overusing the same muscle groups.

Regardless of your starting fitness level, a comprehensive exercise program should address several areas of conditioning:

- strength
- flexibility
- balance
- endurance

Strength is your body's ability to push, pull, lift, or carry a load—very important if your goals involve hiking up or down steep hills, using your upper body for scrambling, carrying a backpack for a multiday trip, or maybe lifting logs and debris for trail maintenance. The best exercises for strength are weight training types, whether you do machines or free weights at the gym or use your own body weight in calisthenics. Exercises such as squats, lunges, jumping jacks, push-ups, and pull-ups, as well as using rowing machines and CrossFit (a style of fitness training with constantly varied, high-intensity, functional movement), complement hiking and outdoor activities. Consult a personal trainer, physical therapist, or exercise physiologist if you are new to the equipment or style of exercise, to prevent injury.

Muscles also work differently depending on the type of activity they are performing, and it is important to include both concentric and eccentric exercises in your routine. In a *concentric* contraction, the muscle shortens as it produces power to move a joint; think about your quadriceps muscle in the front of your thigh as you climb up a steep hill. In an *eccentric* contraction, the muscle lengthens as it works to decelerate your motion; for instance, this is how your quadriceps work as you walk slowly down a hill. You can see how it becomes important to train both types of muscle contractions! It can be more complicated to plan a comfortable trip when you can only tolerate one direction.

Flexibility is your ability to stretch and lengthen. Think of a rubber band. Good flexibility allows the rubber band to stretch and relax and accommodate changing amounts of tension. Poor flexibility leaves the rubber band brittle and more vulnerable to breaking. The less flexible your muscles are, the more susceptible you will be to strains, sprains, and damage. We need flexibility in our legs for stepping up, over, and around things in the backcountry; for taking wide steps in boulder hopping and stream crossings; and even for squatting in the woods when nature calls! We need flexibility in our rib cage for deep breathing, flexibility in our shoulders for taking our packs on and off, and flexibility in our feet and ankles for hiking over uneven terrain such as loose rocks or sand. Yoga, gentle stretching, and Pilates are all good examples of flexibility exercises.

Balance is our ability to maintain upright over our base of support. This is important for our safety when hiking on steep or loose terrain, boulder hopping and scrambling, and staying dry during stream crossings. Tai chi, yoga, wobble board activities, superslow activities, physioball exercises, and eyes-closed activities can challenge your balance.

Endurance is our ability to last over time. Good endurance allows for longer hikes, multiday trips, and multiple activities. Endurance training requires aerobic activities that use oxygen for prolonged periods of time (for example, running a marathon versus sprinting). Walking, cycling, hiking, stair climbing, swimming, running, circuit training, Zumba, Jazzercise, in-line skating, and using an elliptical machine are all good examples of endurance training exercises. Good indicators of aerobic fitness include a resting heart rate of sixty beats per minute or slower, as well as a rapid return to a normal heart rate after exercise.

Tailor Your Fitness Plan to Your Activities

Consider your goals as you design your fitness plan. Different activities will place different demands on your body, and you'll want to tailor your routine to meet your specific goals. For instance, see the activities, their requirements, and suggested exercises in Table 3-1.

You may need to tailor your fitness routine to mimic the nature of your adventure. For instance, if you plan on climbing to the summit of, say Mount Whitney or Mount Rainier, then your training program would include occasional sessions of moderate to vigorous exercise lasting for several hours. Your lungs and heart are under greater stress at higher altitudes because of the reduced oxygen content in the air, and long-duration exercise coupled with frequent, short exercise sessions (such as interval training) will help you attain your highest level of fitness.

The Mayo Clinic (see "Resources" in the appendix) recommends a balanced routine of cardiovascular exercise (aerobic) and strength training.

TABLE 3-1. FITNESS PLAN FOR OUTDOOR ACTIVITIES

Activity	Requirements	Suggested exercises
Rock climbing	Requires a lot of upper-body strength, strong core muscles, lots of gripping and balancing, tremendous endurance for holding up your body weight, hip flexibility for rotating hips out so you can get close to the rock face	Pull-ups, push-ups, lat pull-downs, rowing, reverse crunches, straight leg raises, bicycle crunches, core work, hip flexibility exercises
Boulder hopping	Requires long steps in multiple directions, good balance	Lunges in multiple directions, sidestepping squats, triangle pose and half moon pose (yoga), core work
Scrambling	Requires you to often be on all fours using arms and legs	Downward dog pose (yoga), mountain climbers*, push-ups
Peak bagging	Repeated up- and downhill over several hours, lots of concentric and eccentric quadriceps strength, endurance	Squats, lunges, hill training, stair climbing
Backpacking	Any of the above with a 30- to 45-pound pack on your back! Requires more load on your trunk and pelvis, more leg strength	Squats with weight, hill training with your pack or a weighted vest on, lunges with weights, core work
Flat trails and nature walks	Requires good walking tolerance, balance on uneven terrain, ability to navigate around or over hazards if needed	Exercises that help with hip flexibility, ankle flexibility, and safe balance

* Mountain climbers are a specific type of calisthenic exercise popular in the military or old-school physical education classes.

They suggest 2½ hours per week of moderate-intensity aerobic activity and two days per week of strength training. As a guideline for aerobic activity, you should be able to talk but not sing while exercising. If you can sing and carry a tune, you are not working hard enough. Pay attention to your body, go at your own pace, and progress slowly as you feel comfortable. If you dedicate yourself to quality conditioning, you will be rewarded with the ability to last longer, go farther, and see more wilderness!

Exercise Regularly and Safely

Be creative about building activity into your daily routine. Take the stairs versus the elevator; park farther away from the store; walk on a treadmill or ride a stationary bike while watching TV. Walk to the grocery store and carry your items back in your pack. Include different activities so you can exercise various muscles while others rest. Break things up if you have to; for instance, try walking for twenty minutes two times a day versus forty minutes at a time. Be flexible, and don't let a little bad weather keep you from exercising outdoors. It's bound to rain on a future trip, so why not test out that raingear!

Allow time for recovery and healing, and avoid the old "no pain, no gain" philosophy. If your body is in pain, something is not right, and you could be in danger of hurting yourself. Listen to your body and stop if you feel faint, pain, shortness of breath, dizziness, or nausea. If you have concerns about your fitness or struggle with any preexisting conditions, it's best to follow up with your physician (see the next section).

The right gear can make exercising more comfortable and safer. Choose shoes and boots that best support your foot type. A low or poorly defined arch can lead to *overpronation and plantar fasciitis* as the tissues under the arch are stretched, and you may require an orthotic or motion control shoe. A very high arch or stiff foot may feel better with a less rigid shoe and more cushion. You'll want more cushion for hiking the granite of Yosemite and maybe more support for the sandy terrain of the desert. Also, keep your toenails trimmed to avoid any damage or loss of the nail.

A properly fitting backpack will ensure good body mechanics and minimize back pain. Trekking poles can help redistribute the load on longer or steeper outings so your legs don't fatigue as quickly and your knees don't take as much pounding.

CONSIDERING POSTURE AND STRETCHING

If you sit at a computer all day during the work week, and you intend to be a peak bagger on the weekends, you'll want to consider your posture. Your muscles and soft tissues will tend to "favor" whatever position they are in the most. Prolonged sitting can have negative effects on flexibility, especially the hip flexors, hamstrings, pectoral muscles, and neck. As the muscles shorten to accommodate the sitting posture, it can become more difficult to stretch and extend them when needed, such as stepping over logs or rocks or high stepping up steep inclines or boulders. A lack of flexibility increases the chance of injury, so frequent stretching is important, both on and off the trail.

Most experts agree that some sort of warm-up prior to exertion is helpful for increasing blood flow and oxygen to your muscles. Hiking and outdoor adventures are *dynamic* activities, so an active warm-up is best to complement how your muscles will be used on the trail. This can include marching in place for three to five minutes or taking an easy walk to the trailhead before things get more strenuous.

Simple stretching can be done at the trailhead and during the hike as needed to prevent stiffness and allow your muscles to rest. Stretching after your adventure is also good practice to relax and allow your muscles to cool down in a lengthened position. This will minimize stiffness and soreness through the night and the next days, especially after more strenuous outings. The stretches shown on pages 34–36 address all muscle groups and can be done outdoors on the trail.

Stretching should generally feel gentle and easy, as you relax into the postures. You should not bounce or force yourself to move beyond comfort. Forced aggressive stretching causes your body to guard against that movement and could result in injury.

GETTING HELP FROM PROFESSIONALS

While anyone can enjoy the outdoors, some people may find themselves more vulnerable. Chronic health conditions, preexisting injuries, physical issues, gender-specific issues, and environmental factors should all be considered prior to choosing the right outdoor activity for you. If you are concerned about beginning an exercise program or have a preexisting health condition (such as asthma, diabetes, or high blood pressure), you may want to consult a health-care provider prior to any new outdoor adventures.

Your **primary-care physician** is able to assess your overall health and any current symptoms, as well as perform diagnostic tests such as X-rays, MRIs, and blood labs to diagnose disease. He or she can prescribe medication and also refer you to other specialties such as podiatry, orthopedics, neurology, or rheumatology if your condition requires additional care.

A **physical therapist** has knowledge of anatomy and movement. He or she can help you rehabilitate any existing musculoskeletal injuries and also assess your movement patterns to address any areas of weakness, decreased range of motion, or incorrect body mechanics that could lead to injury.

Top left: *side-bend stretch;* top right: *gluteal stretch;* bottom left: *squat;* bottom right: *lower back stretch* (Photos by Michael Jungling)

Top left: *hip flexor stretch;* top right: *hamstring stretch;* bottom left: *quad stretch;* bottom right: *calf stretch* (Photos by Michael Jungling)

Top left: *chest and shoulder stretch;* top right: *trunk extension stretch;* bottom: *back-relaxing stretch* (Photos by Michael Jungling)

A **nutritionist** specializes in dietary analysis, which can be helpful if you suffer from food allergies or have special dietary concerns. A balanced diet is essential on the trail for fuel and energy.

An **acupuncturist** is an alternative-medicine practitioner who uses thin, solid needles to correct imbalances in the flow of *qi* (pronounced "chi") through channels known as meridians. In Traditional Chinese Medicine, disease is perceived as an imbalance in the functions or interactions of these meridians or in the interaction of the body with the environment. If you experience symptoms such as chills, dry or irritated skin, sweating or clammy skin, chronic runny nose, dry cough, dry or itchy eyes, or headaches when exposed to the elements of nature (such as wind, cold, or dampness), an acupuncturist may be able to help restore balance.

An **exercise physiologist** studies the body's metabolic response to short-term and long-term activity. He or she can help design a safe exercise program to meet your goals without compromising your health, including modifications for high blood pressure, asthma, and other conditions that may be exacerbated by exercise.

A **personal trainer** or **strength-training specialist** can help design a fitness program for you and keep you on target for your goals. He or she generally completes a certification program in exercise and can help you develop a creative and fun program that keeps you interested in fitness.

A **massage therapist** manipulates the soft tissues of the body to restore normal tone, promote relaxation, and reduce inflammation or swelling. Massage therapy can be helpful in decreasing tension, addressing spasms, and assisting with healing and recovery time after strenuous activity.

CONSIDERING HEALTH ISSUES

If you have been diagnosed with any particular health condition, you should consult your physician prior to beginning or changing your exercise regime. Medications are prescribed to stabilize body chemistry or regulate crucial organ activity (such as your heartbeat, blood pressure, and cholesterol), and changes in altitude, stress from the elements, dehydration, and nutrition can all interfere with their effectiveness. It is best to consult with your physician or health-care provider to discuss how your outdoor activity may affect your symptoms so your dosage or use can be adjusted properly. It is also not unusual for people to improve their health with regular exercise, so as you become more fit, you may not need as much medication. Your physician or health-care provider can appropriately monitor your needs.

Diabetes is a disease in which your immune system attacks the cells that make insulin. Insulin is needed to control blood sugar levels, and without insulin your blood sugar levels can rise to dangerous levels. Elevated blood sugar can affect the eyes, kidneys, nerves, gums, and teeth. The most serious complication of diabetes is heart disease. If you are diabetic, it may be helpful to take the following precautions with outdoor exercise:

- Discuss with your health-care provider what exercise activity is most appropriate for you. If you have severe eye disease or nerve damage, some activities will not be safe for you. Your doctor may also want to schedule a test to see how you heart responds to exercise.

- Learn the effects of various types of exercise on your blood sugar, and have carbohydrate-based foods available during and after exercise. You may need to adjust your insulin doses.
- To reduce the risk of hypoglycemia (low blood sugar), follow a regular routine of exercising, eating your meals, and taking your medication at the same time each day.
- Be sure to wear socks and shoes that are comfortable and fit well to help prevent foot irritation. Always check your feet after exercise for blisters, sores, and cuts that could lead to serious infection, which is an especially dangerous problem for people with diabetes. Boots with a wide toe box may be more comfortable and can accommodate swelling on the trail.
- Carry your glucose monitor with you, and monitor your blood sugar before, during, and after exercise so you can adjust your insulin or food intake as needed. Always carry a small carbohydrate snack, such as fruit or fruit drink, or glucose tablets for when low blood sugar occurs.
- Always wear a medical ID tag or carry an identification card that states you have diabetes.
- Never exercise alone in the wilderness. Exercise with someone who knows you are diabetic, and educate them on what to do if you have a low blood sugar reaction.
- Drink plenty of fluids during your outing. Dehydration can cause your blood sugar levels to rise.

Blood pressure can be affected by altitude, diet, and stress. If you currently take medication for high blood pressure or for blood pressure regulation, you will want to consult your health-care provider for guidelines with outdoor exercise. He or she may recommend a particular dosage, lower-sodium trail snacks, and altitude precautions.

Allergies can affect your tolerance for outdoor activity. If you have hay fever or are allergic to dust mites, bees, or grasses, your doctor may recommend an antihistamine prior to exercising outdoors. The type of medication depends on several factors, so it is best to consult with your health-care provider for the prescription appropriate for you.

If you are allergic to certain chemicals, choose your clothing fabrics and supplies carefully. You may do better with cotton or organic fabrics, such as canvas, versus nylon or plastic types (like polyester). Consider this when backpacking and selecting your tent and base layers.

Here are some suggestions for minimizing allergic reactions so that nature doesn't get the best of you in your outdoor activities:

- If your allergies are severe, wear a medical warning bracelet to alert those around you of your condition.

- If you require an epinephrine pen for bee stings, make sure your hiking buddy is aware of where it is located so he or she can assist you if needed. Avoid bright-colored clothing, perfumes, or scented lotions that may attract bees.
- Know your triggers, and avoid activity near those things that affect you. Check the pollen counts and air pollution if needed prior to your outing, and avoid peak hours of the day when pollen can be high (6:00 a.m. to 9:00 p.m.). If you must be outdoors during these times, it may help to wear a bandana or face mask.
- Humidity can trigger mold growth and irritate mold allergies. Be aware that mold allergies can be more troublesome in humid weather. You may tolerate dry or rainy days better.
- Exercise in the rain! Rain clears the air, making it a good time to go outdoors if you have allergies.
- If your allergies are severe, you may consider outings closer to help, with easy access for emergency personnel to get to you if needed.

Asthma can make breathing difficult outdoors or at altitude. An inhaled medication (such as albuterol) can be used before or during exercise to prevent asthma problems, and your physician can recommend the best medication for you.

- Avoid exercising in areas of chemicals or exhaust from traffic.
- Consider how stop-and-go types of activity versus long periods of sustained activity affect you.
- Cold air and very dry air can be irritating to the bronchial tubes, so consider traveling in warmer, moister climates. A face mask or scarf may be helpful in colder weather.

Considering Women's Issues

Typically, men and women are able to enjoy the same types of trips, but women have some inherent characteristics both anatomically (body shape and size) and physiologically (body chemistry) that must be considered when they venture into the outdoors.

Pregnancy should not deter women from enjoying the outdoors, but it is best to consult with your health-care provider prior to starting a new exercise program. Exercise is generally good for both mother and baby, but certain precautions should be taken, especially if you have a history of certain medical conditions, including poorly controlled diabetes, high blood pressure, heart disease, or bleeding.

The Mayo Clinic recommends beginning with as little as five minutes of exercise a day, building up to ten minutes, fifteen minutes, and so on, until you reach thirty minutes a day. In general, you should be able to carry on a conversation while you're exercising. If you can't speak normally during your activity, you are probably pushing yourself too hard.

Precautions women should take during pregnancy include:

* Try not to hike at high altitudes due to decreased oxygen availability.
* Do not take drugs and chemicals used for altitude sickness during pregnancy.
* Do not use iodine for water purification during pregnancy.
* Avoid activities with a high risk of falling, such as free climbing, rock climbing, boulder hopping, or hiking in steep, unstable terrain. Abdominal trauma could be very dangerous to both mother and baby.
* After the first trimester, it is best to avoid exercise that forces you to lie flat on your back. Pressure on the abdominal arteries can restrict blood flow to the baby.
* *Stop* if you experience dizziness, headache, shortness of breath, chest pain, abdominal pain, or vaginal bleeding, and consult your healthcare provider.
* Never venture out into the wilderness alone, and consider outings close to help and medical care if needed.
* Stretch before, during, and after your outing to minimize low back pain and muscle tightness.

A growing abdomen causes a woman's center of gravity to move forward, which can affect balance. Pregnant women generally arch their back to compensate for this anatomical change, and this can cause joint compression, muscle tightness, and low back pain. Sitting periodically or leaning on a bench or tree on the trail can help relieve pain.

Hormonal changes during pregnancy cause ligaments and tissues to relax, which causes muscles to work harder to stabilize joints during activity or sustained postures. Water retention and swelling can also affect balance and activity tolerance.

Pregnant women should listen to their bodies and adjust their activity level as needed. In later months it can be very uncomfortable to wear a backpack, and balance may not permit scrambling or taking wide steps safely. Trekking poles can assist with balance issues, compression socks can help with swelling in the legs and ankles, and supportive boots can help with arch pain. Consider shorter, flatter outings as you become more challenged.

Menstruation is a time of fluctuating hormones, and changing body chemistry can increase the laxity in ligaments that support the low back, knees, and arches of the feet. During this time, women may feel achy, off balance, and less stable.

Osteoporosis is the loss of bone density and thinning of bone tissue over time, and it begins happening long before you have any symptoms.

Women are more at risk for osteoporosis due to the dramatic decrease in estrogen with aging, and advanced osteoporosis can make bones, especially in the hip and spine, more susceptible to fracture. Spinal compression fractures can cause a "stooping" posture, which makes it very difficult to carry a heavy pack.

Your doctor may be able to slow the effects of osteoporosis by recommending a high-calcium diet, resistance exercise, hormone replacement therapy, or even special medications. If you have a family history of osteoporosis, talk to your doctor about awareness and treatment. Osteoporosis is no reason to stay off the trail, but you may need to be more careful and take fewer risks to avoid falling.

Knee pain is more common in women due to wider hip angles and hormonal changes that cause ligament laxity. It can be helpful to strengthen the hip muscles (especially the abductors and external rotators) and stretch any tight muscles (such as the iliotibial band, hip flexors, quadriceps, and hamstrings). During flare-ups it is best to avoid activities that aggravate your knee pain, such as walking up steep inclines or downhill, stair climbing, and squatting.

Achilles tightness is more common in women who wear high-heeled shoes because that footwear places the calf muscle and tendon behind the ankle in a shortened position. Women who wear high-heeled shoes all day and then attempt very aggressive activities such as running, jumping, or step aerobics are more likely to develop Achilles tendonitis (inflammation of the Achilles tendon) due to poor flexibility of the calf and Achilles tendon. Ice and a nonsteroidal anti-inflammatory drug (such as ibuprofen) can temporarily help with pain, but proper calf stretching and supportive flat shoes will address the cause of the imbalance.

CONSIDERING GENERAL ORTHOPEDIC ISSUES

Rotator cuff tendonitis or tears can challenge activities that require upper-body strength and stability, such as rock climbing, boulder scrambling, and putting on or taking off a backpack. The rotator cuff is a group of four muscles that coordinate to stabilize the shoulder's ball and socket joint. Overuse or trauma can cause small tears in the tendons, and over time these tears can worsen or become inflamed, causing pain, swelling, and weakness. Small tears usually respond to rest, ice, and strengthening exercises, but larger tears often require surgery to repair the tendons. If you have shoulder pain, ask for help to put on and take off your backpack, or use a bench or rock to support its weight. Pack as light as possible (see Chapter 5, "Gearing Up"), and minimize overhead re aching or aggravating activities.

Low back pain can be caused by muscle strains, ligament sprains, joint pain or arthritis, d isc bulges, cartilage wear and tear, and nerve compression. Each person has unique reasons for his or her pain, and it is important for you to consult your physician or health-care provider for appropriate diagnosis and treatment. What worked for your friend may aggravate your back. Try to stay in a pain-free range of motion, even if this means modifying your trip planning.

Those with back pain should always consider decreasing the load in their pack and use a rock, tree, or backpacking chair for sitting in camp. Lying on your back with your knees bent or your legs up can be a position of comfort once you reach your destination.

Osteoarthritis can occur in any joint but is very common in the knees and hips due to their load-bearing nature. Over time, the bones rubbing together causes the protective layer of cartilage to wear down and the resulting friction creates swelling, pain, and joint stiffness. In general, arthritis does not need to keep you from the trail, but you should select trips that allow for rest breaks and minimize pounding on your joints (such as downhill on granite). You'll be able to stay out longer with less discomfort if you plan for less mileage per day.

Plantar fasciitis is the most common cause of heel and arch pain. The plantar fascia is the flat band of tissue that connects your heel bone to your toes. It supports the arch of your foot, and if you strain your plantar fascia, it gets weak, swollen, and irritated. The result is heel pain or pain on the bottom of your foot when you stand or walk. Plantar fasciitis is common in people who are on their feet a lot; it can happen in one foot or both feet. Plantar fasciitis can happen over time with poor foot mechanics.

Plantar fasciitis can be aggravated by characteristics such as your feet rolling inward too much when you walk *(excessive pronation)*; having high arches or flat feet; walking, standing, or running for long periods of time, especially on hard surfaces; being overweight; wearing shoes that don't fit well or are worn out; or having tight Achilles tendons or calf muscles.

During flare-ups it's best to choose supportive footwear and flat, even terrain. Wearing flip-flops or walking barefoot in the sand require the foot muscles to work more strenuously and can aggravate symptoms.

GETTING OUT THERE

Preparing for an outdoor adventure is fun and exciting, and your fitness routine should be the same. Start slowly, and start early! Begin training at least ten weeks prior to a big trip, and be realistic. Be consistent, and stick with it. You'll see results, you'll feel better, and you'll enjoy the view from the top!

Planning Your Adventure

Marty Stevens and Dave Moser

Planning a trip into the outdoors can be almost as much fun as the trip itself. Reading books and spreading maps on the floor gives you a thrill of anticipation. In the process, you may also learn about the flora of the area and its history. The time and effort you put into your plans result in greater enjoyment, increased safety, broader knowledge, and fewer unpleasant surprises. Although most of this chapter applies to backpack trips (overnight and longer), the concepts presented here also apply to day hikes. As for a two-person backpacking trip, you would still go through the same planning steps.

RESEARCHING THE TRIP

To help plan your trip, you can rely on five primary resources.

Internet. The foremost planning resource is the Internet. Online you can get detailed information about permits and quotas; trailheads and trail conditions; passes and peaks; lodging and dining; reservations; phone numbers for agencies; ranger stations, campgrounds, and concessionaires; weather forecasts; and links to other useful sites. Some sites contain trip reports and blogs of hikers who have already gone where you are going. One great aspect is the twenty-four-hour convenience of applying for a permit online. Frequently the office that has jurisdiction has limited hours, may be closed on holidays and weekends, or may be unstaffed when you call.

Some of the more useful websites include the US Forest Service, the National Park Service, and the Bureau of Land Management. If you don't know their URLs, see "Resources" in the appendix, or just use a search engine.

Firsthand information. There is nothing like firsthand knowledge and wisdom gained by experience. If you are the trip leader, it is best to scout the trip in advance to get firsthand knowledge about road and trail conditions and the availability of water. Make notes on your maps for future reference. You may discover an interesting side trip or come to the realization that the trip is not appropriate for the group you intend to lead. Of course, scouting for a five-day backpacking trip when the trailhead is ten hours from home might be impractical.

Your friends and acquaintances are also valuable resources. Ask them about the problems they encountered, which areas they liked best, how difficult the trip was, and what they would do differently.

Guidebooks. Another important resource is guidebooks. There are hundreds of guidebooks published for wilderness areas and trails. Some guidebooks are more useful than others, so you will have to look at the table of contents to determine which is best for the area you will be in. Keep in mind that conditions and trails may have changed since the book was written. Note the copyright dates and verify information with local authorities. Also refer to the bibliography and recommended reading lists.

Guidebooks can be found in your local bookstore, but a sporting goods store that caters to hikers and backpackers is a better source. These stores have a much wider selection and are more likely to have a book that covers the area you are interested in. Online resources often have more extensive selections.

Maps. An indispensable resource is maps, which vary widely in types and scale. This includes Forest Service maps, Park Service maps, US Geological Survey topographic maps, and road maps. County maps are good for showing major and minor roads leading to trailheads. Topographic maps allow you to visualize in great detail the topography and trails of the area you plan to explore. Different maps show different features of the same area, so try to collect enough maps to meet all your needs. Obtain detailed maps of the area so that you can meticulously follow printed and verbal descriptions of a trip.

Some maps, such as Forest Service maps, have a wealth of information. These maps have the minor roads, trailheads, trails, campgrounds, regulations, whether a permit is needed or not, which controlling agency has jurisdiction over the area and that agency's contact information, plus a plethora of other information that is very useful for planning.

Remember that even the most current maps may not show newer trails and that existing trails can become eroded, flooded, or overgrown so as to

Maps are essential for successful trip planning. (Photo by Kristi Anderson)

be unusable. Outdated maps are not necessarily useless—they may indicate old mines, defunct trails, historic towns, and other features that you may want to explore that have been left off new maps. A complete research effort might include a trip to a public or university library for a look at old maps in the historic section. Software programs that allow you to print personalized topographic maps of just the area you will be hiking in are a welcome convenience.

Rangers. Rangers are another excellent source of information. However, before contacting a ranger, do your homework so you can ask intelligent questions. A cold call to a ranger asking for a good place to hike may waste both your time and the ranger's. When calling, have your maps and guidebooks in front of you. Ask to speak to someone who is familiar with the area you plan to visit. You may have to wait for a backcountry ranger to return your call, but the information will be worth the wait. Describe your plans and don't hesitate to ask for additional information or suggestions. Rangers will let you know about trail conditions, closures, permitting, quotas, and the availability of water. In some instances, the ranger will recommend an alternate trail that will suit your needs.

DESIGNING THE TRIP

Designing a trip itinerary is exciting! Using the map you plan to hike with, mentally walk along the trail and visualize your intended route. Google Earth, or similar programs, can facilitate this. Study the elevation gains and losses, the distances to be traveled, and the meadows, lakes, forests, glaciers, and other features of the terrain. Identify the best overlooks and the best spots for lunch or snack breaks. Most importantly, identify sources of water, which you will need for camping at night and for refilling water bottles during the day while on the trail. When choosing campsites,

Exploring a spectacular formation like this slot canyon (Buckskin Gulch in the Vermilion Cliffs Wilderness, Utah) makes for an interesting trip.
(Photo by Robert Burroughs)

visualize where the sun will rise and set so you can position your tent for sun or shade. In a similar vein, you may want to plan your trip around a full moon or go when there is a new moon to enjoy the zillions of stars in an inky-dark sky, perhaps catching a meteor shower.

Rather than having to retrace your steps, consider a loop trip. Or design a point-to-point trip (starting and ending at different places) using a car shuttle or a drop-off and pickup service. With these strategies, you will enjoy twice the scenery as you would on an out-and-back trip.

Getting to the trailhead. When deciding how many cars it will take to carry people and gear, keep in mind that backpacking equipment takes up a lot of space. Many compact cars can carry only two people and two backpacks. If someone in your group has a van or pickup, consider using it to haul bulky gear while the participants ride in the passenger cars. If you use a car shuttle for point-to-point trips, remember that everyone and everything will have to fit into half the vehicles.

For a long drive to a distant trailhead, include time for rest breaks or meal stops every couple of hours or so. Carry extra water in the car, and plan to arrive early enough to get a full night's sleep before hitting the trail the next morning. If you are caravanning, cell phones are very useful to make decisions about when to stop for lunch, whether to take side trips, or to notify other drivers if you need to pull over. When caravanning, it is not necessary to stay within sight of one another, which can be unsafe.

Anticipating conditions. Try to anticipate what the weather and trail conditions will be like at the time of your trip. You should know, for example, that snow flurries can occur above timberline in July and August. If there was a heavy snowfall the previous winter, many trails at higher elevations will still be covered with deep snow in late July, necessitating the use of specialized snow equipment or a rerouting of your hike. Rivers swollen with snowmelt can be a problem in the spring and early summer. Sudden rains may turn dirt roads into quagmires of mud. Flash floods can lash the desert and canyon country during thunderstorm season. Desert winds can hit 50 miles per hour or more anytime.

Whenever it has been hot and dry for a long time, wildfires may make large sections of the wilderness inaccessible and may inundate adjacent areas with smoke for many miles downwind. Firefighting efforts can deny you trail access and, in some cases, obliterate trails. Though the fire might have been last autumn and has long burned out, the trail may not have been reestablished by the time you get there. Trees felled by wind or snowstorms may block trails for months. Discuss potential hazards and trail conditions when you talk with a ranger during your research.

Finding water. The amount of water you carry depends on where the nearest streams are in relation to your route and campsites and whether or not they are flowing. The availability of water will also determine where your campsites will be. Ask the ranger when you call. Decide what method you will use to treat water to make it safe to drink. Also, leave some water in your vehicle for use at trail's end.

Caching supplies. Some trips may be made simpler by placing caches (hidden supplies) of water or food in advance, but find out ahead of time if it is legal to do so in the area where you'll be traveling. These supplies must be well hidden and protected from animals and the elements, and remember, the only bear-proof storage container is a bear canister. Leave a note, with the date indicated, stating that you are depending on these supplies for your survival. Never abandon a cache, even if your trip is cancelled. Leave No Trace principles always apply.

Acclimating. When hiking at elevations above 6000 feet, most people benefit from an acclimation period just before the trip. If you are planning on a steep elevation gain the first day, try to sleep at a high-elevation trailhead the night before. Spending a day or two walking or hiking easily at high elevation will let your body adjust more easily to the thinner air.

Formalizing your itinerary. To organize all the details of your trip, create a complete itinerary, starting with the departure. List dates, times, and places and allow some slack time for unforeseen circumstances. Have an alternate trip or route planned in case yours is not doable due to some obstacle like a rock slide, fire, damaged bridge, swollen stream, or an injury to someone in your party. Consider the abilities of slower participants when estimating how long it will take for each section of the hike. And plan to arrive at camp with some daylight left. Once you've determined your route, you can add significant waypoints (campsites, trail junctions, river crossings, peaks, etc.) into a GPS receiver. For more information, see "Navigation by GPS" in Chaper 7, "Finding Your Way: Land Navigation."

Much of the pertinent planning data can be summarized on a trip planning sheet as shown in Tables 4-1 and 4-2.

TABLE 4-1. TRIP PLANNING SHEET

Maximize the enjoyment of your trip by using a trip planning sheet.

Area:	Dates:
Controlling agency:	Phone number:
Ranger station:	Phone number:
Address:	
Permit requirements:	Campfires allowed?
Medical facility:	Phone number:
Address:	
Weather bureau location:	Phone number:
Road maps:	Trail maps:
Guidebooks:	Dates/comments:
Campground:	
Reservations required?	Have them?
Drinking water available?	Toilets?
Tent sites?	Picnic tables?
Sunrise:	Sunset:

TABLE 4-2. SAMPLE ITINERARY

Recording information about your trip in an organized manner will make the information easy to find and will prove a useful reference throughout the trip. The sample below includes data from the Pacific Crest Trail in California.

Day	From	To	Miles	Elevation gain/loss	Estimated hiking time	Water availability
1	Highway 58	Big Tree	10.2	1550	5:40	None
2	Big Tree	Unnamed meadow	15.6	−350	8:40	At Golden Oak Springs
3	Unnamed meadow	Jawbone Canyon Road	10.0	1600	5:35	None
4	Jawbone Canyon Road	Road SC123	15.8	−2050	8:50	None
5	Road SC123	Skinner Peak	16.6	2400	9:15	None
6	Skinner Peak	Walker Campground	16.8	−1850	9:20	None

CHECKING ON PERMITS AND REGULATIONS

The permit system serves several purposes. In some cases it is used to limit the number of people in an area, which helps lessen the impact and guarantees a better wilderness experience for all. In other cases, by issuing permits agencies are able to advise users of regulations and collect data needed to carry out effective management of the wilderness area. Finally, permits allow authorities to keep tabs on your whereabouts in case of an emergency, such as an evacuation of all users due to a quickly spreading wildfire.

Permit policies vary widely. Go online or check your map to find out what the controlling agency is. This is a good opportunity to get accurate contact information to put on your emergency contact sheet. In many areas, permits are free, but most agencies offer an advance permit reservation for a fee of about $10 per person on the trip. Find out well in advance what the permit policy is for the area you are interested in. Agencies may start taking reservations on a certain date of the year or five to six months in advance of the date of your planned hike. Permits can be requested by mail, phone, online, or in person as a walk-in. Except for walk-ins, permits will be mailed to the requestor through the US mail system. If you arrange to pick the permit up in person, be aware that it might be reassigned if you are late picking it up. Some remote trailheads have self-issue permits, and some ranger stations set out self-issue permits after normal hours.

Quite often, the key to getting the permit you want is to apply early and online. Permits for the most popular areas and trailheads have quotas and become available only during a limited time, starting several months in advance of the height of the season, and are quickly taken. Some permits are granted on a first-come, first-served basis, depending on the application date and time, while other permits are granted by lottery. For those trailheads with quotas, ranger districts will always set some permits aside for walk-ins. You might not get the trailhead you want, so be flexible about your dates of entry and try to avoid the most popular days: Fridays and Saturdays, particularly on a holiday weekend.

Fire regulations. Find out the fire regulations, which vary widely from area to area. In some places, campfire permits are required; in others, campfires are banned altogether because of wildfire hazards or scarcity of firewood. Some jurisdictions allow fires as long as you bring your own firewood. Wild areas may have various fire restrictions imposed on them during the hot, dry summer and fall seasons. During extremely hazardous conditions, visitors may be prohibited from using any open flame device or may even be prohibited from entering certain areas. Although campfires are a traditional part of the outdoor experience, they are not always needed for enjoyment. Campfires draw attention to a small world only a few feet across, while the absence of a campfire opens up the infinite majesty of the night sky to sight and mind.

Regulations regarding bears. Some areas require that food be carried in bear-proof canisters, which can be rented or purchased at local retailers that specialize in backcountry gear. Some ranger stations also rent bear canisters, usually on a first-come, first-served basis. Call the ranger station during your planning phase to see whether a bear canister is needed and whether the ranger station rents them. Regardless of regulatory requirements, you may want to take a bear canister with you if your hiking area is in bear habitat. Bears have learned how to snatch food that has been hung in trees, to the chagrin of many backpackers, so this method not only may be unreliable, it also may not be allowed. In addition, it habituates bears to human food, which can result in either forced relocation or execution if the bears become troublesome.

PLANNING TO LEAD A TRIP

Some of the material in this chapter is geared toward those in leadership roles. Even if you never take on the responsibility of leading a large group, you will profit by and appreciate knowing the detailed planning incumbent upon the leader.

Choosing Trip Companions

If you are the leader and are not personally acquainted with prospective participants, it is your responsibility to screen them. Each participant should have the proper equipment and skills, be in good enough physical condition for the difficulty of your trip, and possess the confidence and attitude necessary to handle the trip without depending unduly on other members of the group. In evaluating prospective participants, keep notes on each individual. You will need some of this information for your use during your planning, and you may need some of this information should it be necessary to send for medical help while on the trip. The use of a questionnaire such as in Table 4-3 is a good idea.

Of course, all of this information is confidential, and some is personally identifiable information that is protected by federal law (Title 18 USC, Section 1028). You cannot share this information with anybody except medical personnel, and legally you must destroy, not just discard, all notes when you are finished with them.

Screen participants initially over the phone, and do more screening at the planning meeting (see the next section). Even after someone has been accepted for the trip, something could come up that would change that status. A participant's recent illness or injury might be reason to reconsider his or her participation. It is your duty as the leader to continue screening right up to the beginning of the trip. Dropping an obviously unqualified individual is fair to the group and to the individual, who might end up having a miserable time, and can protect that individual from possible injury. If the trip is to be a backpack over rough terrain, effective screening might include a pretrip day hike over similar terrain. Those who seem to be having trouble should be kindly informed that the trip is not for them.

Planning Meeting

Planning meetings are effective for almost all trips, especially for those lasting two days or longer. At the very least, the participants get to know one another beforehand. During the meeting, the leader explains the trip plan and objectives:

- Driving route
- Campground facilities

TABLE 4-3. PARTICIPANT INFORMATION SHEET

Each trip will have its own unique needs for collecting information about participants.

Name:	Age:
Email address:	Zip code or city (if using carpools):
Home or cell phone:	Work phone:
What do you do for exercise?	How often?

Recent outing experience (when, where, distance, elevation gain, with whom):

Physical limitations or medical conditions:

Allergies:

Medications:

Physician's name:	Phone number:

Health insurance company:

Policy number (carry with you):

Emergency contact person:

Address:

Phone number:	Relationship:

- Hiking route
- Number of miles to be hiked each day
- Elevation gains and losses each day
- Availability of water
- Hazards: bears, rattlesnakes, poison oak, avalanche hazard, thunderstorms, snow, etc.
- Trail difficulties

The following details should be worked out during the meeting:

- Carpools and drivers
- Equipment sharing: tents, stoves, water filters, etc.
- Cooking groups or a commissary wherein all share the same menu, cooking, and cleaning responsibilities
- Food purchases
- Participants' dietary restrictions
- Sharing of costs

All participants must understand what the trip entails and acknowledge that it is something they want to do. The leader should remind the group about individual responsibilities and encourage questions and discussions.

The leader can suggest that drivers take along an extra car key. At the start of the trip, drivers would then give the extra key to another person to carry, a simple precaution that could save the group hours of wasted time at the end of the trip in case a driver loses his or her key on the trail. Before leaving home, all drivers should have their vehicles checked to be sure they are in good working order (check the oil, tire pressure, etc.).

The leader should pass out the following checklists and printed information. The more of these details the leader puts on paper, the more prepared participants will be.

- Trip description or summary
- Itinerary
- Map of driving route
- Map of hiking route (USGS topographic and other maps can be photocopied without violating copyright laws)
- List of required and optional maps (if not provided)
- Water needs
- Packing checklist (see the packing checklist in Chapter 5, "Gearing Up")
- Important phone numbers, including that of the controlling agency, to call in case of an emergency
- List of dos and don'ts (for example, pack out all toilet paper, bury human waste at least 200 feet from water, do not feed animals, *do not let anything get into water sources, including biodegradable soap*)

The leader should remind the group about individual responsibilities. It is up to each individual to develop a personal checklist. Everyone is forgetful to some degree, and there can be quite a number of things competing for your attention when you are packing, so a checklist is a must. After every trip, add to the checklist any item you wish you had taken. You will eventually end up with a very long list, too much for any one trip, but at least you will not overlook anything when planning future trips.

Safety

While safety is everyone's business, there are several things the leader can do to ensure trip participants are prepared in the event of an emergency.

Familiarize everyone with the medical facility nearest the hike area and local emergency phone numbers. In addition to 9-1-1, these numbers include the local sheriff, ranger, or fire department, depending on what agency has jurisdiction.

Leave full written details with someone dependable, such as a family member or a friend, outlining where you are going, how many you are going with, when you expect to return, and what to do and when to do it if

A well-planned trip will leave you smiling. (Photo by Arleen Tavernier)

you don't return on time. This is always important but is vitally important if you will be hiking alone. You should include your own phone number, phone numbers of the local sheriff or ranger station as discussed above, and your vehicle description and license plate number. Ask your family member or friend to report you missing if you are not back by the time you specify. While it is a good idea to give a ranger your itinerary, rangers are accustomed to people neglecting to check back in at the end of the trip, so ask your family member or friend ahead of time whether they would be a suitable emergency contact.

Don't forget to check back in with your emergency contact when you return, or you can forget about a prompt rescue sometime when it might be needed. On some trails, hikers are required to sign in and sign out at the ranger station. After the trip, don't forget to sign out! If you do forget, you may be responsible for costs if an emergency search is conducted.

LAST-MINUTE DETAILS

Some things cannot be done until the final day or final hours before the trip starts. Fill up the gas tank and do a final check on the oil. Check the weather: call the ranger station or check online. If the weather has been nasty, also ask the ranger about trail damage, stream crossings, and wilderness road conditions. Finally, if you notice anything during your trip that authorities should know about, report it. Those who follow in your footsteps may have a better wilderness experience because of it.

Gearing Up

*Mike Fry, Bob Stinton, Jim Matlock, Jan Hawkins, Carolyn Moser,
Priscilla Anderson, Scott Anderson, and Glen Van Peski*

Your life is basic, simple, and clear when you are in the wilderness. This clarity reveals the natural world and how we are a part of it. Backpacking is a minimalist existence of making do with the fewest possible possessions.

The experienced wilderness traveler uses basic skills and equipment to keep trips safe and enjoyable. Individuals new to the sport tend to overload on equipment. This chapter covers what gear is essential, what is not, some tips for where to get your gear, and how to use these skills and equipment to keep trips safe and enjoyable.

BASIC SKILLS AND EQUIPMENT

As you gather your equipment, take each piece out and field-test it with other pieces of your gear to make sure that the pieces work together. Is your nylon shirt so slippery that your pack won't stay in place? Does your hat hit your pack when you turn your head or look up? Test each piece, test the system, and never take something out on a long trek until you know that you can rely on it.

Regardless of the length and nature of the trip, travelers must carry the Ten Essentials. This is a list of items so important that they are considered essential on any hike. Many elements of these essentials do not change from trip to trip, but a few items will change based on a trip's anticipated demands and weather.

THE TEN ESSENTIALS

1. Navigation: map and compass (and perhaps a GPS device)
2. Sun protection: sunglasses, sunscreen, lip balm, hat
3. Insulation: extra clothing
4. Illumination: headlamp or flashlight, spare batteries
5. First-aid supplies: including personal needs and toilet paper
6. Fire starting materials: firestarter and waterproof matches or lighter
7. Repair kit and tools: including knife
8. Nutrition: extra food
9. Hydration: extra water
10. Emergency shelter: raingear, poncho, space blanket, or bivy sack

In addition to the Ten Essentials, you may want to carry a cell phone, two-way radio, or other communication device.

Keeping Things Light

When you carry everything on your back, weight is a major issue. A heavy pack is no fun! It places a load on your joints and feet, can slow your progress, and increases the likelihood of injury. Because of the revolution in lightweight materials, gear is getting lighter. Carrying less weight will make your entire body thank you! It will also extend the years that you can enjoy backpacking. As the weight of your equipment goes down, to some extent the risk goes up. The goal on every wilderness adventure is to maximize enjoyment and minimize discomfort without compromising safety.

How much weight should you carry? One key to managing pack weight is to know how much your gear should weigh. What is the maximum weight an individual should carry? Carry absolutely no more than **one-quarter of your body weight, less for a woman.** For a 150-pound male backpacker, this is 37 pounds. This rule does not factor in the individual's physical condition or trail conditions.

Nonconsumable pack weight is the weight of everything you carry in your pack, not including the consumables of food, fuel, and water. It doesn't include items that you typically wear during the day. *Consumable pack weight* is primarily food, fuel, and water. Food should weigh about 1½ pounds dry weight per person per day. This provides about 2400 calories each day (to find out why, see Chapter 6, "'Eating Out' in the Wilderness"). Stove fuel should weigh about 1.7 ounces per person per day for simple meals or 2.4 ounces per person per day for gourmet cooking. If you have to melt snow for drinking water or boil all your water to purify it, double the amount of fuel.

Water is very heavy—and very important. A gallon weighs 8 pounds 5 ounces, plus the weight of the container. A useful rule is one gallon per person per day for drinking and cooking, and high temperatures can double that. Ideally, water will be available along the trail and in camp, so you will have to carry only two quarts in your pack.

Figure 5-1. *Items from the Ten Essentials*

Another key to managing pack weight is careful choice of nonconsumable items. These are your backpack, shelter, sleeping bag, clothing, cooking gear, the Ten Essentials, and any toys you want to add.

How do you figure out how much weight you're carrying? Let's estimate how much weight you might be carrying. A typical backpack and the average two-person tent each weigh about 5 pounds. The typical sleeping bag weighs in at about 3 pounds. Backpack, tent, and sleeping bag are the "big three." Quick addition brings the total weight of the big three to 13 pounds.

Now let's say the other nonconsumables such as clothing, cooking gear, and Ten Essentials add an additional 12 pounds, and you're sharing the weight of the tent so you carry only 2½ pounds of it, making your base pack weight 22½ pounds. Adding 4 pounds for the two quarts of water you always carry brings your total to 26½ pounds. Now, since you're probably used to eating pretty regularly, add 1½ pounds of food and fuel per day.

For a weekend you'll have a 29½-pound pack. For three days you'll have 31 pounds. Keep adding 1½ pounds of food and fuel per day to figure out your weight for longer trips. For a trip longer than three days, add in a couple of pounds for more clothes and a bit of extra food and fuel. Your pack weight for a week shouldn't start out at more than 37½ pounds.

Be constantly learning safe ways to reduce this weight. You have to carry your brain when you're backpacking, and it doesn't weigh any more no matter how much you stuff into it!

How can you reduce the weight you're carrying? The big three is a place where you can cut pounds and ounces. For example, a lightweight tent for two can weigh only 4 pounds. Lightweight backpacks weigh only about 3 pounds. Usually they are not as durable or comfortable as the heavier backpacks, so they must not be used until the pack weight is quite low. Lightweight tents and sleeping bags have similar trade-offs of durability and sometimes comfort. Lightweight gear is typically made with lighter materials and fewer features, so it requires a higher level of care and more experience to use it safely.

After you have taken into account the weight of the big three, look at the other items that you plan to carry. Minor weights add up quickly. Watch the ounces, and the pounds will take care of themselves. Have a goal to take fewer things, take lighter things, take smaller quantities, make items multifunctional, and leave at home anything you don't really need.

For example, don't carry six months' worth of anything. Comb the stores for small sizes or samples of products, and carry them partially empty. Buy mini containers, label them, and decant products into them. Check out ideas in "Resources" (in the appendix) for items available in tiny or lightweight quantities.

Make a biodegradable soap like Dr. Bronner's peppermint variety work not only as soap but also for shampoo, dishwashing, deodorant, and toothpaste, and leave those other items at home. Don't take the whole bottle—that's two years' worth! Transfer a very small amount into an emptied breath mint bottle.

Don't take a flashlight that can survive being run over—take an LED flashlight or headlamp that uses smaller batteries. Take a separate super-bright pinch light that is lighter than a set of extra batteries. A bandana can serve as a water prefilter, washcloth, towel, bandage, hat drape, mini-tablecloth, dish towel, napkin, hot pad, handkerchief, and more. Rinse it out occasionally.

Here are some other ways to keep your load as light as possible:

- Purchase the lightest equipment that will work for you.
- Lightweight doesn't just involve light gear. Learn techniques for going lightweight. Get an ounce scale and weigh your gear. A major key to managing your pack weight is to know how much your gear weighs. Make a list and put it on a spreadsheet.
- Share items such as a tent, stove, cookware, and water treatment system with a partner, and divide the common load evenly.
- Hike with a partner who carries the lion's share of the weight and keeps you warm at night.
- Carabiners are cool—for climbing, not for hanging things all over your pack. They add unnecessary ounces. Use cord or nylon clips instead, or stow items in a pocket.
- Travel where there's abundant water and good weather, so you don't need to carry as much water or clothing.
- Hike where there aren't bears or where you don't need a bear-proof canister (which weighs 2 to 3 pounds).
- Develop and follow a gear list.
- Pack ahead of time, so you can be deliberate about it.

Figure 5-2. *Use a small scale to weigh and evaluate items.*
(Photo by Jennifer "Spidermonkey" Lanci)

- Ask other wilderness travelers how they trim their pack weight. Find people with lighter packs than you, so you can learn from them.
- Search "lightweight backpacking" on the Internet for information and videos. Peruse the "Resources" in the appendix.
- An inexpensive way to reduce your load by 10 pounds is to lose 10 pounds!

Choosing Products

Look for companies that manufacture high-quality wilderness gear. Some companies design for lighter weight as well as for functionality. Learn about manufacturers' reputations, the quality of their products, the length of time they've been in business, and their warranties and service capabilities. Check the product labels for specifications, care and cleaning, and guarantees. After you've made a purchase, follow care directions to keep your gear performing as intended.

Product Sources

Where you buy your equipment may be just as important as who manufactures it. Ask salespeople if their store offers any guarantees beyond those offered by the manufacturers. Your best bet is to purchase from a source that is reputable, has been in business a long time, offers a product satisfaction guarantee, and has knowledgeable salespeople. A store that also offers rental equipment can be helpful for a backpacker looking to try before buying.

Usually, sports and adventure outfitters attract salespeople who love the outdoors and try out the equipment they sell. Ask lots of questions. Internet and mail-order outfits may offer considerable savings, but you have to know what you want and how to use it. In addition, scan outdoor magazines and ads for bargains. Even the most expensive outfitters have periodic sales to clear out excess stock as well as demo and rental equipment. Not all of your equipment needs to be brand-new. Swap meets, thrift stores, and surplus outlets are all good hunting grounds once you know what you want.

Cost Considerations

When outfitting yourself, you may want to prioritize your purchases. The list is short for day hikers: boots (or appropriate hiking shoes), day pack, and the Ten Essentials. However, accumulating backpacking gear involves major purchases. Fortunately, some of the more expensive items needed for backpacking can easily be borrowed or rented. Personal items such as boots and special clothing are first priority, then sleeping bag, sleeping pad, and backpack. You may be able to share a stove and cookware for some time before deciding what kind to buy. A tent is a key purchase—you may want to rent or share one for a while before investing in your own.

Making your own equipment can be an economical way to collect good gear. Go online to look for ideas and instructions. Lots of shelters and small items can be well improvised, but prices for new equipment are low compared to the amount of time it takes to create a finished piece. But do keep your needle sharp for repairing or modifying equipment and clothing. Always bring your sewing kit, ripstop repair tape, and safety pins.

FOOTWEAR

During a typical hiking day, your feet hit the ground 10,000 to 20,000 times (about 2000 steps per mile). On multiday trips, they must carry you out and back to the trailhead over a wide range of trail conditions. Your footwear must fit well! Your boots must be up to the demands of the trail or routes.

Most outdoor specialty retailers generally divide boots into three primary categories: trail, backpacking, and mountaineering. Better-quality trail and backpacking boots are more suited for most wilderness travel, while mountaineering boots are more appropriate for climbing hard snow and ice (see "Clothing and Winter Equipment" in Chapter 12, "Winter Snow Travel").

Boot Construction

All-leather boots. Full-grain leather is commonly used in higher-quality trail and backpacking boots as well as in some mountaineering boots. To make the full-grain leather truly waterproof, the boot must be treated. Always use products recommended by the manufacturer. Full-grain all-leather boots tend to be heavy and take a while to break in (soften and mold to your feet) but are comfortable and, once broken in, very durable.

Nylon-leather combination boots. The majority of boots on the market are made with a combination of nylon and leather panels, or a combination of leather, synthetic materials, and mesh. These combination boots are generally lighter in weight, ventilate better, and are more flexible and break in more quickly than similar all-leather boots. They breathe well, but combination boots will not be waterproof unless they have a Gore-Tex or eVent membrane.

Considerations When Purchasing Boots

What is the intended use of your boots? They need to match your travel plan. Often a good all-around pair of boots will serve you for both trail hiking and backpacking. If your primary interest is three-season (spring, summer, and fall) backcountry trail travel and backpacking, you are better off purchasing a pair of light, sturdy, well-ventilated boots to keep your feet comfortable. They should be waterproof or have the capacity to be waterproofed.

If your planned activities cover a wider range of environments, you will probably need a heavier pair of boots. If you will be doing a lot of snow travel, you will need to consider a second, heavier pair of boots, which would also allow you to use a thicker sock.

The latest technology is useless if the boots hurt your feet. Use these tips to help you select the appropriate boot for you:

- Go on a short hike before trying on boots, because your feet normally swell a bit when on the trail. If a hike isn't possible, try on boots late in the day after you've been on your feet for a while.
- When trying on boots, bring along the socks, orthotics, or inner soles you plan to use with the boots.
- Look for a retailer with a fit guarantee; the best guarantees allow you to take the boots out on the trail and return them if they don't fit properly.
- Shop at a store with knowledgeable staff.
- Try on several pairs made by different manufacturers. Each manufacturer has its own sizing system, so there are differences between the same sizes made by different manufacturers.
- Go to the footwear department first if you are shopping for other items in addition to boots. When you think you've found the right pair, ask if you can wear the boots in the store while doing your other shopping. The extra time allows you to better evaluate the fit.
- Allow about a half inch of extra toe room. You'll need it for steep downhill hiking when your foot slips forward inside the boot. With the boots on, kick the floor several times. Can you force your toes to hit the front of the boot? If you can, the boots are too short or not laced tightly enough. The back of your heel should slide up and down no more than a quarter inch with each step. Excessive heel slippage is an all-too common cause of blisters. Excessive heel pressure is just as bad. A quarter inch of up-and-down motion is a good compromise.

Resoling. Many boots cannot be resoled since the sole is molded to the boot upper. If you are looking for boots that can be resoled, it is also important to find a resoling service. Do not use silicone sealer on any boot you intend to have resoled.

Break-In and Boot Care

Put some miles on your boots before you take them out for an all-day hike. Wear them at home, on walks, and to work. This will not only soften the boot but toughen your feet.

Generally all models of boots need the same basic general care. Clean after use with running water and a brush to remove mud and dirt. Dry them in a place with good ventilation, but do not expose them to elevated temperatures. If the boots are very wet, a good means to dry them is to stuff them with newspaper and roll them up in newspaper. Change the paper every day until they are completely dry.

Socks

The best all-around socks for hiking and backpacking are wool-blend socks. Wool-blend socks hold their shape better, dry more quickly, and are easier to care for than 100 percent wool socks. Blends are generally made with 70 to 80 percent wool, plus nylon and an elastic material such as spandex. Avoid cotton socks; wool blends provide more cushioning than cotton, are less abrasive than cotton, and are warmer when wet than cotton.

Synthetic socks made of performance fibers do not provide quite as much cushioning as wool, but they do wick moisture away from the skin, dry more quickly, and can be a very good choice.

Many individuals prone to blisters use liner socks under their outer socks. Liner socks are thin and are made of blends consisting primarily of nylon, polyester, or silk. Pick a sock or sock combination before purchasing your boots. You may have to change your sock combination as your boots stretch and your feet change.

For cold weather, it's better to wear a heavier sock. However, if this results in a tighter boot fit, which reduces blood circulation to the feet, the result will be colder feet. To use a thicker sock, you might need a larger boot for cold-weather hiking.

Gaiters

A gaiter is a fabric cover that closes the gap at the top of your footwear, keeping out trail debris, snow, and rain. Ankle-high gaiters are lightweight, stretchy, and breathable for trails in mild weather. Knee-high gaiters are breathable or waterproof-breathable for warmth and protection when hiking, skiing, or snowshoeing. Mountaineering gaiters are insulated for the very low temperatures of high altitude.

TREKKING POLES

Trekking poles are used for both balance and propulsion. Most are made with either aluminum alloy or carbon fiber. They are adjustable for a person's height. Most people choose a short length that reaches just to their elbow or a long length that reaches to their armpit. You can then adjust them for differing terrain (shorter for going uphill, longer for going downhill). You can collapse them completely to stow them in or alongside your pack. The length is adjusted either by twisting or by means of a clamp; the ones that lock with a clamp are sometimes a little easier to lock and unlock.

The grips are usually made of either cork or foam rubber, and some are set at an ergonomic angle to reduce wrist strain. Some poles have antishock springs that absorb shock; your wrists will appreciate it. Get the lightest poles that will work for you. Before you buy, try a pair on a short hike. If you can feel the benefits, it's time to buy your own.

CLOTHING: THE LAYERING SYSTEM

Your clothes must shelter your body from sun, wind, rain, and cold—sometimes all in the same day! Each article of clothing must continue to function wet or dry. As you move, body heat and water vapor (perspiration) need to escape, while wind and rain need to be repelled.

The well-equipped wilderness traveler needs to assemble a lightweight, compact outfit that will do the job, rain or shine. This is done most effectively through the layering system (see Figure 5-3). This is a clothing system in which each item of clothing works well with any other piece so you can quickly adapt to changing temperatures and conditions by adding or taking off layers of clothing.

Figure 5-3. *The layering system*

Materials

Cotton is not recommended for any cold or wet weather conditions. Cotton absorbs water readily and, once wet, is cold and slow to dry. Blue jeans and other heavy cotton items such as sweatshirts may seem ideal for outdoor use, but the combination of cold conditions with wet clothing will create a deadly rapid drain of your body heat. On warm, dry days, though, thin, light-colored cotton shorts, shirts, and bandanas can keep you comfortably cool.

Wool and performance fabrics (polyester, nylon, acrylic, and polypropylene) make good insulating garments that retain much of their insulating ability even when wet. Wool is a natural fiber that can retain as much as 30 percent of its dry weight in water and still be comfortable to wear, but it is slow to dry. Performance fabrics are synthetic fabrics or fabric blends that are engineered to provide functional qualities such as temperature regulation, moisture management, UV protection, and wind and/or water resistance. They absorb almost no moisture into the fibers and are easier than wool to wring out and dry in case they do get wet. This type of fiber can be knitted and used in long underwear or made into fleece for use in shirts, pants, gloves, and hats. Nylon is used in shirts and pants that come with sun protection factor (SPF) ratings, providing a lightweight alternative to sunscreen. Tighter-woven nylons are used in wind jackets and pants. Polyester fibers make up the vast majority of fibers used as synthetic down replacements in garments and sleeping bags.

Down, typically the fluffy inner feathers of geese, is a very effective insulator when dry and is preferred over synthetics for its warmth-to-weight ratio and the fact that it can be packed into a small volume. However, down provides no insulation when wet and is difficult to dry in the field, making it a poor choice for conditions where it might get wet.

Waterproof-breathable membranes such as Gore-Tex and eVent have revolutionized raingear. These membranes are perforated with tiny pores that allow water vapor from perspiration to pass through but resist the passage of liquid water. The amount of water vapor these materials can pass is more than that exuded by a person at rest, but with increasing activity or in wet conditions, additional venting is needed.

Waterproof fabrics such as nonbreathable, coated nylon are treated with polyurethane, silicone, or polyvinyl chloride (PVC), providing a less-expensive alternative to waterproof-breathable materials used in raingear. *Silnylon* is nylon infused with silicone, giving it much better tear strength, allowing thinner and lighter fabrics to be used. These materials block wind and rain but also trap in the moisture generated by the body. This can lead to a buildup of moisture in clothing worn under the coated layer, so effective ventilation is absolutely necessary.

A **vapor barrier** is a thin, water-vapor-impermeable layer worn next to the skin (or over lightweight undergarments) to block perspiration and evaporative heat loss from the skin. This system is most effective at very cold temperatures when you're not very active. At higher temperatures or levels of effort, these layers become saunas.

The Layers

First, or base, or wicking, layer is the layer that touches your skin. It is mainly chosen for comfort, but it does provide some insulation. It normally consists of long underwear, usually made of performance fabrics that absorb little moisture and keep the skin dry. Cotton should be avoided. Polyester has become more popular than polypropylene, which tends to trap odor. For most activities, thin underwear is more versatile than medium- or expedition-weight underwear. Some people take a clean, dry set to sleep in, both to stay warm and to keep their sleeping bag clean.

Middle, or insulating, layer(s). While the first layer keeps the skin comfortable, the middle layer provides most of the insulation needed to protect against the cold. You'll likely have to adjust the ventilation to this layer often, as the temperature rises and falls and as your activity waxes and wanes.

You may carry several items to function as middle layers. In warm weather, this is your shirt and pants or shorts. In cooler weather, your middle layer could be a long-sleeved wool or lightweight fleece shirt—but not cotton flannel. In colder weather, this layer may be replaced with, or layered over, either a wool or synthetic sweater or a fleece jacket. Fleece pants go under synthetic hiking pants to protect the legs in very cold weather or when lounging around camp (fleece has no wind protection of its own). Down-filled or synthetic-filled vests, jackets, or parkas (a long jacket with a hood) can be used next, but remember that down does not insulate when it gets wet. Avoid middle layers that also have a heavy, bulky outer shell. You lose versatility and add weight.

Your best insulating layer is your sleeping bag. If you get cold, it becomes apparel. Save the weight of another layer and go to bed!

Outer, or shell, layer. In cold or wet weather conditions, the outer layer is extremely important. The outer shell of your layering system blocks wind and sheds rain and snow. Adequate ventilation (zippered openings) must be provided so plenty of air can reach the middle insulating layer when needed, so a zippered jacket is better than a pullover, and underarm zippers ("pit zips") help a lot. Pants with full-length leg zippers provide for both ventilation and ease of putting them on over boots. The fit should be loose to allow room for all the inner layers. Coated nylon is inexpensive and very effective in shedding rain, but it traps moisture and requires a great deal of ventilation. A low-cost outer-shell system could consist of wind-repellent (uncoated) nylon pants and jacket, plus a two-piece coated-nylon rain suit. Use the coated garments over the uncoated ones when it is cold. Under warmer storm conditions, you could use the coated layer alone. A more expensive solution is a jacket or parka and pants made of Gore-Tex or eVent waterproof-breathable or similar material. This can keep you a little drier but still requires fully adjustable ventilation.

When you are hiking with a backpack, a coated-nylon poncho worn over both your body and pack is sometimes the best solution for warm, no-wind rain protection because of its good ventilation, and it can also serve as an emergency shelter. Ponchos can act like sails in a wind, but you can install grommets and use a string along the edge of the poncho to run a tighter ship. Use rain chaps with the poncho to keep your legs dry. Ponchos are more difficult to use off-trail or in the desert because of snagging and because the poncho can obstruct your view of your feet.

Shop carefully for your outer garments. Some rain and wind shells contain too many pockets, extras, or styling features that simply add to the weight of what should be a lightweight, functional article of clothing. When you buy, ask whether the garment has factory-sealed seams or whether you will have to seal them, and if so, with what.

Fabric Care

The coating on coated nylon can peel with age or machine washing. You can prolong the life of coated raingear by hand-washing and air-drying only when necessary. Raingear is cleaned every time it rains!

Most of the technical outerwear we buy comes with a durable water-repellent (DWR) coating, but it is removed by wear or laundering; rain will bead up and roll off when the jacket is new but will soak in after you have washed it several times or when it is dirty or abraded. You can buy products that will temporarily restore the DWR coating. The products cost about $10 for one washer load, so wash several jackets and share the cost, then machine dry or iron on a low setting. Make sure the DWR product is recommended for the type of fabric or membrane used to waterproof your garment.

Headwear

Did you ever hear the maxim "If your feet are cold, cover your head"? It's true. In fact, the whole body benefits when you contain the heat that leaks skyward from the blood-rich vessels of the head. Use the layering system here as well. A lightweight balaclava (hood) that covers your head and mouth but allows you to breathe also allows you to reclaim warm moisture from your breath. A second hat or knitted cap adds middle-layer insulation.

The outer layer is simply the hood of your parka or other shell garment. It should have enough of a brim to keep rain off your face, but if it doesn't, wear a visor underneath. Pulling the drawstring narrows the opening to your face, helping to prevent heat loss.

Handwear

Use the layering system for your hands by wearing gloves and mittens. Mittens are warmer than gloves but must be removed for dexterity. A combination of a thin liner glove with thick wool or fleece gloves or mittens solves this and provides insulation.

Wet conditions are a real test for handwear. When you're active, mittens or gloves can easily soak up water, but not enough body heat is delivered to your hands to evaporate it, so waterproof mitten shells are your outer defense. Gloves and mittens are easily lost, so the almost negligible weight of an extra pair of lightweight gloves is good insurance. To quickly find both of your gloves or mittens in your pack, safety-pin them together if they don't include their own fastener. Chemical heat packs are excellent for all-day hand and foot warmth in the cold.

SHELTER: TENTS AND TARPS

Sleeping under the stars on a clear, bug-free night is a glorious experience. But when there's wind, snow, rain, or annoying insects, a tent is most welcome. In extreme situations, your survival may depend on a sturdy shelter. One that's large enough to hold packs as well as people is convenient, but you'll have to balance the comfort of having a bigger shelter against the discomfort of carrying it.

Tent costs vary dramatically. Cost is based on materials, quality of construction, design, features, and options. When shopping for a tent, consider the following features:

- anticipated seasons of use: three- or four-season
- size and weight
- ease of setup
- ease of entry and exit
- ventilation efficiency: doors, windows, bug screening, storm flaps
- cost and durability
- freestanding or nonfreestanding
- double-walled or single-walled (or a hybrid of these two)
- vestibule(s) for cooking and storage: a vestibule is a space created where the rain fly extends away from the tent body like a porch roof over each door of the tent; it is useful for cooking in bad weather, storage of gear, and keeping the inside of the tent dry when you are entering or exiting during rain or snow

Types of Tents

Freestanding. With a freestanding tent, the framework of the poles will hold up the tent without it being staked to the ground, and the tent can be moved. Freestanding tents tend to be heavier than nonfreestanding tents because of the greater number of poles. All tents should be staked down anyway—don't count on the weight of your gear to hold down the tent in a strong wind. A sudden wind may blow your unstaked tent and your gear into a lake or over a cliff!

Nonfreestanding. A nonfreestanding tent needs to be staked down or it will collapse, and so it can't be easily moved once set up.

Double-walled. A double-walled tent consists of a tent body, usually with a floor, and a separate waterproof cover called a rain fly. Because of the protection of the rain fly, part of the tent body can be netting to allow for the ventilation needed in any tent to reduce condensation inside. The rain fly can be left off in fair weather for better ventilation or a better view outside. Because of their two separate parts, double-walled tents tend to be heavier than single-walled or hybrid tents, but they ventilate best.

Some double-walled tents have a fast-pitch option in which the rain fly, poles, and a separately available ground cloth called a *footprint* are used together without the tent body to make an open shelter (more like a tarp tent) that is lighter than the entire tent assembly would be.

Single-walled. Single-walled tents have eliminated the rain fly to save weight and bulk. The tent body itself is waterproof, with its ventilation netting being protected from rain or snow by storm flaps or covers instead of a rain fly. Because there is less area of netting, condensation can be more of a problem than in double-walled tents or in hybrids, and you can wake up to find little drops of water falling on you from moisture condensing on the walls inside the tent. Single-walled tents made of a waterproof-breathable fabric perform a little better in this regard. They generally work best in dry climates.

Hybrids. Hybrid tents use the good features of both double-walled and single-walled tents: they have a waterproof tent body with a permanently attached partial rain fly placed where it is needed most, which allows for much more ventilation than is available with a single-walled tent, with a savings of some weight.

Tent Tips

- If the tent seams are not factory sealed, you will need to seam-seal them before use and every few years after. High winds will loosen the seams. Don't forget to buy the seam-sealer if it doesn't come with the tent.

- When comparing tents to buy, use the "trail weight"—the combined weight of the tent body, rain fly, and poles only—to make sure you are comparing exactly the same parts.
- A ground cloth can be used under the tent to protect the floor. You can buy one made to fit your tent, called a footprint, or you can just make your own from inexpensive 2-mil or 4-mil plastic sheeting. Cut it slightly smaller than the tent floor so it doesn't catch rain and cause a pool beneath your tent.
- Always pitch a tent (especially a floorless tent) in a spot with good drainage and use LNT techniques. See Chapter 2, "Leave No Trace: Outdoor Ethics," for how to do it right!
- Always set up your new tent at home before heading out into the backcountry. You need to practice in good conditions, and there may be a missing or broken part that could totally disable the tent.

Tarps, Tarp Tents, and Bivy Sacks

Tarps are the simplest and usually the lightest form of shelter. A simple tarp is a flat piece of waterproof or waterproof-breathable fabric with grommets to fasten lines to suspend it or to guy it out. Tarps may use trekking poles for support. They are inexpensive, pack up small, and give more living space than a tent. They do not provide as much protection from insects and the elements, and they take some practice to learn to pitch correctly.

Tarp tents are more like very lightweight single-walled tents without a floor. They may have their own pole, or you can use trekking poles to save weight. Cuben fiber, a strong and thin nonwoven laminate, is popular for this category of shelter. Large, lightweight, floorless pyramid tents that give a lot of room for their weight are also available (the ultimate tarp tent).

Bivy (short for bivouac, an unplanned overnight stay) sacks are one-person bags that slip on like raingear over your sleeping bag. They can be very light but usually don't have much room inside for your pack, boots, or gear. If they have any pole at all, it will be at your head, so the rest of the bag lies on top of your sleeping bag, which means waterproof-breathable fabrics are useful here. Bivy sacks make your sleeping bag warmer.

SLEEPING SYSTEM

Comfort on the trail is much different than comfort at home. Your tent doesn't have a heater, so you must rely on a good sleeping bag and sleeping pad. Increase warmth by wearing a warm hat when you sleep or taking a bottle of hot water to bed. Avoid restless or chilly nights by discovering the right combination of clothing, keeping-warm routines, and sleeping equipment.

Sleeping Bags

Your sleeping bag is the most important component of a warm night's sleep. The warmth of a sleeping bag depends primarily on the amount of loft, or thickness, of the insulating layer. The more dead (trapped) air there is between you and the cold, the warmer the bag.

Shape. Another factor is the shape of the bag. Most efficient are close-fitting bags that keep your body heat close to you. A bag that is too roomy will have air moving inside, and extra area to heat, so it will be colder. "Try on" the bags when shopping, being sure to roll over and mimic your regular sleeping behavior, and purchase a bag that is just your size.

A woman should consider buying a sleeping bag designed for a female. It will be cut narrower in the shoulders and wider in the hips, will have more insulation in the footbox and torso, and will come in shorter lengths (up to about 5 feet 10 inches—then it's on to a men's or unisex bag). Its temperature rating will also take into account that women often sleep colder than men.

Mummy bags are the lightest and warmest style because of their narrow, tapered design. Rectangular bags weigh more but offer more room—an advantage for the warm-blooded. They also open flat so that two bags can be zipped together for a twosome (bags used for this purpose must have mating zippers, so check before you buy) or used flat as a quilt. Semirectangular (modified mummy) bags are a good compromise between roominess and warmth. They are more open at the top, as opposed to the contoured hood of a mummy bag, for a less-restricted feel and easier breathing. Figure 5-4 shows the differences in shape.

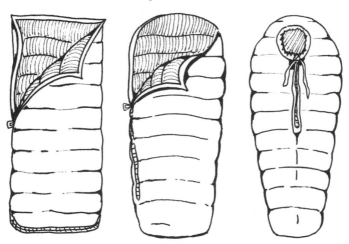

Figure 5-4. *Sleeping bags:* left, *rectangular style;* center, *semirectangular style;* right, *mummy style*

Features. Common sleeping bag features include an insulated draft collar that helps keep shoulders and neck warm, a draft tube over the zipper to prevent heat leakage through the zipper, and possibly a DWR coating or waterproof outer shell.

Temperature rating. The temperature rating on a sleeping bag tells the lowest temperature at which the average sleeper can sleep comfortably. Summer-weight bags are rated down to 35 degrees F, three-season bags are rated from 35 degrees F down to 10 degrees F, and winter bags are rated from 10 degrees F to as low as -50 degrees F. These ratings are of help in comparing bags but may not guarantee your comfort at those particular temperatures. If you tend to sleep cold or sleep without a tent, consider getting a bag with a rating 5 to 15 degrees F lower than the minimum temperature you're likely to encounter.

Using overbags or bag liners, and inserting a thin closed-cell foam pad inside your bag (between you and the top of the bag) will increase the warmth of any bag. They allow you to use a single bag to cover a broader range of seasonal conditions, but as with boots, you still may need a separate bag for winter.

Fill. Down-filled sleeping bags are lighter and more compressible than synthetic bags of the same temperature rating. They are warmer for their weight, rejuvenate better after laundering, are far more durable, and are much more expensive. When wet they're practically useless, and down is almost impossible to dry in the field, so you'll have to keep the bag dry. Some are available with waterproof-breathable shells to protect them from dew, tent condensation, and wind. These shells increase the bag's weight slightly. Down bags don't need to be cleaned very often, but when they do, they can be washed with special down soap or professionally cleaned by a company familiar with down cleaning. Check with your local outdoor-equipment outfitter for advice, and they may also offer this service.

Bags filled with synthetic materials (primarily various forms of polyester such as Polarguard, Primaloft, Climashield, etc.) are heavier and less compressible than down-filled bags, but they insulate even when wet and so are more reliable in wet conditions, can be machine-washed and dried, and are less expensive. They are not as durable. Cramming a synthetic-filled bag into a stuff sack, washing it, and exposing it to heat in a hot car or a dryer breaks down the fibers that create loft, and warmth depends on loft. Synthetic bags are great for extended winter trips, kayaking, and other outings where the bag will almost certainly get damp.

Tips. Here are pointers for getting the best performance out of any sleeping bag:

- Always fluff your bag before using it to get the maximum loft.
- Perspiration often condenses on the fibers of the insulating fill

during cold weather. Your bag, particularly if it is down, may need some drying time during the day to keep from getting heavier and colder each succeeding night.

* At home, store your sleeping bag by hanging it in the closet or uncompressed in a large bag; never keep it compressed in its stuff sack. Make sure it's fully dry before putting it away in a ventilated place.

Sleeping Pads

Sleeping pads are the foundation of your wilderness bed. No sleeping bag keeps you warm on a cold night unless you are thermally insulated from the ground. Thick pads have more insulating ability at the cost of greater weight, bulk, and expense. Short pads (48 inches long or so) under your torso are fine for summer camping if you don't mind sacrificing a little comfort. The standard 72-inch pads are best for winter. If you're using a short pad, place your pack or some clothing under your lower legs and feet for extra comfort and insulation.

Closed-cell foam pads (see Figure 5-5) are excellent insulators, do not absorb water, are lightweight, and come in several styles, thicknesses, densities, and materials. Some have ridges or a waffle pattern that reduce weight and volume while maintaining good comfort. Closed-cell foam pads are the best value for providing excellent, durable, lightweight insulation. Avoid open-cell foam pads such as mattress cushions. They're too heavy, bulky, and water-absorbent for backpacking.

Self-inflating pads (see Figure 5-5) are quite comfortable to sleep on, but they are more expensive and heavier than closed-cell foam pads of

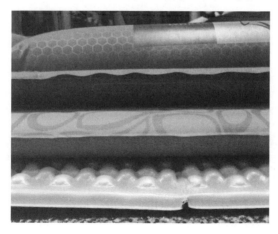

Figure 5-5. *Sleeping pads:* bottom, *closed-cell foam pad;* middle, *self-inflating pad;* top, *inflatable air mattress* (Photo by Jennifer "Spidermonkey" Lanci)

the same insulating value. They require more care on the trail to prevent punctures and valve failures (repair kits are available). If you use a ground cloth underneath and avoid punctures, they last for years.

Insulated air mattresses (see Figure 5-5) have become popular because they are lighter and more compact than self-inflating pads but are thicker and more comfortable when inflated. They are inflated by blowing into them, but they differ from earlier air mattresses by being insulated to prevent internal air circulation every time you move, so they are much warmer. They require the same care as self-inflating pads.

Pillows. Any number of soft items can be used as a pillow; place them in a stuff sack or tie them up in a bandana. Remember that on a cold night, that fleece jacket you hoped to use as a pillow might already be in use as one of your layers in your sleeping bag. Lightweight inflating pillows are available. If a pillow is important to you, figure it out at home, and test it to make sure it works with your sleeping pad.

STOVES

When choosing a backpacking stove, first consider its performance under the conditions of temperature, wind, and elevation you'll likely encounter during your trip. Also consider the stove's weight, ease of fueling and operation, reliability, stability, and availability of the fuel it uses. To help you choose the right stove, talk to people who use them and to salespeople at outdoor stores. Several outdoor magazines have published comparative information about stoves and reviews of new models. Stoves are classified by the types of fuel they burn. Stove performance is usually compared by the length of time it takes to boil one liter of water.

Stove Fuel

Various types of backpacking stoves use liquid fuels, pressurized fuel in canisters, or solid fuels. Never carry stove fuel on an airplane; you'll need to buy it locally when you reach your destination.

Liquid fuel stoves are economical to operate and have a high heat output. These stoves burn gasoline (white gas) or alcohol. Kerosene and unleaded gasoline stoves are available but are better suited for international travel, where fuel availability is an issue. In most cases, liquid fuel stoves have a start-up procedure known as priming that makes them a bit more complicated to use than canister stoves.

White gas is very flammable (which is why it's a good stove fuel), burns cleanly, and evaporates quickly when spilled. Kerosene is safer because it is less volatile than white gas and slower to ignite and evaporate, and it produces more heat per volume of fuel. However, it has a greasy feel, a lasting odor, and a tendency to give off smoke and soot when burning—more good reasons to use white gas instead. Some stove manufacturers claim that their stoves can use unleaded gasoline, but avoid it, because it will gum up your stove.

Denatured alcohol (ethanol) is the fuel of choice for homemade stove enthusiasts. They use empty soda cans to build lightweight stoves. These stoves have no moving parts, making them very reliable (but nonadjustable). There are many home-built designs available on the Internet and a few for sale ready-made. Alcohol burns clean but has the lowest heat output of the liquid fuels. Homemade stoves are more suitable for warming small meals than for group cooking or melting snow. Avoid methanol for its toxicity and low energy-to-weight ratio.

Liquid stove fuel should be carried in special fuel bottles with tight-fitting caps and special seals. Mark them clearly. For some models of liquid-fuel stoves, the tank is an integral part of the stove, while for others the stove has no tank but is designed to be connected to a fuel bottle. Some stoves have small tanks, while others run full blast for more than three hours on a single tank. Some operate from simmer to full heat, while others operate only at full blast and sound like a roaring blowtorch.

Canister fuel stoves (see Figure 5-6) have become more popular than liquid-fuel stoves. They burn propane, butane, isobutane, or an isobutane-propane mixture in a small pressurized canister. Before it is lit, the burner of the stove is attached to the metal fuel canister. Operating the stove is easy, and no priming is required. Propane is excellent in the cold, but its canisters are much heavier than butane canisters and are not recommended for backpacking. Butane and isobutane must be warmed to operate at cold temperatures, so you may have to store the canister in your sleeping bag with you overnight. Instead, use a canister filled with an isobutane-propane mixture.

Canister stoves have a built-in valve that allows for detachment from the burner between uses. It's hard to tell how much fuel is left in a canister without weighing it, so weigh the canister and mark the weight on the bottom before and after your trip, and you will soon learn how much burn time you will get out of each canister. If there is any doubt as to how much fuel you will use, always carry one or more spare cans.

Using a canister stove is quite simple in warm weather—just light a match and open the single valve. Most of these stoves have less heat output than liquid-fuel stoves that use white gas or kerosene, are a little more sensitive to the cold, and cost more to operate, but they are easy to set up and use.

There are cooking systems that combine the canister stove, windscreen, cooking pot, and fuel canister together into one unit and boil water very rapidly, but these are rather heavy and bulky.

Figure 5-6. Left, *a canister stove;* right, *a liquid fuel stove* (Photo by Henry Wilson)

Solid fuels include jellied alcohol (Sterno), waxlike heat tablets, and charcoal. These fuels are safe to handle, but all have a low heat output. With a windscreen, a very lightweight setup using homemade fuel tabs (such as Esbit) is a reliable cooking method suited to simple meals for one or two, but it is not sufficient for melting snow. They do take additional skill to use effectively, but you can make your own for free!

Windscreens

Many stoves feature a windscreen that is either part of the stove or an accessory. The fuel tank should be below or outside the windscreen, and the windscreen should never allow the fuel tank to overheat. Because all stoves are very sensitive to wind, a windscreen should be considered a mandatory piece of backpacking stove equipment.

Fueling Stoves

All stoves must be considered dangerous, but with a little knowledge and common sense, it is possible to minimize this danger. The most important thing you can do is *understand how your stove works.* **Read the instructions!** Some models have instructions printed on the stove itself. Test the stove's operation outside your home (never inside). You need to learn how to use it before you go on your trip.

Liquid fuel stoves. Here are some tips for using liquid fuel:

- Never refill a liquid-fuel stove when the stove is hot.
- Use care when pouring liquid fuel into the stove, and add fuel slowly. Check the level in the tank and don't overfill. A filter funnel or pouring cap helps keep the fuel where it's supposed to be.

- Leave an air space above the fuel. Don't fill all the way to the top of the tank.
- Refuel away from flame sources.
- Don't ever refuel inside a tent or building.
- Check the fuel level before lighting the stove to ensure that you don't run out while you're cooking.
- Replace the cap on both the fuel bottle and the stove before lighting the stove.
- Always store fuel bottles away from the cooking area to keep them from exploding.

Canister stoves. Here are some tips for using pressurized canister fuel:
- When attaching the stove to a canister, be careful. Make sure the on-off valve is closed and the gasket surfaces are clean. The screw threads should be easy to turn until tight. If you strip or damage the fittings, both the burner and canister can be ruined.
- After the canister is attached, make sure it doesn't leak by listening for a hissing noise.
- Light the match or lighter and hold it next to the burner before turning on the gas. If a butane lighter won't work in cold temperatures, warm it with body heat.
- Never throw an empty canister into a campfire. Pack it out.
- Always store canisters away from the cooking area to avoid explosion.

Using the Stove

Operating a backpacking stove can be simple and easy but hazardous if done improperly. By observing these guidelines, you can prevent accidents and end up with a warm meal:
- Never cook inside a tent. A burning stove consumes oxygen and gives off deadly carbon monoxide; many stove bases get hot enough to melt nylon tent floors and foam pads, and if the stove flares up during lighting, it can melt your rain fly.
- Make sure that the stove is in a safe place and is on a stable, level surface. Stove stability varies quite a bit among models.
- Place a full cookpot on the stove to check the stability of both together before lighting.
- Never leave a burning stove unattended.
- Carry spare parts, tools, cleaning kit, and instructions on how to repair your stove. Clean the fuel jet hole on the burner regularly.
- If your stove has a pump, oil it before each trip.
- If your stove uses a fuel tube, keep the open end covered to prevent dirt from getting in when it is not connected.

Know how to operate your stove before setting out into the wilderness.
(Photo by James Glenn Pearson)

Using Your Stove in Cold Weather

Insulate the warm bottom of the stove from the snow with a piece of plywood, high-temperature plastic, cardboard wrapped in duct tape, or something similar. A foam pad might melt.

Use caution with white gas, since if it is spilled on your skin it can cause frostbite by its rapid evaporation. For canister stoves, use an isobutane-propane mix. If frost forms on the canister while the canister is in use, you will soon burn off the propane, and you will have only butane left. You will not be able to light your stove at your next meal. To prevent this, use the stove with the canister in a shallow pan of an inch or two of warm water. Add hot water to the pan to keep the canister from frosting. A few canister stoves allow the canister to be inverted after the stove has started. This gives better cold-weather performance and more consistent output over the life of each canister.

WATER TREATMENT

It is best to assume that all water in the backcountry is unsafe to drink due to possible contamination by bacteria (*E. coli,* salmonella, etc.), parsitic protozoa *(Cryptosporidium or Giardia lamblia)* or, less commonly in North America, viruses. You can either kill the contaminants (by purification) or you can remove them (by filtration). Both methods are called "treating" the water. Neither is expected to remove odors or chemicals such as heavy metals or chlorine. Choose your water treatment method based on effectiveness, how good you want the water to taste, and the equipment's ease of use, weight, size, and cost.

Purification
Purification is done with either chemicals or ultraviolet (UV) light or by boiling. These methods of treatment are effective against all waterborne pathogens, with the exception that treatment with iodine will not kill *Cryptosporidium.*

Chemicals. The types of chemicals used are either tablets (iodine—get the kind that has a vitamin-C flavor neutralizer) or liquid in dropper bottles (chlorine dioxide). Common household bleach can also be used. All have a wait time for the chemicals to work, usually thirty to forty-five minutes, longer if the water is cold or cloudy or if crypto is suspected. Try some treated water at home to see if the chemical taste is acceptable to you.

UV light kills 99.9 percent of all bacteria, viruses, and protozoa. UV light is supplied directly into a bottle of water by a device called a SteriPEN. It is small and light, and one set of batteries will purify about fifty quarts of water.

Boiling is effective against all water-borne pathogens and does not introduce any chemicals into the water.

Filtration
Filtering removes contaminants by hand-pumping water through a cleanable filter element, which is why people often call the filtering process "pumping." In general, filters do not remove viruses, but this level of protection is considered safe for backcountry use in

Find a comfy place to sit with a view to make filtering water an enjoyable task. (Photo by Dan Girard)

the United States and Canada. One brand of filter, FirstNeed, does remove viruses and is considered a purifier.

Sip-and-squeeze bottles have a filter element in the cap or straw so as you drink, the water is filtered. Gravity filters save you the work of pumping by using gravity to pull the water through the filter element.

COOKWARE

Economize, but don't skimp, on your cookware and utensils, and be alert to keeping weights down. You can modify ordinary pans by removing or shortening their handles, but backpacking pots made of thin stainless steel or titanium will probably be much lighter. Some come with a nonstick surface and heat-absorbing black exteriors. Some cook sets consist of two pots nested together with handles that fold aside or no handles at all (a pot gripper is used). A pot lid can sometimes be used as a frying pan. One small pot or a cup per person may suffice for one or two people, but fancier meals and larger cook groups will require two pots.

It is very helpful to have your cookware marked with common intervals of volume measurement (1 cup, 2 cups, etc.). If your pots are not already marked, carefully do it yourself by making small dents with a hammer and screwdriver.

If you're cooking only for yourself, simply eat from the pot or pan. Otherwise, each person needs a cup or bowl to eat from. Try disposable plastic bowls and cups for permanent use, but make sure that hot food or liquid won't melt them or burn your hand. As a minimum for utensils, use a pocketknife for cutting food and a lightweight, unbreakable spoon for eating—a fork is nice but not necessary. A cook group also needs a large, lightweight spoon for stirring and serving. An insulated plastic cup, with or without a lid, keeps your beverage or soup hot. Any cup can have its volume measured and marked at home.

A few other useful items, depending on what you cook, include resealable plastic bags, which are handy for mixing beverages, pancake batter, and pudding; a spoon takes the place of your mixer back home. Don't forget a *small* can opener if you have canned food, a measuring cup (if you're not using your cup for this), aluminum foil for a variety of uses, and a spatula if you need one.

For cleaning up, you might want a very small pot scrubber. Some people just use very hot water without soap for washing dishes, and for a one-night trip you can just wait and wash them at home. But if your food is particularly greasy, the bears will love you, so you may want to use a very small amount of biodegradable soap and wash well away (200 feet, equivalent to eighty paces) from any water source.

PACKS

The pack you choose greatly affects how much you enjoy the sport. Fit and style are as personal with packs as they are with shoes, and what works great for one person may not work for you. The types of packs are these, from smallest to largest:

- **Fanny pack:** can hold 120 to 1000 cubic inches or 2 to 16 liters; weighs ½ to 1½ pounds. This is simply a bag on a waist belt, so all the weight is on your hips with none on your shoulders; your back stays cooler, but fanny packs (also called waist packs) are often too small for the Ten Essentials.
- **Hydration pack:** carries a water reservoir and sometimes not much else. Often too small for the Ten Essentials.
- **Small day pack:** can hold 1200 to 2000 cubic inches or 20 to 32 liters; weighs 1 to 2 pounds. These can be used not only for day hikes but also for day hikes on backpacking trips.
- **Full day pack:** can hold 2000 to 3000 cubic inches or 32 to 49 liters; weighs 1½ to 4 pounds. These are suitable for longer day hikes or for short backpacking trips (with gear strapped to the outside).
- **Backpack (internal frame or external frame):** can hold 3000 to 6000 cubic inches or 49 to 98 liters; weighs 3 to 8 pounds. These are best for overnight trips.

Figure 5-7. *Frame packs:* left, *internal-frame pack;* right, *external-frame pack*

Day Packs

For day hikes or peak climbs, you'll need a day pack. These vary from light and simple bags with quick-dry mesh straps to fully constructed load haulers with internal frames. You may need a pack holding as much as 2500 cubic inches (40 liters) to carry your Ten Essentials and other necessary gear. Low bulk is important if the smaller pack has to fit inside a backpack. A large day pack (3000 cubic inches or 32 liters) can be used for multiday backpacking if you strap your sleeping bag and pad on the outside. The pack is then small enough to also use as a day pack, and this can save 2 pounds or more.

Backpacks

Your backpack is a key component of your gear. For recreational (as opposed to expedition) backpacking, you'll need a pack capacity of 4000 to 5500 cubic inches (65.5 to 90.1 liters) in an internal-frame pack and 3000 to 3500 cubic inches (49.2 to 57.6 liters) in an external-frame pack. Don't be tempted to buy too big a backpack. What you choose to put in your pack always seems to exceed the capacity anyway. Choose the size that fits your needs most of the time. You can always securely strap items to the sides or rent a larger pack when you require extra capacity.

Women choosing a backpack should consider not only men's or unisex packs but packs designed specifically for a woman's shape. A pack designed for a woman has shorter torso lengths available, has narrower shoulder straps set closer together, and has a hip belt designed to accommodate the curve of the hip. Packs designed for women are not women's packs; they are just designed for a woman's shape and will also fit some men perfectly.

Internal-frame backpacks are currently very popular. As their names suggest, internal-frame packs and external-frame packs (see Figure 5-7) differ from each other in that internal-frame packs have vertical stays (curved, rigid bars) inside the pack sack, and external-frame packs have the frame on the outside of the pack sack. Internal-frame packs are relatively compact and streamlined, and they should fit snugly against your body; if properly designed and adjusted, they will feel more balanced than external-frame packs. Internal-frame backpacks are equally well suited to trails and rough terrain. They're designed to hold sleeping bags, tents, pads, and all your gear inside. Adjustable straps compress the load and keep it from shifting.

Drawbacks of internal-frame packs include generally higher cost, heavier weight, more difficulty in getting to your gear (in top-loading models, particularly, but a top compartment helps), and less air circulation for your back.

External-frame backpacks have a rigid, exposed frame structure that keeps the load slightly away from your body, allowing for more air circulation to your back and for vertical weight to be transferred to the hips so you can stand more upright. These packs need, and have, fewer adjustments. Sleeping bag, pad, and tent strap onto areas provided for them outside of the pack bag on the frame, and most other gear fits inside the pack or the pack's many outside pockets. External-frame packs are easier to load and handle heavy loads better than most internal-frame packs.

Since weight is carried high, they can feel tippy and off-balance, so they are best suited for trails. Most external-frame packs are light but bulky, a drawback when trying to fit several packs in the trunk of a car.

Manufacturers of both styles are working to blend the best features of each. Many internal-frame models now have divided compartments for easier access to gear, and they now handle heavier loads with more comfort. Some newer lightweight internal-frame-style backpacks have a minimal frame, and some have no frame but use a sleeping pad as an internal stiffener. The newer external-frame packs are becoming less boxy and more contoured, to enhance their stability while maintaining their carrying volume.

Features and Fit

More features mean more weight, so do pay attention to the overall weight of the empty pack, but the weight of the load is much greater than the weight of the features that make the pack carry a load more comfortably: wide, padded shoulder straps; a padded hip belt; load lifter straps at the top of the pack; a sternum strap across the chest (not only takes the load off your shoulders but also helps you stand more upright). Backpacks can have adjustment for torso length, a pocket and port for a hydration reservoir, side pockets for water bottles or snacks, elastic cords or gear loops for stowing gear on the outside, and a top compartment that might be detachable to use as a fanny pack. Some will have a front pocket, waterproof fabric and zippers, or a suspended ventilation panel to keep your back cooler. And remember, features are nice, but fit is king.

Correct fit is the most important factor in pack comfort. Don't try to correct bad fit with adjustment. Never buy a pack without trying it or a similar rental first. Have your torso measured, select the right size for your body frame, load it up with thirty pounds, and walk, climb up and down, tip, turn, and twist. Try the pack on while wearing your hiking hat and clothing to see if there is any interference. Make sure the top of the pack doesn't hit you in the back of your head and your arms don't rub the shoulder straps or side pockets. If the pack feels like an extension of your body, moves with you, and doesn't poke or gouge, you've found a winner! If you can, rent it for a weekend backpack trip. The pack shouldn't cause excessively sore spots on your shoulders, hips, back, or elsewhere.

Once you've been fitted and have made your choice, ask that your pack be adjusted properly to fit the exact size and contours of your body. Ask if there is someone in the store who specializes in this and, just as if you were fitting boots, speak up if something doesn't seem right.

Packing

When you try out a backpack, understand that the perceived load may vary by as much as 10 pounds, depending on how you distribute items inside. Place the heaviest items in the bottom, close to your back. Don't hang anything swinging out from the back of the pack. Adjust the hip belt first and then the shoulder straps to distribute weight slightly more on the hips than the shoulders.

Pack Covers

If your pack is not waterproof, you can either rainproof the contents by lining your pack with a large trash bag, or you can rainproof the whole pack with a pack cover. Pack covers come in different sizes and are made of coated nylon or silnylon. They are also helpful for keeping your pack dry if you have to leave it outside the tent during the night. Another alternative is to hike with a poncho over both you and your pack. (See "The Layers" earlier in this chapter.)

GETTING LIGHTER

There are advanced techniques for dramatically lowering your pack weight, but they are outside the scope of this book. The goal for your base pack weight might be half that of a traditional system. Trips of limited duration, with more experienced leaders, are perfect opportunities for trying out lighter gear systems. One of the main things you are doing when lightening your load is trading knowledge and experience for weight and safety. You don't want to go too crazy on lightening your pack before you have that knowledge.

Table 5-1 is a sample equipment list that you can use to make sure you bring everything you need. This list can be adjusted for different types of trips. It is not intended that a person pack everything on the list. This checklist covers a wide variety of different types of trips and a variety of seasons, weather, and trail conditions. Use it as a framework for personalizing your own packing checklist.

TABLE 5-1. PACKING CHECKLIST

- ❑ Trail permit
- ❑ Ground cloth (footprint)
- ❑ Tent, poles, stakes, and rain fly
- ❑ Sleeping pad
- ❑ Sleeping bag and waterproof stuff sack
- ❑ Backpack and pack cover
- ❑ Day pack
- ❑ Fanny pack
- ❑ Pack and tent repair kit
- ❑ Trekking poles
- ❑ Sunscreen and lip balm
- ❑ Insect repellent
- ❑ Skin cream
- ❑ First-aid kit, field medical guide
- ❑ Pocketknife
- ❑ Candle
- ❑ Matches (waterproof) or lighter
- ❑ Flashlight or headlamp
- ❑ Extra batteries
- ❑ Whistle
- ❑ Signal mirror
- ❑ Maps and compass
- ❑ Large trash bag or other emergency shelter
- ❑ Wallet or plastic bag with driver's license, credit card, health insurance information, emergency contact, and money
- ❑ Guidebook and/or excerpts
- ❑ Nylon cord or rope
- ❑ Pencil and paper
- ❑ Needle and thread (or dental floss)
- ❑ Extra water in car at trail's end
- ❑ Clean clothes in car for drive home
- ❑ Toilet paper, plastic bags, trowel, and disinfectant
- ❑ Toothbrush, toothpaste, and floss
- ❑ Towel or washcloth
- ❑ Personal items and prescriptions
- ❑ Socks: outer and liner
- ❑ Boots or hiking shoes
- ❑ Lightweight camp shoes
- ❑ Snow and ice traction devices
- ❑ Glacier glasses (for snow travel)
- ❑ Gaiters
- ❑ Pants: long, short, and warm pullovers
- ❑ Underwear: regular and long
- ❑ Shirts: long-sleeved and short-sleeved
- ❑ Sweater, warm jacket, or parka
- ❑ Wind gear: jacket and pants
- ❑ Eyeglasses, sunglasses, and retainers
- ❑ Sun hat
- ❑ Cold-weather hat (wool or fleece)
- ❑ Gloves and shell overmitts
- ❑ Hand warmers and foot warmers
- ❑ Bandana
- ❑ Raingear
- ❑ Swimsuit
- ❑ Extra clothing
- ❑ Pot and pot gripper
- ❑ Cup, bowl, and utensils
- ❑ Biodegradable soap
- ❑ Stove, windscreen, repair kit
- ❑ Fuel
- ❑ Water reservoir, water bottles
- ❑ Water treatment: chlorine, iodine, filter, or ultraviolet light
- ❑ Collapsible water carrier
- ❑ Breakfast, lunch, dinner, and trail snacks
- ❑ Warm beverage
- ❑ Electrolyte replacement
- ❑ Extra food and water
- ❑ Paper towels or moist disposable towelettes
- ❑ Plastic bags (for wet clothes, trash, used toilet paper, water or vapor barrier for feet)
- ❑ Bear canister or stuff sack and rope
- ❑ Duct tape
- ❑ Extra car key for another hiker to carry
- ❑ Sit pad or chair
- ❑ Walkie-talkies
- ❑ Cell phone
- ❑ Wristwatch
- ❑ GPS device
- ❑ Camera
- ❑ Binoculars
- ❑ Altimeter, thermometer, or pedometer

chapter
6

"Eating Out"
in the Wilderness

Pauline Jimenez, Priscilla Anderson, Scott Anderson, and Carolyn Moser

Old photographs of large group outings such as those by the Sierra Club or The Mountaineers show people cooking great quantities of food in cauldrons, with wooden tables lined up beneath giant trees and piled high with freshly baked bread. But John Muir, founder of the Sierra Club, wrote, "My meals were easily made, for they were all alike and simple, only a cup of tea and bread."

You can emulate John Muir and subsist quite comfortably on a variety of uncooked foods. Or you can bring along a small camp stove, lightweight cookware, and a variety of ingredients to whip up a great feast at the end of each day. Your choices of what to eat in the wilderness and how to prepare it have never been broader.

NUTRITION BASICS

Some people believe backpacking is a good way to lose weight, and some may fast in the outdoors for health or spiritual benefits, but wilderness travel usually demands more calories, not fewer. Poor nutrition can decrease your endurance and limit your body's ability to repair itself after a hard day of hiking. Lack of food or energy reserves lowers your morale and clouds decision-making skills, which could be dangerous if an emergency arises.

Symptoms of malnourishment include more than just hunger and weight loss. Not enough food (or the wrong kinds of food) can cause depression and lack of energy, leaving you incapable of a positive outlook. Use good nutrition to keep your body healthy and your mind alert, especially when out in the wilderness.

On a hike or backpack, you will need to modify a low-calorie diet. The number of calories you need depends on factors such as your body size, metabolism, length of the trip, pack size, pace, terrain, temperature, etc. For a short, leisurely trip you may need to raise your caloric intake only slightly, but your intake will increase on long, strenuous trips.

If you know you have special nutritional requirements, take them into account. For instance, a pregnant woman may need to increase her protein intake. A person with diabetes may need to bring hard candy for medical emergencies (see "Diabetic Emergencies" in Chapter 13, "Ouch! First Aid in the Backcountry"). If you're on a medically supervised diet, consult with your doctor to determine how to adjust your program. Important nutritional components include the following, which are covered in more depth below:

- water
- carbohydrates
- proteins
- fats
- fiber
- vitamins and minerals

Water and Fluids

Always remember that water is the most important thing to drink and carry with you. Drink before you start your hike, and keep yourself hydrated throughout the day. Remember that thirst comes *after* your body begins to dehydrate, so it is not the best indicator of your needs.

Fluid intake is critically important during strenuous exercise. Most of us have experienced the discomforts of "cotton-mouth," dizziness, weakness, and headaches when exercising heavily on hot days. These conditions are symptoms of dehydration—the loss of water and minerals from the body. Dehydration impairs your judgment and coordination, and it makes you more vulnerable to altitude sickness, hypothermia, and heatstroke (and, of course, death).

Lost body fluids must be replaced by drinking water or other fluids and by eating *sodium- and potassium-rich foods* such as these:

- soy sauce
- cottage cheese
- tomato juice

- cheddar cheese
- beans
- spinach
- raisins
- potatoes
- oranges
- bananas
- milk

You should generally consume one gallon (four quarts) of water or other fluids per day. In the desert or with heavy exertion, you may need much more, and in cool or wet conditions you may need less. With experience, you'll learn what your body requires. Drink small amounts at frequent intervals rather than a large amount at one long gulping session. Drink regularly and often. Some beverage choices include these:

- teas
- hot cocoa
- powdered fruit drinks (such as Kool-Aid, hot Jell-O mix, and spiced cider)
- powdered electrolyte or vitamin supplements (such as Emergen-C)
- soups and broths

Sports drinks. For vigorous hikes lasting longer than an hour, you need to *replace carbohydrates as well as fluids*. Unlike water, some sports drinks can replace both. The drinks that work best during exercise contain 13–21 grams of carbohydrates per cup. Those with more carbohydrates slow digestion and can cause cramping, nausea, bloating, and diarrhea during exercise. Those with less won't get enough fuel to your muscles fast enough.

Check the ingredients list for sugars (such as sucrose, fructose, glucose, and maltodextrin). Avoid those with a high concentration of fructose because this can slow hydration and upset your stomach. Some fructose is fine, but make sure it is not the first or only ingredient listed. Other ingredients to check for include sodium, potassium, minerals, and electrolytes. A small amount of sodium (less than that found in sweat) encourages you to drink more and helps you retain water (to prevent dehydration). Choose a drink with 100–110 milligrams of sodium and about 30 milligrams of potassium per 8-ounce serving.

Coffee drinkers should be aware that caffeine is a diuretic that increases urine output, so it is worse than useless as a fluid replacement. It is also a stimulant that increases your heart rate and causes blood pressure to rise.

Alcohol is an even stronger diuretic than coffee, and it decreases your appetite. Taken in excess, it generates a feeling of warmth for a short time, but it actually promotes a net loss of heat in cold conditions. Alcohol impairs your judgment, balance, coordination, and awareness. These effects are multiplied at high altitude. Simply put, excessive alcohol consumption puts you at risk in an unforgiving environment.

Carbohydrates

Carbohydrates are the staple of a hiker's diet; they come in two forms.

Complex carbohydrates are high-nutrient foods that include whole-grain products (such as rice, wheat, quinoa, and buckwheat), vegetables (such as carrots, potatoes, and sugar-snap peas), beans, fruits, and berries. Complex carbohydrates are high-energy calories that are stored in the liver and muscles as glycogen. Generally, you have enough stored glycogen to last through about one and a half hours of vigorous exercise. To keep your body working effectively, you must replenish these reserves with frequent snacks throughout the day. *Somewhere between 50 and 70 percent of your total daily calories should be from carbohydrates.*

If you forget to eat frequently or skip meals, exhaustion may come within only a few hours. When this happens, it usually takes more than twenty-four hours to restore your glycogen reserves. This means recovery for tomorrow's hike will be slow. Even with frequent snacks, your glycogen reserves can be depleted. Complex carbohydrates enter the bloodstream faster than animal protein, so remember to eat complex carbohydrates and hydrate well within thirty to sixty minutes after you stop hiking. You can stoke your reserves again later with a wholesome evening meal.

Simple carbohydrates include sugar, honey, agave nectar, jams, and candy. Since most of these are metabolized quickly, they can be beneficial in very small amounts or when combined with other foods. These are quick but nutritionally vapid calories. In some people, they can cause a "sugar-high, sugar-low" syndrome, which is a chain reaction that leads to an over-reaction of the pancreas and low blood sugar levels.

Protein

Protein is best eaten regularly in small amounts because it is either used immediately for muscle renewal and repair or it is stored as fat. A complete protein contains twenty-two amino acids. Fourteen of these are produced in the body, but eight essential amino acids are not. Amino acids combine in various ways to produce proteins, which then combine to produce cell components, structural fibers, organs, and tissues. You need protein to help fight disease; build, repair, and maintain body tissue; and keep your brain cells thinking and your blood flowing.

There is debate about how much protein is too much. Some researchers believe that high consumption of protein could result in kidney disease, osteoporosis, and some forms of cancer.

The World Health Organization notes that people need to consume

5 percent of their calories from protein, and some experts recommend a safety margin of 10 percent. Others assert that 20 to 30 percent of your daily calories should be from proteins.

Some backpackers base their entire diet on plant proteins because these also supply important vitamins, minerals, carbohydrates, and fiber. Even if you are not a vegetarian at home, plant-based proteins add variety to your meals and make sense on a backpack because they are usually lighter, cheaper, and more colorful than animal proteins. Eaten regularly and in variety, plant-based proteins (complex carbohydrates such as whole grains, fruits, nuts, legumes, and vegetables) give your body a double benefit of quickly absorbed glycogen *and* complete protein. Examples of complex carbohydrate partnerships that combine all twenty-two amino acids to form complete proteins include the following:

Grains and legumes:
- rice and beans
- lentils and rice
- tamale pie (beans and cornbread)
- refried beans and tortillas
- peanut butter sandwich
- cornbread and lentil soup
- hummus and wheat crackers
- baked beans and Boston brown bread

Legumes and seeds:
- peanuts and sunflower seeds in your trail mix
- three-bean salad topped with toasted pecans
- hummus or tofu with tahini (ground sesame seeds)

Dairy products and complex carbohydrates (animal proteins derived from dairy products can combine well with many kinds of complex carbohydrates):
- macaroni and cheese
- cheese and wheat crackers
- pasta with cheese
- milk and cereal
- rice pudding
- bread pudding
- pancakes (whole wheat flour and milk-egg batter)
- bean chili with cheese
- yogurt topped with chopped nuts

Animal proteins (products such as jerky or canned meat, fish, eggs, and powdered milk) are complete proteins, but their nutrients are slower to enter your bloodstream than those of plant-based proteins because they digest more slowly. Some types of animal proteins may not be practical for longer trips or for hiking in hot weather (due to spoilage and weight). These proteins (typically meats) are slower to digest and leave you feeling satisfied longer, but they can also make you sluggish when eaten at the wrong time.

The US Department of Agriculture and the US Department of Health Services have affirmed that all of the body's nutritional needs, including protein, can be met through a plant-based diet. Eating a wide array of nuts, seeds, beans, vegetables (such as dark leafy greens), sea vegetables (such as kelp, kombu, and wakame), fruits, and sprouted grains (such as quinoa and wheat berries) will easily meet your protein needs. Good protein supplements also include spirulina (a freshwater blue-green algae superfood) and nutritional yeast (a plant-based culture generally extracted from molasses that contains up to 50 percent protein). Two heaping tablespoons of nutritional yeast (also called brewer's yeast) contains 110 calories and 17–18 grams of protein, B vitamins, and iron. It adds a unique flavor to sauces, grains, and beans.

Fats

Fats provide more energy per ounce and keep you satisfied longer than either carbohydrates or proteins, but they take even longer to digest. When eaten with a meal, foods such as avocados, ground flaxseed, almonds, and olives contain oils that help your body absorb fat-soluble vitamins (A, D, E, and K). Essential fatty acids (omega-3 and omega-6) are also vital for blood clotting, brain development, and controlling inflammation. Heart-healthy unsaturated fat sources include almonds and other nuts, ground hemp seeds, corn oil, and olive oil. Saturated fat sources include butter, cocoa butter, margarine, coconut oil, palm oil, dairy cheeses, and animal fat.

It is best to include the majority of your day's fat in the evening because fats are easier to digest when you are at rest. Eating small amounts of healthy fats keeps you from becoming hungry during the night and helps you stay warm. You should increase fat consumption when dealing with extreme cold (snow camping), but also be aware that fats eaten in large quantities at high altitudes may cause indigestion. *For backpacking, about 20 to 25 percent of your daily calories should come from fats.*

Vitamins and Minerals

Vitamins and minerals enable your body to make the best use of the food you eat. Eating a variety of foods is the best way to ensure that you get all the vitamins and minerals your body requires. Commercial supplements are usually a good idea, especially if you are uncertain about your vitamin and mineral needs.

Calcium. Foods that are high in calcium are especially important to

long-distance hikers. Examples include the following:
- dark leafy greens
- soybeans
- white beans
- raw tahini (sesame seed butter)
- blackstrap molasses
- kelp
- some fish (such as sardines, salmon, perch, and rainbow trout)
- oatmeal
- some breakfast cereals

Fiber

Fiber in foods is important because it increases the efficiency of your digestive tract, lowers blood cholesterol levels, promotes weight loss, and helps you feel more satisfied with a smaller quantity of food. Sources of fiber include whole grains, nuts, fruits, berries, and vegetables.

TYPES OF FOOD

Compared to explorers like John Muir, today's hikers and backpackers have a world of tasty choices available for food provisions. You can decide whether you should take fresh, frozen, canned, dehydrated, or freeze-dried foods using factors such as the availability of water, weather conditions, difficulties of terrain and pace, number of hiking days, and pack weight. Your meals will be more appetizing if you incorporate a variety of foods.

Fresh and frozen foods are the healthiest foods you can bring, but most of them spoil easily and weigh a lot. They are great for weekend trips but less practical for longer trips. Some homemade breads, energy bars, and cereal mixes will keep for days or weeks and also have high energy-to-weight ratios.

If you make your own foods in advance, you can control the ingredients and/or reduce additives such as preservatives. Some ultralight backpackers make it a practice to carry only foods that yield at least 100 calories per ounce.

Canned foods expand your choices because they do not spoil. However, the weight of the packaging is a consideration on longer journeys (remember that you'll have to pack out the empty cans). Certain flavorful items that will enhance your versatility in meal planning are available in small cans.

Dehydrated food can be bought as prepackaged meals (turkey tetrazzini, beef amandine, etc.) or as individual-item packages. Commercial freeze-dried processes remove about 96 percent of the moisture, whereas home dehydration removes about 90 percent. That's not bad, considering the money you will save for the little time invested and the control you have over what goes into the food. Almost any kind of food can be dehydrated.

If you have the inclination, you can dehydrate your own food at home. The process is fairly simple and can be done in an oven, but best results are obtained from a food dehydrator. You can home-dry fruit leather, spaghetti sauce, chili, salsa, thinly sliced fruit, vegetables, jerky, and stew. You can even double a favorite meal at home, eating half and dehydrating the other half for a future trip. Home-drying gives you variety, nutrition, your own choice of ingredients, and homemade taste.

A disadvantage of dehydrated foods is that some can be slow to rehydrate. You can start the process several hours before making camp by mixing the dehydrated food with water to soak in a carefully sealed container or water bottle (allow space for the food to approximately double in volume as it rehydrates). When you arrive in camp, simply heat your dinner and eat!

Freeze-dried foods offer good alternatives for longer trips because they are light in weight, offer lots of variety with little fuss, and almost never spoil. They are widely available at grocery stores and camping supply stores and by mail order. Some of these foods are laced with chemical additives, but some companies offer healthier alternatives.

Freeze-dried foods tend to be expensive and may need longer cooking times than the package indicates, and the servings are generally on the small side. A "large" packet (four 8-ounce servings) will usually feed only two people. The foil packaging does not burn in a campfire, so be sure to carry out the trash. Some specialty foods, such as freeze-dried strawberries or precooked, freeze-dried beans, can be well worth the cost.

Wild foods that you forage can in some cases supplement your diet. However, this requires specialized knowledge of plants and their uses. Learning about nonpoisonous and edible plants and gathering them in the right areas can add a new appreciation of nature's bounty and beauty. However, foraging takes time and work, and you may not always find what you are looking for.

Always check with the local rangers to see if harvesting wild plants is legal in the area you plan to visit. In many parks, cutting or picking any plant is illegal. Even if foraging is permitted in the area you're visiting, consider the effects of overharvesting and limit your gathering to what the environment can tolerate. If huge quantities of people visit an area, it likely cannot tolerate even minimal foraging. Under no circumstances should you gather endangered or rare plants, nor should you gather plants for commercial sale.

CHOOSING WHAT FOODS TO CARRY

On weekend backpacking trips, you can eat almost anything as long as you are reasonably healthy and consume enough calories to cover your energy expenditures. Longer trips require more planning for maximum nutrition with the least amount of pack weight. As you plan your meals and develop a repertoire of ideas, you might create a menu and then check off each item as you purchase it and pack it. To decide which foods will fit your trip, consider the following points, which are covered in more detail below:

- availability of water
- itinerary: terrain, pace, and difficulty of your trip
- weather conditions
- volume and weight of your food
- cost
- variety and taste
- ease of meal preparation and cleanup

Availability of Water

Water is heavy and bulky (one gallon weighs 8.3 pounds), but it is the most important thing in your pack. Availability of water will significantly affect your selection of which foods you will carry with you. For instance, it would not be practical to bring freeze-dried food on a desert trip because extra water would be needed to rehydrate it.

Study a map for the area where you intend to hike and camp to determine where the nearest water source is. Make observations as to whether you will have plentiful water along a trail or in camp or will need to carry water with you for a "dry camp."

Itinerary: Terrain, Pace, and Difficulty

Ponder your estimated mileage and elevation gain and loss for each day. For a short, leisurely trip, you may need to raise your calorie level by only 10 to 20 percent. But weeklong, strenuous trips with a heavy pack may require 50 to 75 percent more calories. Depending on the terrain, incline, weight of your pack, and hiking speed, you can easily burn 500 or more calories per hour.

Consider known conditions. Will you be carrying your backpack to move camp every day? Is the trip cross-country or on trail? Are there technical challenges such as boulder-scrambling? These factors will affect not only your caloric needs but the time and energy you have available for meal preparation.

Weather Conditions

Cold increases your need for calories, so it's a good idea to eat small carbohydrate snacks even more frequently in extreme cold. You'll need the quick extra energy. Add extra water to turn all your dinners into soups (instant potato soup, couscous soup, etc.). Hot foods and liquids are more appetizing in cold conditions, and they help you stay warm. In colder weather or at higher elevations, you may need to melt snow for water. This requires extra work, fuel, time, and planning, especially in severe conditions.

Heat reduces your appetite but significantly increases your water needs. For a hot overnight trip, try freezing a juice pack at home before you leave.

Snow camping requires extra fuel to melt snow for water. (Photo by Pauline Jimenez)

Stored deep in your pack, the juice will ice the foods you want to keep cold, and you will have a refreshingly cool drink later in the day.

Never underestimate your needs for food and water. *Even on the simplest trails, always* carry at least a quart more water than you think you will need. Drink early and often, and never ration your water. It will do far more good in your stomach than on your back.

Volume and Weight

The National Outdoor Leadership School recommends about one and a half to two pounds of food for the average person during moderate outdoor activities and two and a quarter to two and a half pounds for extreme mountaineering. By choosing mostly dried or dehydrated foods that are low in water content (selectively avoiding most heavier fresh and canned foods and removing all cardboard and excess packaging at home), most backpackers are quite satisfied with less than two pounds of food per day (28 ounces of a judicious mix of dried, freeze-dried, and whole foods contains about 3000 calories).

A 3000-calorie day assumes a caloric density of about 125–150 calories per ounce. If you also consider the volume of your food, you will need to make decisions about what is most important to you (such as a Snickers bar or a larger bagel, which each contain 270 calories). If your food takes up a lot of space, it may not fit in a bear canister or in your backpack. With experience, you will learn what your body requires for different kinds of wilderness experiences.

Cost

Keeping costs down is another consideration when preparing a trip menu. Perhaps you would put this high on your importance list, but food cost should never be the primary factor in choosing what is right for a trip. If a trip requires a great expense, you should consider whether or not you should go, not how little food you can bring to survive.

Variety and Taste

Choose a variety of colors, textures (chewy, crunchy, soft, creamy, rich) and tastes (sweet, salty, spicy) to make appetizing meals and snacks that meet your nutritional needs. For instance, a handful of smoked almonds (crunchy and salty), a strip of barbecue-flavored beef jerky (chewy and salty), an energy bar (chewy and sweet), and chocolate-covered raisins (chewy and sweet) might all taste fine individually, but all of those choices are "brown" and the flavors are similar. You might substitute or add another taste-texture combination such as cheese (chewy and rich) or homemade and beautifully colored fruit leather (chewy and sweet).

The same snacks on every day of a backpacking trip are boring, which makes you tend to not eat all of your food. This can compromise your nutritional needs and cause you to carry useless weight in your pack. There is no single food that will meet all of your nutritional needs. Try to ensure that each meal has "something special" that you will look forward to eating and/or sharing with others.

Ease of Preparation and Cleanup

Depending on your preference, meals can be quick and require minimum preparation, allowing maximum time on the trail, or a meal can be more elaborate, with several courses requiring extra preparation and cleanup.

When you don't want to spend time cooking, you need to walk all day, or only one stove is available, one-pot meals are the best choice. Always pack at least one "little or no effort" meal. When people are cold, tired, and hungry, they appreciate simple, quick meals. It is also a good idea to pack a small amount of a lightweight "bland" item, such as instant butter-flavored potato flakes or lightly seasoned instant rice. These items are useful for situations such as illness or extreme fatigue, for thickening stews, or for adding a few extra calories to a meal.

If you need to get an early start, pack some breakfast flakes or instant cereal and powdered milk handy in a plastic bag before you start your hike. During your first break, add water to the bag, stir, and have a quick meal before continuing. Continue with high-carbohydrate snacks every hour or so. If you return to camp late in the day, hot soup and a dehydrated meal are quick and easy.

On rest days, on fishing trips, or in places where wood fires can be built, you might consider fancier meals. You could enjoy a more elaborate breakfast such as eggs, pancakes, sausage, and biscuits. Pancakes contain no surplus water and are efficient in the ratio of weight to calories. A day hike could start at midmorning and you could return by midafternoon. A decadent dinner meal could include soup, a special beverage, fresh fish, sautéed vegetables, and dessert.

Your choice on the continuum of quick to elaborate meals may depend on weather, water, energy levels, or other circumstances that are beyond your control. Remember that advance preparation at home can save hours out in the wilderness, where you will lack the conveniences of a modern kitchen.

MEALS AND SNACKS

Planning meals and snacks is an important part of backpack preparation. Consider the following details when choosing foods: water availability, itinerary, weather conditions, volume and weight, cost, variety and taste, convenient preparation and clean up, and how *you* like to eat. Are you a nibbler, or do you prefer to eat three traditional meals? The suggestions in this section will help you as you plan your menu.

Breakfast

A substantial breakfast is important. It gives you much of the energy you'll need for the first half of your day's activity. Generally, this meal should consist of carbohydrates (both simple and complex) to get you going and some protein or fat to help sustain you for several hours. A whole-grain cereal, sweetened with berries, jelly, or a squeeze of honey, is a good choice.

Millet and quinoa are the fastest-cooking whole grains. For two servings, presoak a cup of grain in two or three cups of cold water overnight. Bring it to a boil in the morning and simmer for three minutes (stirring frequently). Take the pot off the stove, cover it to hold in the steam, and let the grains finish cooking for five minutes. Instant hash browns, instant oatmeal, and instant grits are less nutritious, but they are easier and more convenient options.

Cold cereal can also work well. Pack about one cup of cereal in a plastic freezer storage bag (tougher and safer than ordinary plastic bags), adding about one-quarter to one-third cup of powdered milk and two or three tablespoons of nuts and/or dried fruit. You might sprinkle in a little nutritional yeast for extra protein. Many pellet-sized cereals (such as Grape Nuts or Ezekiel 4:9 cereal) can be eaten hot or cold. In camp simply add water to the bag, stir, and eat. No cleanup!

Round out your morning meal with a hot or cold beverage to make sure you are fully hydrated before starting the day's activities.

Lunch and Snacks

Lunch may not be a "square," sit-down meal. Instead, you may find yourself snacking while you move along the trail on "no cook" high-carbohydrate, low-fat foods that digest quickly. Since about half your daily food allotment should be for lunch and snacks and therefore needs to be portable hiking food that is not cooked in camp, coming up with a varied menu for this part of the day can present challenges. Below are some suggestions; also see Table 6-1.

Dried foods do not spoil, pack easily, and are lightweight. These include dried fruits and vegetables, nuts, chocolate, granola, or muesli (mixed with powdered milk and water).

Other ideas include fresh fruits and vegetables; cheeses; sandwiches made with whole-grain breads, bagels, or crackers; and spreads such as cream cheese (smaller packets do not spoil if you eat them as soon as the seal is broken), jam, honey, peanut butter products, and instant hummus powder (mixed with a little water and olive oil). Mustard does not need to be refrigerated, and you can even bring mayonnaise (sealed packets from fast-food restaurants tend not to spoil).

Some foods that are traditionally refrigerated will keep for several days: sausage, cheese, hard-boiled eggs. Foods that contain water (most fruits and many vegetables) are heavy for their calorie content but make refreshing treats on the first day or two of your hike. Less-perishable fruits include apples and oranges. Vegetables that carry well include cabbage, corn, potatoes, onions, and carrots.

GORP, which stands for "good old raisins and peanuts," is a common trail snack. GORP (also called "trail mix") comes in a variety of combinations of nuts, seeds, small crackers, dried fruits, and candies. Most prepackaged mixes are loaded with fats. You may wish to create your own GORP combinations. Here are some ideas:

Melba toast, animal crackers, goldfish crackers, mini pretzels, smoked almonds, nuts (peanuts, cashews, almonds, etc.), sunflower seeds, dried fruits (raisins, papaya, banana chips, figs, prunes, dates, etc.), candied ginger, shredded coconut, chips, strips of roasted and salted nori seaweed sheets, snack-type crackers, sesame sticks, pumpkin seeds, dry breakfast cereals (cornflakes, Rice Chex, Cheerios, etc.), malt balls or other small candies, butterscotch chips (don't carry these in your pocket), carob chips, gummi bears, or gourmet jelly beans.

Energy Bars and Gels

Energy bars and gels have become common trail foods. One energy bar or two gel packets per hour (30 to 60 grams of carbohydrate) is about right. Keep in mind that no single bar or gel supplies the wealth of nutrients found in whole foods. These foods should be only one of the kinds of snacks you bring, and they are not meant to take the place of regular meals. You can get the same carbohydrate value from a banana, four graham crackers, or four fig bars.

Energy bars. For hiking, opt for bars with no more than 8 to 10 grams of protein and 4 or fewer grams of fat per for every 230 calories. Higher fat content than this can slow digestion and make you feel nauseated. Also, choose bars with 5 or fewer grams of fiber because too much fiber may also slow digestion and may trigger the urge to defecate. Make sure to consume at least 12 to 16 ounces of water for each bar you eat.

Energy gels typically weigh about an ounce per packet and are very portable. Choose packets that contain 70 to 100 calories and 17 to 25 grams of carbohydrate. Remember to drink about 8 ounces of water for each gel packet you swallow. Since some gels contain caffeine, be careful. For some people, these can have a laxative effect.

TABLE 6-1. TRAIL LUNCH AND SNACK IDEAS

For backpacking, about half (50 percent) of your daily calories should come from lunch and snacks. Of these, 60 to 70 percent should be from carbohydrates such as whole grains, fruits, and vegetables. The squares

Breads and Grains	Fruits and Vegetables	Dairy Products
Bagels, pitas, English muffins, hard rolls, flatbreads, tortillas, cornbread	Fruit leathers, dried fruits (peaches, pears, apricots, cranberries, pineapple, mangos, raisins, figs, dates), and chocolate-covered raisins	Hard cheeses (string cheese, cheddar, Parmesan, and Gouda)
Pretzels, crackers, pilot biscuits, rye crackers, Wheat Thins, saltines, Pringles	Fig bars and fruit bars	Yogurt
Pasta salad (made with oil, *not* mayonnaise), couscous, or tabbouleh salad	One piece of fresh fruit (apple, orange, or banana) *or* one can of fruit (peaches, apricots, etc.)	Powdered milk (1/3 cup plus 1 cup water for granola, etc.)
Animal crackers and graham crackers	Bean salad sprinkled with sesame seeds or bean and cheese burrito	Cream cheese packets (these keep for 2–3 days if protected from heat and seal is unbroken)
Trail breads (fry-breads, pancakes, biscuits, and bannock)	Carrot salad, fresh vegetables (broccoli, carrots, cauliflower, cabbage, green beans, Chinese pea pods, small zucchini, jicama, celery, and bell peppers); fresh vegetables should be stored in paper, *not* plastic.	Mayonnaise and/or mustard packets (these keep for 2–3 days if protected from heat and seal is unbroken)
Granola and cereal	Precooked baked potato with butter and brown sugar or relish, cheese, bacon bits, etc. (try a sweet potato or Yukon Gold; seal well so it doesn't leak)	

within each column contain similar ideas to help you focus your thinking. Aim for a variety of textures and tastes by choosing at least one food from each column.

Animal Proteins	Spreads and Dips	Miscellaneous
Hard-boiled eggs	Bean spread, hummus, pesto, and olive oil	Recovery drinks, gel packets and powders, boxed fruit juices, instant breakfast, hot Jell-O, and tea
Jerky, salami, and bacon bits	Honey packets	Hard candy and lemon drops
Condensed mince-meat (in a box, *not* in a jar)	Jam packets, fruit spread, and apple butter	Trail mix (nuts of all kinds, raisins and other dried fruits, granola, melba toast, croutons, goldfish crackers, mini pretzels, corn nuts, sesame sticks, pumpkin seeds, sunflower seeds, Rice or Wheat Chex, M&M candies, granola, shredded coconut, malt balls, gummi bears, gourmet jelly beans)
Canned seafood: tuna, sardines, shrimp (choose only one can per trip and eat immediately after opening)	Nut and seed butters (peanut butter or tahini)	Chocolate bars, mints, orange candies, licorice
Canned chicken, Vienna sausages, and deviled ham (choose only one can per trip and eat immediately after opening)		Energy bars (best ones have 40 grams carbohydrate, 8–10 grams protein, less than 5 grams fat)
Foil packet of salmon, tuna, or chicken	Salsa	Fruitcake, pound cake, and toaster pastries

Dinner

Dinner should include carbohydrates, protein, and fats for your body to digest while you sleep. This is also the time to replenish the salts and liquids you have lost during the day. Start with a hot beverage or soup (unless it's a warm evening when something cool might be more refreshing).

To conserve fuel and save time, try "one-pot" meals. Choose a carbohydrate base (angel-hair pasta or ramen noodles, rice, grains, stuffing,

Mealtime is the payoff after a long day on the trail. It's a time to share stories, company, and good food. (Photo by Pauline Jimenez)

instant potatoes, couscous, polenta, beans, etc.) and then build a full meal with additional ingredients for protein (cheese, jerky, crumbled bacon, canned or dried chicken, canned shrimp, dried vegetables), fat (butter, olive oil, coconut oil, etc.), and flavor (dehydrated soup; taco, spaghetti, curry, or pesto sauce mixes; onion, garlic, a sprinkle of basil, etc.). Hearty pilafs (made with lentils, wheat, or rice) and soups (such as minestrone, multibean, beef, barley, or chicken) are also good choices. Add cheese and crackers, biscuits, or bread to round out any of these meals.

Add spices and seasoned mixes to enhance the flavor of many prepackaged meals. A pinch of curry powder livens up a rice dish, and onion flakes add a home-style touch to stews. Sprinkle a little sage and basil in the butter or oil before cooking your freshly caught trout. Top the meal off with a satisfying dessert (such as instant pudding, instant cheesecake, cookies, or an easy-bake cobbler) and social gathering around a small campfire.

Remember to pack extra foods that could see you through an emergency. Pack foods that keep well and need little or no cooking, in case you run out of fuel. Depending on the length of the trip, your emergency supplies might include jerky, granola bars, dried fruits, instant soups, and an additional dehydrated prepackaged meal. Don't pack emergency foods that are too enticing, or you may be tempted to dig into them unnecessarily. Wrap the food up tightly, store it in the bottom of your bag, and forget about it. You can use the same batch of emergency food for multiple trips, as long as it remains fresh.

Menu Planning for Groups

You can increase camaraderie and cut pack weight by forming a "cook group" with people who will share the same menu or cook their evening meal together. This system has less duplication of cooking equipment, and the weight is distributed among those who will eat it. Since most backpacking pots hold only about six cups of liquid and most stoves are made for this size pot, cook groups of two to four people usually work quite well. For larger groups, consider arranging a "central commissary" where two or three stoves and several large pots serve about ten people, with cooking and cleanup chores rotated among the members of the group.

To simplify menu planning, you can create a chart with each day's itinerary notes, allergy notes and modifications, meals required for each day, number of servings, and space to list the foods for each meal (see Table 6-2, Sample Menu). Include which meals will be eaten on the way to and from the trailhead, whether certain meals will need to be eaten hot or cold, whether you will be snacking on the move or stopping for a "real" meal, etc. Consider both nutritional value and weight, and, as mentioned above, remember to pack a little extra food for emergencies.

TABLE 6-2. SAMPLE MENU

This sample menu is for a summer backpack in the Sierra Nevada at 9000 feet with readily accessible water; forecast is pleasant daytime weather around 70°F with possible thundershowers and night lows just above 35°F. The itinerary is for easy backpacking on trails, setting up a base camp, and rambling day hiking on trails with no technical difficulties.

	Breakfast	Lunch and Snacks	Dinner
Thursday	Eat at home	Purchase en route	Purchase en route; sleep at trailhead
Friday	Cold breakfast to get on the trail fast: granola mixed with 1 cup water, 1/3 cup powdered milk, dried fruit, and nuts; hot cocoa; water	Eat on the move: prebaked sweet potato (with butter and brown sugar), jerky, dried apricots, salty trail mix, sports drink, water	Set up camp: instant miso soup, one-pot (canned) shrimp dish with rice (spiced with instant soup packet, toasted seaweed, toasted almonds, grated cheese, sliced, hard-boiled eggs); fortune cookies (packed carefully in your pot); hot tea
Saturday	Powdered eggs with rehydrated hash-browned potatoes, rehydrated fruit compote, instant chai (tea with powdered milk)	Couscous salad (made with hot water at breakfast), pita bread, string cheese, salty trail mix, fig bars, sports drink, water	Instant soup, quesadillas (vegetarian or not), salsa (rehydrated), beans and rice, chocolate bar (or instant pudding if you have a snowbank to chill it on); hot tea or cocoa
Sunday	Hardest hiking day; hot whole-grain cereal fortified with dried fruit bits, nuts, and powdered milk; hot tea; water	Peanut butter and crackers (or whole-grain bagel with low-fat cream cheese), raw carrot, fruit leather, sweet trail mix, energy bar, sports drink, water	Instant tomato soup, freeze-dried entrée or pasta (with chicken, sun-dried tomatoes, pine nuts, and powdered sauce); bread sticks, brownies (made at home); hot tea
Monday	Break camp, hike out; instant potatoes with smoked sausage and cheese bits; instant hot broth	Eat on the move: sweet trail mix, oatmeal-raisin cookies, jerky, energy bar, dried apricots, sports drink, water	Purchase en route

Emergency Food: One packet of electrolytes, an energy bar, instant corn chowder, instant potatoes (with salt, pepper, and butter powder), 2 ounces shelled sunflower seeds, small packets of hard candy

Meal planning also involves equipment considerations. How will you measure the amount of water you need to cook your dinner? Do you have a bandana or metal gripper to lift the pot when it is hot? Do you have a ladle or clean cup so no one needs to dip dirty dishes into your pot? Remember that three quarts of food won't fit in a six-cup pot, and a massive kettle will not balance on a tiny stove.

SHOPPING AND REPACKAGING

You can browse recipes, speed through a local grocery store, explore ethnic and health-food stores, or discover new freeze-dried ingredients at some sporting goods stores. Camping stores and mail-order catalogs (such as Adventure Foods, AlpineAire Foods, the Baker's Catalogue, Spices, etc.) are good sources for dehydrated foods and meals. Once you have planned your meals, create a list of what ingredients to buy. Check off each item as you get it and again as you pack it for the trip.

Repackaging

Reduce weight by removing unnecessary commercial packaging. Freeze-dried products are often packaged in moisture-tight foil packets that serve as good containers for rehydrating food, so don't repackage these.

Weigh and/or measure to decide how much food you need, what containers will work best, and how you will organize your ingredients to make them easily accessible. The process takes some time at home, but it will lighten your pack, shorten preparation time in camp, and make it almost impossible to forget anything or run out of food on the last day of a trip. Don't forget to *label your food and include brief written instructions* in case someone else needs to take over. (If you need one cup of water for your couscous, just write it on the plastic bag with a permanent marker pen or tuck a simple note inside.)

If your food supply ends up too heavy, then examine each meal carefully. Ask yourself if the portions are correct, if there is an ingredient that could be substituted, or if a lighter container is available. Most of the containers you'll need are probably around the house already:

Plastic bags. Most food items can be repackaged in plastic or cloth bags. Plastic freezer-storage bags are safest for boil-in-bag meals. Plastic bags with twist ties are good for carrying powders (such as milk) because nothing will catch in a zipper to make the bag hard to seal. Bags that can be vacuum-sealed at home are also a nice option for longer trips. Plastic bags are economical, convenient, light, and reusable, but they don't meet every backpacking need.

Paper. Fresh vegetables need to be kept dry and stored in paper (not plastic). If you plan to have a campfire, you could cut paper grocery bags to wrap some dry food items, writing weight, number of servings, and cooking instructions on the outside. Use the paper to ignite your fire, or recycle it to use on another trip.

Plastic wrap. To save space in a bear canister, you can compact some foods (such as cereals and powders) into small balls and wrap them in plastic wrap. Put the food in the center of a square of wrap, bring up the corners to compress the food, and form a ball, pressing out as much air as you can. Then wind the excess wrap into a small "tail," and tape the tail securely to the package. Write the weight and brief cooking instructions on a small file label and attach it on the outside of the ball, opposite the "tail." To guard against accidental puncture, repeat the process to wrap the ball again.

Plastic bottles and jars. Dry seasonings can be packaged in pill containers or small plastic bottles. Use wide-mouth plastic jars and other plastic storage containers when necessary, but keep these to a minimum because they are bulky and do not compress when empty. Thoroughly clean plastic containers between trips to avoid fostering bacteria or absorbed odors, flavors, and oils. Make sure that the lids are leak-proof. If the contents are a liquid or powder, it is good insurance to enclose the container in a self-sealing plastic bag to contain any possible leakage.

Squeeze tubes. Reusable squeeze tubes (as opposed to squeeze bottles) are great for semiliquid or semisolid foods such as honey, peanut butter, jam, and mustard. Squeeze tubes are filled from an open end that is later sealed tight by a plastic clip. They can be obtained at camping supply stores and by mail order.

Egg cartons. Plastic egg cartons come in sizes that hold as little as two and as many as a dozen eggs. You can use one to carry fresh eggs as long as you place it in a self-sealing plastic bag—just in case. If you plan to use fresh eggs very early on the trip, you can break them into a plastic bottle at home and then simply pour them out when it's time to use them. Egg cartons can also be used to transport delicate items such as chocolate-covered strawberries (if the weather is mild and you eat them on the first day).

Final Organization

For the final packaging on longer trips, follow one of these suggested methods:

Package by day—the "series" method. Group all breakfast, lunch, and dinner foods for a given day in a stuff sack. Pack a separate bag for tea bags, powdered beverages, spices, and other items that could be used during any meal.

Package by common meals—the "three-bag" method. Select a different-colored stuff sack for each type of meal—breakfast, lunch and snacks, and dinner. You might still pack a separate sack for coffee, tea, sugar, condiments, and seasonings that could be used during any meal.

THE WILDERNESS KITCHEN

Once you're out in the wilderness, pretrip planning and preparation will pay off.

Establish Your Campsite

Establish your campsite and pick a cooking area nearby. The Leave No Trace Center for Outdoor Ethics recommends that your site be located at least 200 feet away from any water sources or established trails (see Chapter 2, "Leave No Trace: Outdoor Ethics"). If in bear country, you should also restrict all cooking, eating, cleaning activities, and food storage to at least 200 feet downwind of tents.

A large, flat rock or rock ledge or a low area next to a large fallen tree works well for setting up your wilderness kitchen. Look for a flat, wind-protected spot for your stove. If the soil is sandy or soft or if you're camping on snow, you may need to put some support under your stove to steady it.

Hygiene

Remember to *wash your hands* before handling and cooking food. Hands are the vehicle for one of the most common ways that illnesses are spread in the backcountry: fecal-oral transmission. Fecal-borne pathogens get into your system through direct contact (even if you use toilet paper, you will still have germs on your hands), indirect contact (letting someone with contaminated hands dip into your bag of trail mix instead of shaking it into their hand), contact with insects that have rested on feces, and contaminated drinking water.

The best way to reduce the risk of contamination is to wash your hands and to use clean cooking and serving implements. The *best camp soaps are both biodegradable and germicidal* (such as Klenz Gel Blue), but they are hard to find. Many biodegradable soaps (for example, Campsuds or Dr. Bronner's Magic Soap) don't kill germs, and many germicidal soaps (including Betadine or Hibicleans) are not biodegradable. One idea is to use a biodegradable soap and then, after your hands are dry, use a tiny amount of antiseptic, waterless hand lotion. Never use soap directly in any water source, and keep in mind that "biodegradable" means that the soap will eventually decompose, not that it has zero impact.

Getting Ready to Cook

Take a moment to *get organized*. Find a safe, comfortable place to sit. Read the package directions or mentally run through the steps to cook your meal so you can decide what needs to be done first. Make sure the water you need is handy, and locate your matches and flashlight before dark. Set out the ingredients, instructions, pot, stove, fuel, ladle, knife, and any other equipment you will need before you begin.

Freeze-dried and dehydrated foods. Read the instructions carefully. These foods can be quite inedible if not properly rehydrated. Many freeze-dried foods have a dessicant (drying agent) packet in the package—don't forget to take the packet out before you add the hot water! Presoaking of some foods may take fifteen to sixty minutes, so allow enough time. Food that has been shredded, grated, or powdered usually takes a short time; whole chunks take longer. The higher the water temperature, the shorter the time it takes to rehydrate the food.

High-altitude cooking always takes a few more minutes. As elevation increases, the boiling point of water decreases due to the change of atmospheric pressure. This means that at higher elevations, even though water will boil more quickly, more time will be required to cook your food because water will be at a lower temperature upon boiling (see Table 6-3). Cooking time doubles for most boiled or simmered food at about 10,000 feet, so remember to use a pot cozy (see "Conserving Fuel" below) and/or take extra fuel if you will be cooking at high altitudes. Some packaged-food instructions give cooking-time adjustments for various altitudes. For foods that cook in twenty minutes or less at sea level, add one minute of cooking time for each 1000 feet of elevation. For items that take more than twenty minutes at sea level, add two minutes of cooking time for each 1000 feet of elevation. You may want to keep notes on the cooking time of your favorite foods for reference on future trips.

TABLE 6-3. BOILING TEMPERATURE OF WATER AT VARIOUS ALTITUDES

Elevation	Temperature
Sea level	212°F
5000 feet	203°F
10,000 feet	194°F
14,000 feet	187°F

Conserving Fuel

A fat, squat pot is the most efficient kind for conserving fuel because it captures the most heat under your food instead of up the sides of your pot. A one-quart pot (with a lid) or a backpacking teakettle is a good choice for a single hiker, and a two-quart pot usually works for two or three people. Titanium and hard-anodized aluminum are the favorite materials for light or ultralight backpacking pots. Even if all you do is heat some water, remember to cover your pot with a lid or aluminum foil to conserve fuel and increase stove efficiency.

Pot cozy. For worry-free cooking, you can use a *pot cozy*. A cozy allows you make many foods that you might not bring on a backpacking trip such as uncooked rice, beans, and thick pastas. If the food you are cooking normally requires twenty minutes of simmering, bring it to a boil and simmer for five minutes. Then remove the pot from your stove, place it in a covered pot cozy, and let the food "cook" for the remaining fifteen minutes. Depending on conditions, the cozy may keep your food piping hot for up to three hours. The pot is then insulated, so you can hold it in your hand or lap while you eat.

Pot cozies also allow you to keep your food warm while it rehydrates. Bring your food to a boil; turn off the stove, then transfer the pot to a cozy for ten minutes. For smaller pastas, simmer for two minutes before transferring to the cozy.

Commercial pot cozies are available from companies such as AntiGravityGear, or you can make your own with a 3/8-inch closed-cell foam pad (cut up an old foam pad or buy a cheap one), two-inch-wide aluminized furnace tape (or duct tape), and heavy-duty aluminum foil. Excellent do-it-yourself instructions for pot cozies and bag cozies are available on the Brasslight Backpacking Stove website (see "Resources" in the appendix).

HOW NOT TO DIRTY A POT

Most lightweight backpackers don't do "fancy" cooking, but they can still eat well. With hot water, a plastic freezer-storage bag (tougher and safer to use than ordinary plastic bags), and a *bag cozy*, you can reconstitute dried and freeze-dried meals and make hot beverages, soups, and hot cereal—all without dirtying a pot.

Figure 6-1. *A titanium pot (with easy-grip handles), bag cozy, and long-handled spoon are fuel-efficient kitchen equipment. Note the burned spot on the lid. Never melt snow without any water in the pot!* (Photo by Pauline Jimenez)

Making a Bag Cozy

A bag cozy is an insulated envelope that fits around your plastic freezer-storage bag. You can buy postal envelopes made with bubble insulation. These are cheap, come in different thicknesses for different sizes, and are easy to cut if you decide to customize them.

You can also make bag cozies with foil bubble insulation (polyethylene bubble wrap sandwiched between two sheets of aluminum—available at most hardware stores) and reflective foil tape. Another material choice is a cheap car windshield shade and clear two-inch-wide mailing tape.

Using household scissors, cut two pieces of insulation about a half inch wider than the freezer bag you plan to use. One piece should be about a half inch longer than the freezer bag, and the second piece should be about four inches longer. Evenly stack the shorter piece of insulation on top of the longer piece, matching the bottom and sides. Cut three lengths of tape to join the sides and bottom together, forming an insulated envelope. Cut off any excess tape around the edges, and tuck the longer edge inside the envelope to close it (or add some adhesive Velcro dots to the inside of the flap and outside of the envelope to keep the cozy closed).

Bag Cozy Cooking

To cook your meal with a bag cozy, here is all you need to do:

1. Bring your water to a boil in a cookpot (usually about a cup of water for every cup of dry uncooked food).
2. Open your freezer-storage bag of food and slide it into the bag cozy.
3. Pour the boiling water into your cup to measure it, and then pour the water into your freezer-storage bag of food. (Always measure first to avoid painful burns, adding too much water, or melting the bag by touching it with a hot metal pot.) Stir the food with a long-handled spoon to mix it well with the water; don't use a spork (spoon-fork) or a fork, which could puncture the bag. Carefully move air out of the bag and seal it tightly.
4. Let your food "cook" in the cozy for five to fifteen minutes. (Freeze-dried meat and slower-cooking grains such as dry elbow macaroni will take about fifteen minutes). Then carefully open the bag (watch out for hot steam), stir, and eat. The bag is your bowl!

You can adapt many one-pot meals for bag-cozy cooking. Fast-cooking ingredients that work well include ramen noodles, angel hair pasta, instant rice, couscous, instant refried bean flakes, dried flaked tomatoes, dried minced onions, instant soup mixes, gravy packets, stuffing mixes, meat pouches, etc. Here are some suggestions for single-serving portions:

Freeze-dried meat: ½ cup (2 ounces)

Pasta: 2 to 4 ounces (use two or three parts water; pasta should tumble freely as it boils)

Rice or grains: ⅓ cup (use two parts water for rice; other grains require two or three parts; cornmeal requires four parts)

Dried vegetables: ½ cup

CAMPFIRE COOKING

Sitting around a warm, crackling campfire can inspire treasured memories. If you are camping in an area that has designated fire pits, you can make wonderful food with a humble, no-impact fire. Traditional foods to enjoy include wieners on a stick, popcorn, s'mores, and grilled steaks.

Before you start, gently clear nearby fallen leaves and/or pine needles, have a shovel handy to stir the glowing embers, and make sure water is available to help extinguish the fire. Do not cut down trees or break off branches to use as firewood. (For more information on responsible Leave No Trace techniques, see Chapter 2, "Leave No Trace: Outdoor Ethics.")

Never leave your fire unattended. Make sure it is completely extinguished by dousing it with water or dirt and, if it is not in a fire pit, scattering the ashes carefully. Make sure your campsite is not a source for noise pollution, and always leave your campsite cleaner than you found it.

DUTCH OVEN COOKING

Dutch ovens are large kettles that European settlers used for hearth cooking, and pioneers used them on long wagon-train journeys. Today's Dutch ovens are still used at campfires and barbecues. You can use a Dutch oven to provide a variety of meals for small groups, such as roasts, stews, soups, biscuits, steamed vegetables, coffee cakes, and gooey fruit cobblers with crusty tops. Although the preferred use of the oven is for baking, you can also pan-fry, broil, or deep-fry foods. If you do a lot of outdoor cooking in a camping environment, a Dutch oven is one of the most versatile pieces of kitchen equipment you can own.

Dutch Oven Equipment

The most versatile size for a group of six to ten people is a 10-inch to 12-inch (six-quart) Dutch oven, made of either cast iron or aluminum. It should have legs that are at least 1½ inches high, and the lid should have a lip that seals well. You will also need a metal lid lifter, hot pot pliers to grip the oven lid, a metal shovel to stir the coals and lift them out of the fire pit to the oven, and thick welder's gloves to protect your hands and forearms when handling the coals, removing the lid, or holding onto the bail handle while moving the hot Dutch oven.

Charcoal briquettes, rather than wood or twig fires, are easier for beginners to use while getting the feel of using a Dutch oven. You can purchase a chimney-style coal starter or start the briquettes at the edge of your campfire. If you are in an area where the soil is too moist or the ground will be scarred by hot coals, use a metal coal tray large enough to support the base of your oven. Setting the oven legs on a tray or brick surface protects the cooking site, preserves your briquettes, and prevents direct contact with the coals under the oven as a result of settling.

Cooking Temperatures

To prevent charred food, keep the coals from touching the sides or bottom of the oven, and avoid stacking your food so high that it touches the inside of the lid. Here are some cooking guidelines:

- **Roasting:** heat should come from the top and bottom equally (coals should be placed under the oven and on the top of the lid at a 1:1 ratio).
- **Baking:** use a 3:1 ratio with most of the coals on the lid.
- **Stewing and simmering:** use a 4:1 ratio with most of the coals underneath.
- **Frying and boiling:** place all of the coals under the oven.

Allow twenty or thirty minutes for the coals to burn before lifting them to the oven with tongs that are at least a foot long or with a metal shovel. Each charcoal briquette provides about 25 degrees F (see Table 6-4). That means twenty briquettes will give you about 500 degrees F, sixteen briquettes gives 400 degrees F, etc. Temperatures are approximate because charcoal varies in heating quality, and high winds will make them burn faster. In a high wind or in rain, use a windscreen made from heavy-duty aluminum foil or sheet metal.

Avoid raising the lid while baking because heat will be quickly lost. When you do raise the lid, do it slowly to avoid burns and carefully to prevent ash from falling into your food.

For every fifteen minutes of cooking time, rotate the oven one-quarter turn over the coals, and also rotate the lid one-quarter turn relative to the base (to keep the heat in, try to avoid lifting the lid completely from the oven).

Add new briquettes as older ones begin to burn down and deplete.

Cleaning Your Dutch Oven

To clean your Dutch oven, place some clean warm water in it and heat until it is almost boiling. *Do not* use soap. Using a plastic mesh scrubber or a coarse sponge, gently break loose any stuck on food and wipe the pot clean. Allow the oven to air dry, then heat it until it is just hot to the touch. Apply a thin coating of oil to the inside of the oven and the underside of the lid, allowing the oven to cool completely.

TABLE 6-4. DUTCH OVEN BAKING TEMPERATURE CHART*							
Oven Temperature		325°F	350°F	375°F	400°F	425°F	450°F
8-in. Oven Diameter	Total Briquettes	15	16	17	18	19	20
	On Lid	10	11	11	12	13	14
	Under Oven	5	5	6	6	6	6
10-in. Oven Diameter	Total Briquettes	19	21	23	25	27	29
	On Lid	13	14	16	17	18	19
	Under Oven	6	7	7	8	9	10
12-in. Oven Diameter	Total Briquettes	23	25	27	29	31	33
	On Lid	16	17	18	19	21	22
	Under Oven	7	8	9	10	10	11
14-in. Oven Diameter	Total Briquettes	30	32	34	36	38	40
	On Lid	20	21	22	24	25	26
	Under Oven	10	11	12	12	13	14
16-in. Oven Diameter	Total Briquettes	37	39	41	43	45	47
	On Lid	25	26	27	28	29	30
	Under Oven	12	13	14	15	16	17

* Conversion data from the Lodge Manufacturing Company

Good Rules to Remember about Cast Iron

Never allow cast iron to sit in water or allow water to stand in or on it. *Never* use soap on cast iron. Do *not* place an empty cast iron pan or oven over a hot fire because it will crack and warp, ruining the pot. Also, *never* pour cold liquids into a very hot cast iron pan or oven because the temperature difference will instantly crack it.

CLEANING UP

Cleaning up after a meal should be done immediately to discourage growth of bacteria and unwelcome pests (raccoons, skunks, mice, and even bears). Dried-on food is usually much harder to clean. For some foods, a simple rinse in hot water is sufficient. For meats, greasy foods, or foods that stick to cookware, a squirt of some biodegradable soap is recommended in your biggest pot of warm water. If you don't have a cloth or sponge to scrub with, try using sand. Finish with a clean rinse.

Water used for washing should be scattered well away from camp, among stones or by a bush, and at least 200 feet from any water source. As you dump the water, it is a good idea to strain it to catch any small, loose food particles. Pack these out to minimize environmental impacts.

Waste Disposal

Disposing of food waste is a simple matter—pack it out. Most packaging and paper trash degrades very slowly, and food garbage can take months or years to rot away. Keep your camp clean and free of garbage scraps to discourage animal visitors. Trash and food garbage in or near a camp is unsightly, habituates unwelcome or dangerous animals, and trains them to become camp thieves.

A cute but unwelcome camp guest: a golden mantled ground squirrel
(Photo by Richard Belesky)

SAFE FOOD STORAGE

It may be impossible to stop hungry critters from visiting your campsite at night. To accommodate them in a way that is safe for both them and you (some human foods may be tasty but harmful to animals), remove all food from your backpack. An animal that wants access to a pocket that smells of food may simply chew or tear into it, so leave everything unzipped for curious noses.

Remove all food away from your pack to a safe place. To protect against the usual bandits such as rodents and raccoons, you may store your food in a protective container. In bear country, always store your food in protective bear canisters or use bear lockers if they're provided in camp. *Never* store or leave any food in your tent.

TRAIL FEASTS

Napoleon is reported to have said, "An army travels on its stomach," and the same is true for hikers and backpackers. With today's menu choices and variety of kitchen equipment, "eating out" in the wilderness has never been more fun. Now that you know about how to choose tasty, nutritious food, have some ideas about what foods work best under different conditions, and know how to pack your food and how to cook it, it is time for some delicious experiments. *Bon appétit!*

Who cares if I'm late for dinner?! (Photo by Jerry Schad)

Finding Your Way: Wilderness Navigation

Nelson Copp, Ted Young, and Bill Edwards

Many people are seeking more remote trails and cross-country routes without a good command of the navigation techniques and skills that make such outings safer, more predictable, and more rewarding. Navigation skills require relatively little in the way of equipment. Navigation is primarily a mental effort that keeps a person constantly aware of position, direction, and speed of travel. Like the mental effort required in driving an automobile, it requires plenty of practice but gets easier with time.

In normal life, you're continually faced with challenges of navigating. You're probably quite accustomed to using navigation tools and cues such as road maps, street signs, and verbal directions. Wilderness navigation is simply an extension of the same routefinding skills you use in the urban world. Instead of road maps and signposts, you use a topographic map, a compass, the physical features of the land, and possibly a Global Positioning System (GPS) receiver.

Since landmarks indicating precise locations are not always visible in the wilderness and you won't necessarily be meeting other travelers very often, you have to get used to being a little uncertain about your exact position from time to time. This does not mean you'll be "lost" but, rather, somewhere in transit between one known position and the next. The more you practice reading the lay of the land, the more comfortable you'll be in the wilderness.

MAPS

Most maps, and all topographic maps (or *topos*), are printed with the direction of true north toward the top of the map. Topographic maps are almost always best for wilderness navigation purposes. These maps are drawn to scale with a unique feature: contour lines indicating elevations above (or in some cases below) sea level. Topo maps also show bodies of water and watercourses, vegetation types, named geographical points of interest such as mountain peaks, and human-made features. A skilled user of a topo map is able to visualize the topography (shape of the land) by carefully studying the patterns made by the contour lines.

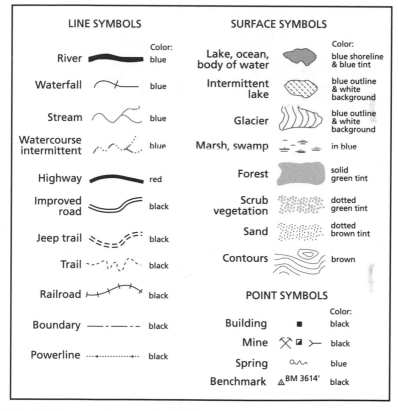

Figure 7-1. *Some symbols used on USGS maps*

Topo maps published by the US Geological Survey (USGS) can be purchased at backpacking and map stores or directly from the USGS. They can be printed or photocopied without violating copyright laws. Private publishers often use USGS maps as a base and update the human-made features, such as roads and trails. Distance scales at the bottom of the map allow you to measure a distance on the map directly in feet, miles, meters, and kilometers. In cases where a route spans several maps, the names of adjoining maps (usually eight of them) can be found on the sides, corners, and bottom of the map or in a small icon at the bottom of the map.

Other maps, such as road maps or trail maps without contour lines, may be of some use for navigation as long as they are drawn to scale. Also useful to some degree are shaded relief maps, giving some rough indication of the topography.

The locations of most benchmarks (survey markers) are shown on topographic maps. A USGS benchmark at the summit of Clouds Rest in Yosemite.
(Photo by Richard Belesky)

Map Scales

USGS topo maps come in two scales: the more detailed 7.5-minute scale (1:24,000) in which one inch on the map equals about 2000 feet, or one centimeter equals 240 meters, and 15-minute scale (1:62,500) in which one inch on the map equals about one mile, or one centimeter equals 625 meters. It takes four 7.5-minute maps to cover the same area shown on one 15-minute map.

These "minutes" refer not to time, but to distance in latitude and longitude. One minute of latitude (latitude is the top-to-bottom direction of your map) is a little more than a mile, so the 7½ minutes covered on your map is a little more than 8.5 miles. Longitude (that's side-to-side on your map) varies with how close you are to the equator and poles, so your map would be nearly square at the equator and narrower the closer you get to one of the poles. USGS topo maps are called *quadrangles*—they have four angles but vary in shape.

Map Symbols and Contours

Figure 7-1 provides a close look at the symbols appearing on USGS topo maps. There are four classes of map symbols:

- point: single-location features such as buildings, springs, benchmarks, mines, etc.
- line: continuous features such as rivers, highways, trails, railroads, powerlines, boundaries, etc.
- surface: large single-location features such as lakes, glaciers, forests, marshes, etc.
- contour: see the following pages.

Contour lines, typically printed in brown ink on topo maps, are imaginary lines of constant (unchanging) elevation. If you could actually see these lines on the ground, they would curve around the terrain but always remain level.

The elevation difference between adjacent contour lines on the map is called the *contour interval*. The contour interval is listed at the bottom of the map. Depending on the type of terrain and the scale of the map, the contour interval can vary from 20 to 200 feet, or 5 to 40 meters. A map with a contour interval greater than 80 feet or 20 meters is generally not very useful for critical navigation. Some contour lines are drawn thicker than others and are labeled with the elevation. These are called *index contour lines.*

Visualizing the terrain represented on a topo map involves understanding the patterns of the contour lines. Figure 7-2 shows several types of terrain and their corresponding contours.

Although topo maps reflect a great deal of information about the terrain, it is impossible to show every detail. Certain features too small to be detected in the pattern of contour lines may still be insurmountable to the traveler. For example, on a map with a contour interval of 80 feet, a cliff or waterfall 60 feet high may not be shown at all if it happens to fall between

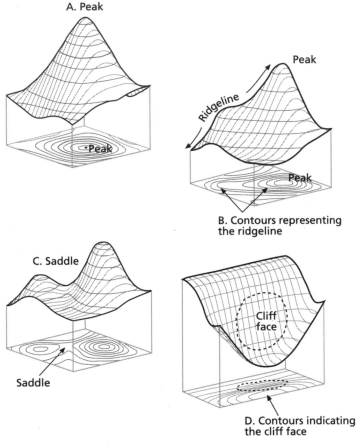

Figure 7-2. *Two- and three-dimensional representations of various landscape features:* A, *peak;* B, *ridgeline;* C, *saddle;* D, *cliff face;* E, *valley;* F, *complex terrain*

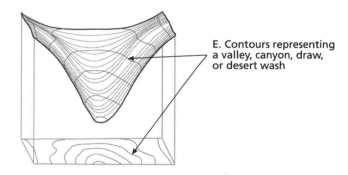

E. Contours representing a valley, canyon, draw, or desert wash

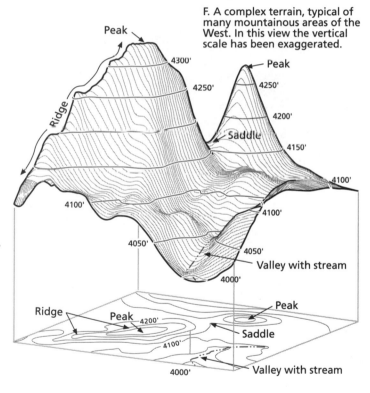

F. A complex terrain, typical of many mountainous areas of the West. In this view the vertical scale has been exaggerated.

Peak

4300'

4250'

Peak

4250'

Ridge

4200'

Saddle

4150'

4100'

4100'

4100'

4050'

4050'

Valley with stream

4000'

Ridge

Peak

4200'

Peak

Saddle

4100'

4000'

Valley with stream

contour lines. On a map with 40-foot contours, cross-country travel over a gently sloping hillside may appear simple, but it really will not be so if the slope is strewn with 20- or 30-foot-high boulders.

Additionally, a vegetation pattern indicating forest may represent anything from scattered trees to a dense redwood forest. The pattern indicating scrub vegetation could mean scattered bushes or impenetrable chaparral. A desert wash could be filled with anything from sand to boulders. Streams indicated by a thin blue line could be 1 foot wide or 50 feet wide.

The topo map allows you to plan your route before you arrive on the scene. Once you are there, you can refine your path, identify spots to visit, locate the land-marks in the field for triangulation, highlight easy or difficult terrain, and estimate your travel time. This terrain photograph shows the Sierras' Seven Gables Peak in the distance; Little Bear Lake is in the foreground. (Photo by Ted Young)

Therefore, it is important to pay attention to all the information a topo provides. Always take note of a map's publication date and the information in fine print at the bottom of the map. Significant changes may have occurred since then. Landslides or simple neglect may have obliterated roads and trails; buildings may be reduced to nothing but half-buried foundations; vegetation may have changed as a result of a fire, logging activity, or urban development; flooding may have rerouted streams or carved new watercourses; timber may have been blown down by a windstorm; and even ephemeral occurrences such as high water or recently fallen deep snow may block your path. Given these unpredictable changes, it is always important to consider a backup route in case unplanned obstacles prevent you from traveling on your intended course.

One method to help fill in the details and get yet another view of the terrain and vegetation is to look up the area on Google Maps (see "Resources" in the appendix).

Finding Where You Are on the Map

A map alone may be all you need to determine your location and plot your course. This works particularly well when distinct features such as roads and trail junctions, peaks, saddles, lakes, or uniquely shaped topographic features are within view. However, the map alone might not be effective in limited visibility or ambiguous topography. In those cases, a compass or GPS receiver is often necessary as well.

Figure 7-3. *Locating your position by map alone*

Finding where you are on the map begins with aligning the map until the features are in the same relative position on the map as they are in the view around you; with this accomplished, you can now begin to determine your exact location on the map.

For example, if you recognize a peak in front of you and a known river junction just below on your left, the map should be rotated and aligned so that when it is held between you and the peak on the horizon, the peak on the map lies in front of you, while the river junction on the map appears to the left but closer than the peak (see Figure 7-3). Then find the spot on the map where the river junction is at the same angle to the left of the peak as is the river junction in your view. That's your approximate location.

To further confirm your position, look for other nearby distinctive features. Are you standing on top of a ridge, somewhere along a slope, or in a valley? Is there a meadow or a lake in view? Are you in a forest area or in brush? Are there any other high points, cliffs, or gorges around you that may help to confirm your position? Can you see a bend in the stream and find that bend on the map?

Navigation Using the Map

Once you have found where you are, mark your position on the map. Select a possible route to your destination based on the elevation gain, difficulty of terrain, abilities of your group, and what you can see in front of you. Draw your intended route on the map. Then, as you travel, keep the map within easy reach to mark the progress along the route so that you can keep yourself located. Write observation notes and revise your route until you reach your destination. You may want to enclose your map in a resealable plastic bag to protect it from rain, perspiration, and abrasion.

COMPASS

The compass has developed over many centuries from a simple direction finder to a sophisticated tool. In most modern versions used for land navigation, the compass needle (a bar-shaped small magnet) turns freely while suspended in a bearing ring filled with a clear liquid.

There are many different types of compasses, but for land navigation, you should use an *orienteering compass* like the one shown in Figure 7-4. The bearing ring rotates on a base plate. The perimeter of the bearing ring is inscribed with abbreviations for the cardinal directions (N, E, S, and W for north, east, south, and west) and a 360-degree scale, typically in 2-degree increments starting at 0 (north) and increasing in a clockwise direction. Inside the bearing ring is an orienting arrow (some compasses have other markings used to orient the needle) and the magnetic compass needle. The north-pointing end of the needle is usually painted red (it is shown in black in all diagrams in this chapter, except Figure 7-4), and there's a prominent arrow on the base plate that is used to indicate the direction of travel. On some compasses, the direction-of-travel arrow is labeled *Read Bearing Here.*

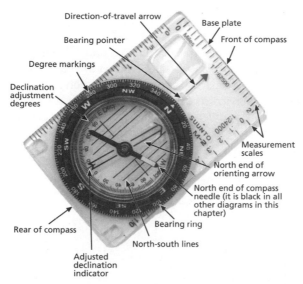

Figure 7-4. *Parts of an orienteering compass* (Photo by Bill Edwards)

In some compasses, the needle's north end is coated with phosphorescent paint, allowing readings to be made at night. Most compass base plates include a small ruler in inches or centimeters to facilitate measuring distance on maps and have a 1:24,000 scale for measuring distance directly on a 7.5-minute map. Features shown in the illustration are explained later in this chapter.

Magnetic Declination

True north is the direction toward the *geographic* North Pole—the north end of the earth's spin axis. Magnetic north is the direction toward the *magnetic* North Pole, which is located some distance away from the geographic North Pole. For most places on earth, there's a correction called *magnetic declination that indicates the number of degrees of difference between true north and magnetic north.* For the continental United States, magnetic declinations range from about 20 degrees east to 22 degrees west.

Adjusting Declination Compass

Some compasses include a feature to automatically correct for declination. This type of compass is called an adjusting declination compass (ADC). This compass includes a declination adjustment scale and adjusted declination indicator inside the bearing ring (see Figure 7-4 above). In keeping with the model portrayed in this book, our instruction focuses on the ADC, which this book simply calls "the compass." Non-ADC notes follow in parentheses.

Navigation by Compass

Basic compass skills involve setting, taking, and following bearings. A compass bearing is simply *the angle,* as measured by your compass, *between the direction of true north* (magnetic north if using a non-ADC) *and the direction of an object or destination.* An angle is formed when two lines start at one point and go out in different directions. The number of degrees of the angle (and bearing) is read at the *bearing pointer,* which is at the end of the direction-of-travel arrow.

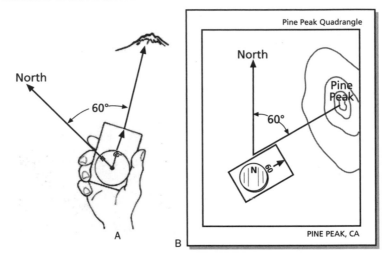

Figure 7-5. *This is the angle that you are measuring with your compass:* A, *in the field;* B, *on the map. The angle (and bearing) is 60 degrees.*

Setting a Bearing

Let's say some friends tell you that their favorite fishing hole is on a true north bearing of 60 degrees (or a magnetic bearing of 40 degrees if using a non-ADC) from a certain parking area. (The 20-degree difference is the *declination* in the area. Since declination is the number of degrees of difference between true north and magnetic north, the two compasses will read 20 degrees different if one has had the declination adjusted.) Without a compass, you might have only a vague idea of which direction to hike after you park your car. But if you *set a bearing* of 60 degrees on your compass, you can simply follow the compass's direction-of-travel arrow to head in the right direction.

To set that 60-degree bearing, hold the compass flat in the palm of your hand and turn the bearing ring until the 60-degree mark (40-degree mark if using a non-ADC) lines up with the direction-of-travel arrow on the base plate (see Figure 7-6).

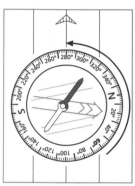

A. Compass before setting bearing. Now rotate the bearing ring to align the 60-degree mark with the direction-of-travel arrow.

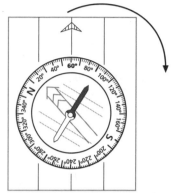

B. Compass after setting bearing. Don't turn the bearing ring again! Turn the *whole compass* until the magnetic needle lines up with the orienting arrow.

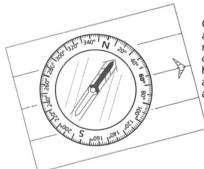

C. Compass with bearing set and compass oriented to north. Follow the direction-of-travel arrow to the fishing hole. Note that the orienting arrow has been adjusted for a 20-degree east declination.

Figure 7-6. *Setting a bearing*

Now turn both yourself *and* the compass (Don't move that bearing ring again! You just set it!) until the north end of the magnetic needle lines up with the orienting arrow in the bearing ring. *Your compass is now oriented to true north* (magnetic north if using a non-ADC), the direction-of-travel arrow is pointing toward the fishing hole, and you are facing in the direction you want to go!

Orient means to turn toward a specified direction. *Orienting your compass* can also be called *trapping the needle* or *boxing the needle*. Because the north end of the needle is often painted red, and because the orienting arrow looks like a tall, thin house, some people even call this *"putting red in the shed"!* Remember that when the magnetic needle is used, the orienting arrow is always used with it.

Be aware that nearby metallic objects, such as mechanical pencils or pens, a magnet on a water bladder hose, a pack frame, a metal watch or ring, or a car can affect the pointing accuracy of a compass needle. Always take compass measurements away from these kinds of objects.

Taking a Bearing

Taking a bearing is the opposite of *setting a bearing.* In setting a bearing, your friends told you what the bearing was, so you already know it. In taking a bearing, you don't yet know what the bearing is, and you use your compass to find ("take") it.

For example, let's say your goal is to reach a peak visible in the distance. You can see a good route straight ahead, but you realize that much of the time you'll be hiking in a forest where your view of the peak will be obscured. You need to take a bearing on the peak so you can refer to that bearing to maintain a correct course at times when you can't see the peak.

To take a bearing, hold the compass in your hand in front of you with the direction-of-travel arrow pointing toward the peak (see Figure 7-7). Keep the compass level. With the direction-of-travel arrow fixed on the

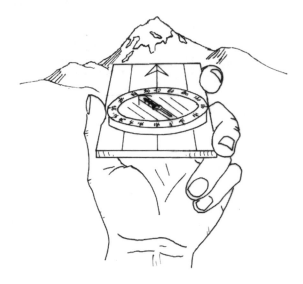

Figure 7-7. *Taking a bearing: The north end of the magnetic needle, shown in black in most diagrams in this chapter, might be painted red on your compass.*

peak, turn the bearing ring until the orienting arrow lines up with the north end of the magnetic needle. *This is called taking a bearing.* You are taking a measurement of the angle between true north (or magnetic north using a non-ADC) and the peak (the direction indicated by the direction-of-travel arrow). Review Figure 7-5A.

As you walk through the forest, keep the compass *oriented* (keep the north end of the needle lined up with the orienting arrow), and the direction-of-travel arrow will be pointing your way. Refer to your compass often to maintain your course. The degree reading (number of degrees) of the bearing is not really important, as long as you don't rotate the bearing ring and lose that number. Still, it's a good idea to memorize or jot down the degree reading in case your bearing ring is accidentally reset.

Using Intermediate Points to Follow a Bearing

In the previous example, you took a bearing on a peak. You're now ready to start hiking through the forest toward that peak. Since the bearing is already set on your compass, all you have to do is hike in that direction. But how easily can you follow this bearing? What happens if you must skirt obstacles like a pond or large boulders? To answer these questions, use *intermediate points.*

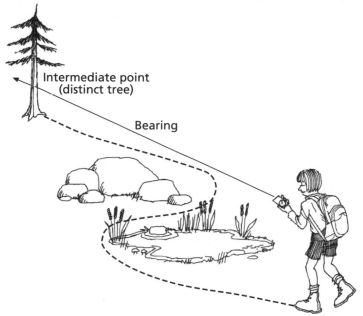

Figure 7-8. *Using an intermediate point to follow a bearing*

Before you start hiking, orient your compass. An imaginary line extends along the direction-of-travel arrow from where you are to the peak.

Now look along that line for an object in the near distance that is between you and the peak, such as a distinctive tree or a pile of rocks. This is your first intermediate point (see Figure 7-8). Walk toward it without losing sight of it. Moving a little to the left or right to avoid obstacles will not make you lose your original line. Just keep heading toward the intermediate point. You should not have to check your compass again until you reach it. Intermediate points keep you from having to look at your compass all the time.

Let's assume that at the first intermediate point, just as you'd thought, you can't see the peak. Which way do you go now? Easy—just orient your compass and look along the direction-of-travel arrow. Pick out a second intermediate point on that line. Continue leapfrogging in this manner until you reach the peak.

Back Sighting

You may lose sight of your intermediate point. To make sure you are still on the right line, you can use the technique of *back sighting* to find the previous intermediate point if it is still visible.

Turn around and orient your compass backward by aligning the *south* (black) end of the needle with the north (red) end of the orienting arrow (since you have turned around and are now looking backward). Now the direction-of-travel arrow points back toward the previous intermediate point.

If the direction-of-travel arrow points off to one side of the previous intermediate point, move in a direction either left or right until it does point directly to it. Now you are on the correct line again, so turn around, orient your compass the regular way with the north (red) end of the magnetic needle in the north (red) end of the orienting arrow, and follow the direction-of-travel arrow to the intermediate point you lost sight of.

It's a good policy to back sight often to make sure you stay on course. It also helps you to recognize the terrain for the trip back if you plan to return using the same route.

Back Bearings

Let's say you've spent an enjoyable hour on the summit, and now you want to return to your car. How do you find your way back? There are two methods you can use.

The first method is to do exactly what you just did with back sighting: orient the compass backward, and walk with the *south* end of the needle lined up with the *north* end of the orienting arrow, following the direction-of-travel arrow.

The second method is to determine the number that is 180 degrees from your original bearing (halfway around your compass's 360-degreee scale), since your return bearing will be the opposite direction, or 180 degrees, from your original bearing.

If your original bearing is less than 180 degrees, then add 180 degrees to it. If your original bearing is more than 180 degrees, then subtract 180 degrees from it. Set this new bearing, orient your compass, and start the journey back (see Figure 7-9).

To mountain

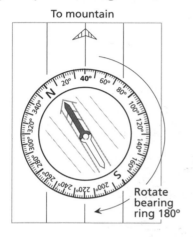

Rotate bearing ring 180°

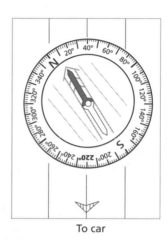

To car

Figure 7-9. *Back bearings:* left, *the original bearing of 40 degrees;* right, *180 degrees has been added to the original bearing of 40 degrees to produce a back bearing of 220 degrees, the compass has been turned around, and the compass direction-of-travel arrow is now facing the car.*

Navigating around Obstacles

When using intermediate points, you will sometimes encounter obstacles that you can't cross or don't want to climb over or that block your view ahead. You could just walk around them, but you should be aware that you might not be able to find your original line again. (What is the difference between bearing and line? A street has the same *bearing* as the street next to it, but it is on a different *line*—that is, the street goes in the same direction but is in a different place.)

One solution to this dilemma is to navigate on a right-angle course around the obstacle. Let's say it's a hill (see Figure 7-10). First determine whether going to the left or the right of the hill will be easier. Okay, the right looks easier. Orient the compass and face your original bearing. Notice that the rear and front ends of the compass base plate are perpendicular to your original bearing. This will be your new direction. Keeping the compass oriented, sight across either end of the compass, instead of down the middle like you normally do, and pick out an intermediate point on that line. Start walking in this new perpendicular direction as far as you need to go to clear the obstacle, counting your paces as you walk.

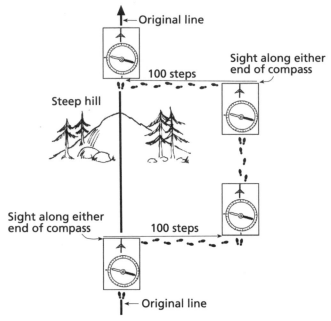

Figure 7-10. *Navigating a right-angle course around an obstacle*

Let's say you have to walk 100 paces to the right, and now you have a clear shot past the hill. Turn left. Orient the compass again and look down the direction-of-travel arrow. This will be the same direction as your original bearing. Find an intermediate point so you don't have to keep your eyes on the compass, and walk until you are past the hill (any distance—you don't have to keep track). Then sight across either end of your compass to the left (to go back toward your original line), find an intermediate point so you don't have to keep looking at your compass all the time, and follow a course 100 paces back to your original line. Turn right. Orient your compass, find an intermediate point, and head off again toward the peak!

An Exercise in Compass Navigation: Following a Circuit

This circuit exercise gives you and your friends some practical experience in taking and following bearings.

First, find a rather large, open outdoor area with at least a few obstacles (see Figure 7-11). Pick out five or ten points on the landscape that can be linked together in a more-or-less circular course. It's more interesting if some of the points can't be seen from the starting point.

Number and describe the points on a sketch map and give everyone a copy. The object is to take bearings on each successive point and to navigate to each successive point using compass techniques. Each participant should record the measured bearing on each leg of the circuit. After completing the circuit, the participants can compare their bearings and discuss any wins, problems, or discoveries.

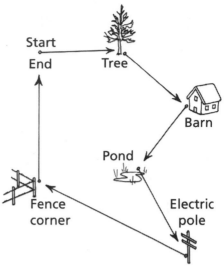

Figure 7-11. *Circuit exercise*

NAVIGATION BY MAP AND COMPASS

To review, you have learned that *magnetic declination indicates the number of degrees of difference between true north and magnetic north.* Maps use true north, and compasses use magnetic north.

Magnetic Declination

If you are using a compass merely as a direction finder independent of a map, magnetic declination is not relevant because the declination difference will never have to be corrected. However, when you are using a map and a nonadjusting declination compass together, any declination exceeding one or two degrees should be taken into account. In short, to stay found and find your way in the wilderness, you need to know how to correct for magnetic declination if you are not using an adjusting declination compass (ADC) that does the adjusting for you. If you are using an ADC, you can skip this next section and go to "Determining the Declination of Your Map Area."

Correcting for Declination with a Non-ADC

To make true north and magnetic north equal in degrees, you need to either subtract or add the declination each time you go from map to field or from field to map. (*Field* means the physical world, as though you're outside in a field, where you use the compass's magnetic needle. *Map* means a paper map—it's not magnetic, so you don't use the compass's needle with the map.) Whether you add or subtract depends on:

(a) whether you have an *east* or a *west* declination and

(b) whether you are *converting a map bearing to a compass bearing* (going from the map to the field) or *converting a compass bearing to a map bearing* (going from the field to the map).

To help remember whether to add or subtract the declination on your compass, Table 7-1 and the following examples may be helpful. This mnemonic rhyme may also help you remember: From map to field, correct the yield! East is least, and west is best.

TABLE 7-1. CORRECTING FOR DECLINATION WITH A 15-DEGREE DECLINATION AND A 95-DEGREE BEARING

Direction of Declination	Map to Field	Field to Map
East		
East is least = *subtract*	95° subtract 15° = 80°	95° add 15° = 110°
West		
West is best = *add*	95° add 15° = 110°	95° subtract 15° = 80°

Map to field. Here is an example of going from the *map* to the *field:* Your declination is 15 degrees east. You want to hike to a small lake you see on the map. You take a bearing on the lake from the map (you'll learn how in "Taking a Bearing off a Map and Using It in the Field," later in this chapter) and you get 95 degrees. You want to use that bearing to find the lake out in the field.

Start with your map bearing of 95 degrees and *subtract* (east is least) 15 degrees, which gives you 80 degrees, then set that on your compass. Pick up the compass from the map, orient your compass (rotate your body and compass together until the north end of the magnetic needle lines up with the orienting arrow) and follow your direction-of-travel arrow to the lake.

If your declination is 15 degrees west instead, you would *add.* You want to hike to a small lake you see on the map. You take a bearing on the lake from the map (you'll learn how below) and you get 95 degrees. You want to use that bearing to find the lake out in the field. Start with your map bearing of 95 degrees and *add* (west is best) 15 degrees, which gives you 110 degrees, then set that on your compass. Pick up the compass from the map, orient your compass (rotate your body and compass together until the north end of the magnetic needle lines up with the orienting arrow) and follow your direction-of-travel arrow to the lake.

Field to map. Here is an example of going from the *field to the map*. Let's suppose you have just taken a bearing on a peak, and you want to put that bearing as a line onto the map. You are going from the *field* to the *map*, so you do the opposite of what you did when you went from the *map* to the *field*. If your declination is east, now you add. If your declination is west, now you subtract.

Determining the Declination of Your Map Area

You need to know the magnetic declination for the area you are considering. On topographic maps, magnetic declination is usually indicated by a symbol at the bottom left. The symbol includes a vertical line pointing toward a star representing true north and an arrow labeled "MN"(for magnetic north), indicating magnetic declination. The angles portrayed are not intended to indicate the *actual* angle but only the direction of change. Only the written degrees indicate the actual declination. More recently updated topos have a written description of the declination instead. Figure 7-12 shows a magnetic declination of 15 degrees east of true north.

UTM GRID AND 2013 MAGNETIC NORTH DECLINATION AT CENTER OF SHEET

Magnetic declination is constantly changing. Although this change is typically only one or two degrees over a period of years, check the map date to make sure your data is less than about ten years old. Declination calculators for any area can be found online (see "Resources" in the appendix).

If declination calculators provide fractions of a degree, round off the number to the nearest degree. For example, 11 degrees 21 minutes rounds off to 11 degrees; 11 degrees 57 minutes rounds off to 12 degrees. (Minutes are 1/60 of a degree.)

Figure 7-12. *Topographic declination icon: The icon depicts variation between true and magnetic north on a topo map. It includes a vertical line pointing toward a star representing true north and an arrow labeled "MN" indicating magnetic declination. The declination shown is 15 degrees east of true north. West declination would be shown to the left of the true-north line.*

Adjusting the Declination of an ADC

Adjusting the compass declination of an ADC is typically very simple and, once done for a given area, needs no further change. Figure 7-13 shows a Suunto Model M-2 compass face down, with the declination adjusted to 12 degrees east; the adjusting set screw is shown by arrow A, and the adjusted declination indicator is shown by arrow B. Other ADCs have different parts and adjustments, so consult the directions that come with your particular ADC.

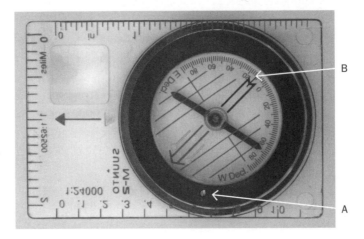

Figure 7-13. *Looking at the back side of an ADC: the declination has been adjusted to 12 degrees east;* A *is the adjusting set screw, and* B *is the adjusted declination indicator.* (Photo by Bill Edwards)

UTM Grid Lines for Use with the Compass

The UTM grid is a system that uses a grid of 1000-meter squares to easily and accurately specify places on the map. The north-south lines of this grid are also very convenient to use to align a compass to true north when using the compass and map together. The grid is recognizable on a 1:24,000 topo map as solid black lines spaced approximately 1⅝ inch (42 mm) apart. These lines are often printed on a topo map, and if they are not printed, they can be added by the user. The UTM grid is covered in more detail later in this chapter.

Orienting the Map

Once you know the declination for your map (and have set the declination on an ADC), orient your map to north so that when you look around, the map and the ground features will match. *Note: The only time you use the magnetic needle on the map is when you are orienting the map.*

Orienting the map with an ADC. First place your map on a flat spot. Orient it roughly by looking at the features around you and turning the map to match these features.

Then set north on your compass: turn the ADC's bearing ring to line up its N (north) mark with the bearing pointer on the base plate. Place the long edge of the base plate along the left or right border of the map, with north pointing toward the top of the map. Don't use any vertical lines drawn inside the map area except the UTM grid, since other lines may represent roads or boundaries that may not go precisely north and south.

Rotate the map and compass together until the north end of the magnetic needle lines up with the orienting arrow (see Figure 7-14A). Make certain that the north end (not the south end) of the magnetic needle lines up with the orienting arrow.

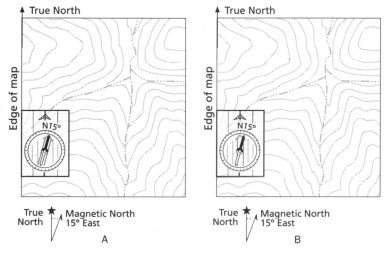

Figure 7-14. *Orienting the map to north: A, the ADC is used to orient the map; note that the orienting arrow is adjusted to point to the declination of 15 degrees east. B, a non-ADC is used to orient the map; note that the declination adjustment is made by pointing the magnetic needle to the declination of 15 degrees east.*

Your map is now oriented to true north, and its orientation is also correct relative to the landscape around you.

Orienting the map with a non-ADC. First place your map on a flat spot. Orient it roughly by looking at the features around you and turning the map to match these features.

Then set north on your compass: turn the bearing ring to line up its N (north) mark with the bearing pointer on the base plate. Place the long edge of the base plate along the left or right border of the map, with north pointing toward the top of the map. Don't use any vertical lines drawn inside the map area except the UTM grid, since other lines may represent roads or boundaries that may not go precisely north and south. (So far both orienting methods are identical.)

Rotate the map and compass together until the north end of the magnetic needle points to the number of degrees on the bearing ring that matches your declination (see Figure 7-14B). You don't have to add or subtract because that is what you are doing when you match the north end of the magnetic needle to the declination. Make certain that the north end (not the south end) of the magnetic needle points to the number of degrees on the bearing ring that matches your declination. Your map is now oriented to true north, and its orientation is also correct relative to the landscape around you.

Taking a Bearing off a Map and Using It in the Field

Let's assume you want to hike to a small lake you see on the map (see Figure 7-15). You'll need to take a bearing on a line between two points—your present position and the lake—then follow that bearing to the lake. Here's what to do:

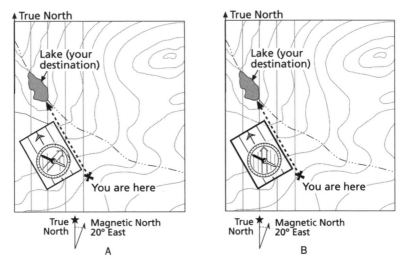

Figure 7-15. *Taking a bearing (map to field): A, using an ADC and the north-south UTM grid lines to take a bearing between two points. Note that the compass north-south lines and the north-south UTM grid lines are parallel and are all aligned to north. The orienting arrow is adjusted to 20 degrees east and hence does not point to north. Remember, the direction of the magnetic needle is always irrelevant on a map except when you are orienting the map. B, using a non-ADC and the north-south UTM grid lines to take a bearing between two points. Note that the compass north-south lines, the north-south UTM grid lines, and the orienting arrow are all aligned to north. Correction for declination is done in a later step.*

1. Make sure the compass declination is adjusted. The map does not need to be oriented.
2. Take the bearing with your compass on the map: place one of the rear (the end closest to you when you hold the compass) corners of the compass base plate on the map at the point of your current known location, and line up the compass so that the long edge of the base plate forms a line between the two points (your current location and the lake). If the distance between the two points exceeds the length of the base plate, you may need to draw a line.
3. Rotate the bearing ring until the compass north-south lines in the bearing ring (to the left and right of the orienting arrow) are parallel to the north-south UTM lines on the map. The ADC will account for the declination. **Reminder:** Ignore the magnetic needle when the compass is on the map. Double-check that the N on the bearing ring still points toward the top of the map.
4. Pick up the compass from the map. (If using a non-ADC, correct for the declination now. You are going from the *map* to the *field*, so if your declination is east, you subtract. If your declination is west, you *add*. Set the corrected bearing on the compass.) Hold the compass level and orient the compass as you have done before by turning both yourself *and* the compass until the north end of the needle lines up with the north end of the orienting arrow in the bearing ring.
5. You can now follow the direction-of-travel arrow to the small lake!

USING A MAP TO CHOOSE YOUR ROUTE

Now that you have successfully taken the bearing to the lake in the example above, you are almost ready to start hiking. First, choose the best route to your destination. If you start hiking without checking the route, you may end up having to climb steep hills or hike through dense vegetation. So take a few minutes to plan your route, using that wonderful tool—your map.

Take note of any obstacles you may detect on the map and mark them. Then plot your course, which may or may not be a direct route. To avoid tough spots, pick out intermediate points, take their bearings from the map, and plot a crooked course with bearings noted for each leg.

Aiming Off

If a destination is not large, such as a small lake hidden in the trees, you could walk right past it. To reduce that possibility, try to find on the map a prominent or obvious stream, road, or trail touching or passing near the lake. If you find some feature like that, aim slightly off (away from) the target lake so that you have to cross the prominent or obvious feature. Then when you do cross the prominent or obvious feature, you'll know which way to turn to find the lake (see Figure 7-16).

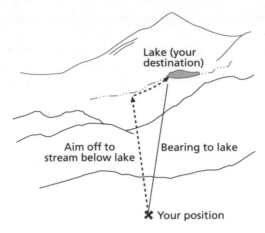

Figure 7-16. *Aiming off: Aim to the left of the lake, then follow the stream to the lake.*

Triangulation (Taking Bearings to Find Your Location)

A good way to keep track of your position is to frequently check your position relative to nearby landmarks and then update your position on your map. You can do that by keeping your thumb on your current position on the map as you walk or by making a series of pencil marks on the map.

If you do lose track of your position on the map, use *triangulation* to determine your location (see Figure 7-17).

First, look around and find three features in the surrounding terrain that you can also identify on the map. With triangulation, you can figure out where you are in relation to these. For the most accurate results, each of the features should approach a 120-degree separation from each other relative to your position. The closer the features are to you, the better.

1. Take a bearing on the first feature. This is described above in "Taking a Bearing," in the example of taking a bearing on a peak visible in the distance (Remember Figure 7-7?). To review: Aim the compass's direction-of-travel arrow at the first feature. Keep the compass level. With the direction-of-travel arrow fixed on the peak, turn the bearing ring until the north end of the orienting arrow lines up with the north end of the magnetic needle. (If using a non-ADC, correct for the declination now.)

2. Place the compass on the map with the N on the bearing ring faced toward the top of the map, with one of the *front* corners of the compass on the *first feature* and, holding it there, *pivot the entire compass until the compass north-south lines in the bearing ring* (to the left and right of the orienting arrow) *are parallel to the north-south UTM lines on the map.* Do not rotate, dial, turn, or twist the bearing ring to match the lines—you have just set that bearing, and you don't want to change it. Double-check that the N on the bearing ring still points toward the top of the map.

3. On the map, draw a line from the first feature back along the long edge of the base plate of the compass, and extend it beyond where you think you are.

4. Repeat steps 2 and 3 for the other two identified features.

5. The three drawn lines should intersect to form a small triangle, and that triangle indicates your approximate location.

A common mistake is to place one of the *rear* corners, instead of the *front* corners, of the compass on the map feature. Remember that your *rear* is not at that feature, so the compass's *rear* should not be there either!

If the triangle seems inordinately big, then you've erred in taking or plotting (drawing the line) a bearing, or you may have misidentified one of your features either on the map or in the landscape. If this happens, retake your bearings and plot them again.

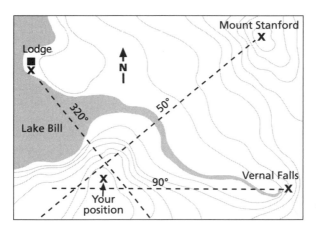

Figure 7-17. *Triangulation*

After getting at least a general fix on where you are, it may be useful to do a second triangulation on closer landmarks to determine your location more precisely. Once you have a better fix, you may be able to determine your location to a precision of just a few yards by examining the contour lines on your map and recognizing around you the features they represent.

Triangulation is also the method you would use to plot the position of a favorite spot onto your map.

Cross Bearings

Suppose you want to hike to a hidden spot, a desert mine you noticed on the map, which is some distance away from a linear feature such as the wash shown in Figure 7-18. Let's further suppose there are no distinguishing features along the wash to indicate the best place to turn off, but the map shows the mine lying directly between a distant peak and the wash (see Figure 7-18).

On the map, draw a line connecting the mine and the peak and extend it backward to where it intersects the wash. Using your compass on the map, take a bearing of this line. This is the bearing you will want to follow when you reach the right spot in the wash. Set this bearing on your compass, and you might want to write it on the map.

Then, as you walk down the wash, stop often and point the direction-of-travel arrow toward the peak, as if you were going to take a bearing. (Don't turn that bearing ring. The bearing is set.) See if the north end of the magnetic needle lines up with the orienting arrow. If not, keep walking down the wash. As you continue, you will reach a place where the magnetic needle lines up with the orienting arrow. You're now on the bearing line you drew on the map. Turn and head toward the mine by following the direction-of-travel arrow.

Using Baselines

A baseline is a linear feature that you use to guide your travel and keep yourself within a specified area. Aiming off, discussed above, involves intersecting a baseline such as a prominent or obvious stream, road, or trail and then following this baseline to the destination. In the example of cross bearings above, you were hiking down a wash (a baseline).

Always be aware of the location of at least one baseline—a stream, a road, or some other fairly linear feature—before you start your excursion. The direction toward this is called your *safety direction*—the direction you go if all else fails.

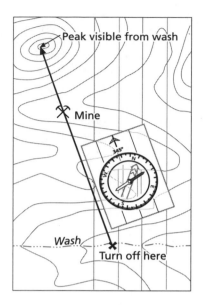

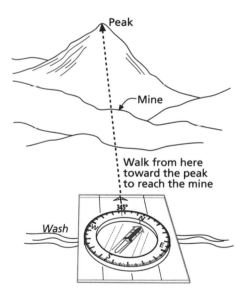

Figure 7-18. *Using cross bearings*

DEAD RECKONING

When visibility is poor, it is often wiser to stay put until conditions improve. However, there may be circumstances in which it is essential to keep moving. You may not have the opportunity to confirm your position very often because of darkness, rain, fog, whiteout, or ambiguous topographic features. In these kinds of situations, you might use the technique of dead reckoning. While you are still certain of your position, plot it onto the map, then find your destination on the map and mark many easily distinguishable points along the way. Draw lines between each of these points, take their bearings, and write them next to each point.

Set the first bearing on your compass and start walking, using intermediate points. If conditions are really bad, you may have to count your paces to determine how far you have gone. A person can be sent ahead to act as an intermediate point, guided onto the bearing line by voice or light signals. In darkness, the light from this person's headlamp can be used as the intermediate point. Continue doing this from point to point.

Dead reckoning techniques are risky, since you can easily lose the thread of your course. If you do, try to retrace your footprints back to the last known location. This is one type of situation in which the GPS is extremely useful in that it is unaffected by darkness or bad weather.

THE UTM GRID

Early maps provided a visual representation of the distribution and spatial relationship of places to one another. It did not take long, however, before users realized that an additional element was needed—some system to easily and accurately specify these places on the map and provide increasing precision in their distances from one another. This need gave rise to the grid coordinate system (see Figure 7-19).

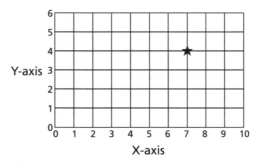

Figure 7-19. *Grid coordinate system: The star represents a position of 7 "easting" ("start at 0 and measure to the east"—the X-axis) and 4 "northing" ("start at 0 and measure to the north"—the Y-axis).*

Latitude and longitude. For centuries an angular (degrees, minutes, and seconds) coordinate system was used to define a position: east-west position (longitude) and north-south position (latitude). This approach was first conceived more than 2000 years ago, launched the Age of Exploration in the mid-1400s, and is still used worldwide by navigators of all types.

UTM grid. A common second approach to defining position is the rectangular system. This is the basis of the much newer Universal Transverse Mercator (UTM) coordinate system that has already been adopted throughout the world, including by a growing number of people in the land navigation community. The major reason for adoption among land navigators is its ease of use with the increasingly affordable GPS technology.

Under the UTM system, the world is divided into sixty east-west *numeric zones,* each covering a 6-degree strip in longitude (see Figure 7-20). These numeric zones are numbered consecutively from 1 to 60 starting at the International Date Line in the mid-Pacific with Zone 1 and progressing eastward around the world.

The lower continental United States is covered by Zones 10 through 19, with Southern California, for example, located in vertical column *numeric Zone 11.*

There are also twenty north-south *lettered zones* designated C though X (missing letters I and O, because they can be confused with the numbers 1 and 0). Each of these zones is 8 degrees in latitude (except the 12-degree-wide Zone X in the far north). Southern California, for example, is in the horizontal row *lettered Zone S.* Therefore, the *grid location* for Southern California is *Zone 11 S*—the intersection of the numeric and lettered zone designators.

The rectangular grid zones are further subdivided into *1000-meter (1-kilometer) squares.* The UTM coordinate system uses a set of coordinate numbers that allow the user to find each 1000-meter square and even the location of any single square meter within it. Grid coordinate numbers can be found at the bottom and top of a topographic map, where each vertical grid line is identified by an "easting" number (for example 577, which is equivalent to line 7 in Figure 7-19), and at both sides of the map by a "northing" number (for example 3629, which is equivalent to line 4 in Figure 7-19).

The numbers found in the bottom and side map margins identify the lower-left corner of each 1000-meter grid. Why is this important? The lower-left corner of each 1000-meter grid is the start point for finding a specific location within that grid; start at that corner and measure to the east and to the north to find a specific point within that grid.

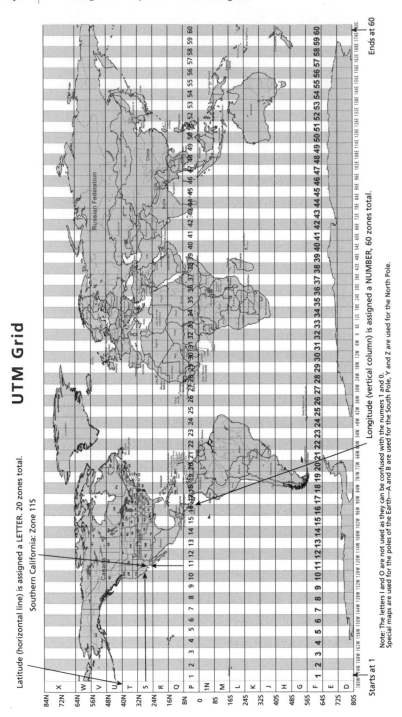

Figure 7-20. *The UTM world grid*

Drawing the UTM Grid on a Topo

If you have an older map without the preprinted UTM grid, you can easily draw in the UTM lines. Connect the small blue UTM tick marks found by careful inspection in the top and bottom map margins, and in the right and left map margins, to the corresponding tick mark across the map, to result in a grid matrix of 1-kilometer squares. To make it easier to use with your compass, you can add intermediate lines where they are needed.

GLOBAL POSITIONING SYSTEM (GPS)

The GPS is a satellite-based navigation system that can pinpoint your position anywhere on the earth's surface. The GPS locates the user's position by receiving signals from a minimum of four of the twenty-four satellites circling the globe; by locking onto these signals, a GPS receiver can triangulate both your horizontal and vertical positions. Depending on the number of satellite signals and their position on the horizon, GPS units have an accuracy of about 10–49 feet (3–15 meters) horizontally and about 115 feet (35 meters) vertically.

GPS receivers work at night and in any weather, but the GPS satellite signals may not penetrate buildings, heavy vegetation, rocks, or other dense objects. Narrow canyons, cliffs, trees, or tall buildings may also interfere with the signals and prevent your receiver from obtaining a location. If this type of interference happens, move away from these areas so your receiver has a direct line of sight to the sky and the GPS satellites.

GPS receivers run on batteries, which are affected by use, age, and cold weather, so always carry spares.

Many models of GPS receivers are available that provide information such as position in terms of coordinates and elevation, direction and distance to waypoints, speed and direction of travel, and estimated time of arrival. Most current GPS receivers provide an elevation; however, the accuracy of these elevations depends on several factors, particularly the positions of satellites relative to one another. Some GPS receivers also display street maps and topographic maps to help you determine position and route.

Other features found on some GPS receivers include a compass, camera, or thermometer. The GPS receiver can be used by itself without a map or as a navigational aid to confirm the position on the map. Use your GPS unit as an additional tool to complement your map and compass rather than relying on it solely.

NAVIGATION BY GPS

Basic GPS navigation skills involve storing positions as waypoints or land-marks in your GPS receiver, traveling to waypoints, and determining the direction and distance to waypoints. Before leaving the trailhead, always save the current position as a waypoint in case you have trouble finding your way back.

As you travel along your route, save waypoints now and then to allow yourself to backtrack if needed. These can be at distinctive features such as trail junctions, stream crossings, lakes, or saddles. GPS waypoints default to numbers that are difficult to remember, so be sure to give your waypoints descriptive names so they will be easy to recognize later.

Storing a Waypoint

The most common use of a GPS receiver is to store specific positions—such as a favorite fishing spot, the location of a secluded campsite, or even a spot you have never visited—as waypoints or landmarks. Waypoints are stored by entering the position coordinates by hand from a map, by using a specific button or function that saves your current position, or (if your GPS receiver is capable), by downloading waypoints from a computer with map-ping software. You can also upload waypoints and routes from your GPS receiver to your mapping software at the conclusion of a trip for future use.

Distance and Direction

Once you have waypoints saved in your GPS receiver, determine the direc-tion and distance from your current position to a given waypoint. Many GPS receivers have a nearest waypoints list that displays the distance and direction to waypoints near your current position. Note that distances rep-resented on your GPS receiver are straight lines, and you have to account for variations in the route or the elevation you will actually travel.

Traveling to a Waypoint

To travel to a waypoint stored in your GPS receiver, use the Go To feature available in most GPS receivers. This function allows you to select a specific waypoint, and the GPS receiver will display a direct path to the location. Once Go To is enabled, a navigation screen provides guidance using a compass or a highway that indicates the direction to travel and provides corrections if you steer off course. En route to a waypoint, a trip informa-tion screen displays your speed, bearing, elevation, and estimated time of arrival. You must be moving for this data to be accurate. The GPS receiver will indicate when you are approaching the destination.

Routes

Navigation using routes allows you to create a sequence of waypoints linked together in "legs" that guide you to your final destination. Simplify routes by automatically switching to the next leg as you approach each waypoint. You can also reverse a route to backtrack to your original starting point. Routes can be created as you travel by including selected waypoints, or routes can be created prior to the trip on a computer by selecting waypoints with mapping software and then transferring them to your GPS receiver. This last method is highly recommended for preplanning your trip. Mapping software allows you to easily create and name waypoints and create routes for easier navigation.

Track Log

Many GPS receivers have a track log feature that automatically saves points at regular times or distance intervals as you travel. You can then navigate, usually back to your starting point, without marking any waypoints.

NAVIGATION BY MAP AND GPS

Navigation using a printed map and a GPS receiver involves two basic operations: translating GPS position coordinates (your current position or any other stored waypoint) from the GPS receiver to a location on the map, and translating physical locations on the map (your destination or any other point along the way) into coordinates that can be used in the GPS receiver.

GPS Receiver Setup

There are a number of setup options in your GPS receiver that affect how your receiver operates and displays information. Some of the settings, including the datum and coordinate system, depend upon the map you are using and must be set correctly. Others such as distance and elevation units and declination mode are based on user preference. To use your GPS receiver with a compass, it is best to set your receiver to use true north if you are using it with an ADC, or magnetic bearings if you are using it with a non-ADC. Contour intervals and distance units are normally set to feet and statute miles, unless your map uses the metric system.

Map Datum

In order to use your GPS receiver with a map, you need to make sure the GPS datum matches that of your map. A datum is a reference system that coordinates your GPS receiver to the map, and the datum is printed on the bottom of your topographic map. Most topo maps in the United States and Canada use the North American Datum 1927 Continental, or NAD27 or NAD27 CONUS for short. Some newer maps use NAD83 or WGS84. Make sure you change the datum in your GPS receiver setup to match that of your map, or your positional information will be incorrect by as much as a mile.

Translating GPS Coordinates to a Map

One of the primary operations you perform is translating GPS position coordinates (your current position or any other stored waypoint) from the GPS receiver to a location on the map. This is easy using the UTM coordinate system.

To find your location on the map shown in Figure 7-21, if your GPS receiver reads 11S 0559264mE ("meters east") and 3652428mN ("meters north"), look on the bottom or top margin of the map for the blue UTM grid tick mark with the number 559. Then look on the left or right side of the map for the blue UTM grid tick mark with the numbers 3652. The intersection of these two lines marks the *lower-left corner* of the 1000-meter square you are in.

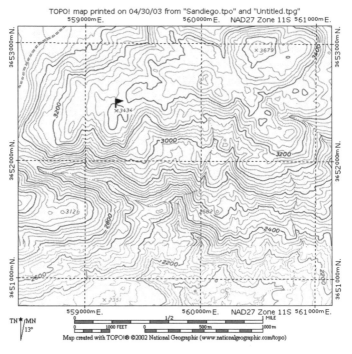

Figure 7-21. *Finding a location on a map using UTM coordinates*

Then, using the last three numbers of each coordinate, measure "right" (east) and "up" (north)—the rule for UTM is always "read right, then up"—to find your exact position (within the accuracy of the GPS receiver) in the

1000-meter square. In this example, that exact position is 264 meters right and 428 meters up. Plastic templates are available with 1000-meter scales along the edges that overlay these squares to make it easy to determine this exact position. In Figure 7-21, the position is shown with a flag icon at a peak with elevation 3434.

Translating Map Coordinates to a GPS Receiver

To translate a map coordinate (your current position or another location) to the GPS receiver, you need to reverse the preceding procedure: determine the UTM coordinate values from the map and enter them in your GPS receiver using the waypoint entry mode.

Locate the position on the map that you want to transfer to the GPS receiver, and then look on the top or bottom margin of the map for the blue UTM grid tick mark closest to, but to the left of, the position. Then look on the left or right margin of the map for the UTM mark closest to, but below, the position. The intersection of these two lines marks the lower-left corner of the 1000-meter square the point is in. Next, read meters "right" and "up" to find the exact location. Proceed to the waypoint entry screen on your GPS receiver and enter these coordinates.

OTHER NAVIGATIONAL TOOLS

In addition to a map and compass and GPS device, an additional tool used in navigation is the altimeter.

Altimeter

An altimeter can be a useful tool in hilly or mountainous areas where navigation is critical. Altimeters can be used to fix your position relative to the contour lines on a topographic map.

Altimeters are really barometers calibrated to measure altitude. Thus, altimeter readings are affected by changes in the weather, so it's important to calibrate an altimeter's reading whenever you arrive at a point of known elevation.

FINDING NORTH WITHOUT A COMPASS

Carrying a compass is a necessity on any trip in the wilderness. There are, however, a few navigation tricks that don't use a compass that will make you feel like an explorer.

Navigating by the Sun, Moon, and Stars

The path of the sun can be used as a general direction indicator. For example, at middle latitudes in the northern hemisphere, the sun always lies toward the south at midday. Therefore your shadow points north at approximately 12:00 p.m. (noon) standard time or 1:00 p.m. daylight saving time. In late June, the sun rises more or less in the northeast, passes high overhead in the south at noon, and sets in the northwest. In late December, the sun rises more or less in the southeast, passes low in the south at noon, and sets in the southwest. In late March and late September, the sun rises due east and sets due west.

A good technique, if you're patient, is to put a stick in the ground and mark the point at the end of its shadow (see Figure 7-22). Do this several more times at intervals of ten or fifteen minutes. A line connecting these points will be generally east-west; a line perpendicular will be generally north–south.

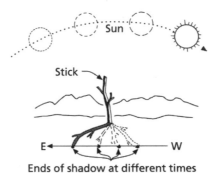

Ends of shadow at different times

Figure 7-22. *Using the shadow of a stick in the ground to determine general north–south direction*

Like shipboard navigators, you can also use the stars and moon to indicate directions. The stars and moon move across the sky in the same direction as the sun, east to west. So stars that climb in the sky are somewhere near east, and stars that sink in the sky are somewhere near west. Polaris (the North Star), however, holds one position in the northern sky and is a reliable north indicator.

Find Polaris by first looking for the Big Dipper. A line extended through the two outermost stars (the "pointers") of the Big Dipper's bowl points to Polaris (see Figure 7-23). When the Big Dipper is not visible, Cassiopeia usually is. The top of Cassiopeia's W-shaped form points toward Polaris. A further hint is that Polaris's altitude, or angle above the horizon, very nearly matches an observer's north latitude. An observer at Yellowstone National Park (latitude 45 degrees north), for example, would locate Polaris 45 degrees above the horizon, or halfway up in the sky.

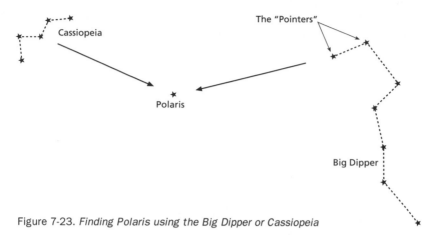

Figure 7-23. *Finding Polaris using the Big Dipper or Cassiopeia*

From simple day hikes to longer wilderness trips, it's important to keep your sense of direction and maintain an awareness of where you are. Carry a map and a compass when you travel in unfamiliar areas, and refer to your map often. With practice, navigational skills become natural everyday habits.

chapter
8

How's the Weather?

Earl Towson, Mark Mauricio, Keith Gordon, and Skip Forsht

My friend said, "It's only a 10 percent chance of rain, and we're already here. Let's just go for it." We had gotten a permit through the lottery system to head up Mount Whitney; it was a "go now or wait until next year" situation. We started up the Mountaineers Route, but by the time we got up near Iceberg Lake, the sky had changed from blue to dark purple and then to black. The temperature had dropped from the mid-sixties to the low fifties, and the wind had picked up to twenty-five-miles per hour.

Then the hail started, and next the rain—torrential rain, the kind where you can't see more than fifteen feet in front of you; blowing, big, stinging droplets of rain. After turning around, we prayed not to fall or to have to stop for any reason as we descended. The temperature had dropped to the upper thirties with the wind chill, we were soaked, and hypothermia had become a very real possibility.

The weather can make or break any hike or trip. Understanding it better, predicting it, and preparing for it are all part of responsible overall trip preparation. The weather can be just a nuisance factor, such as clouds obscuring a meteor shower, or a life-and-death situation, as with hypothermia in high country. Humans have a very small range of core body temperatures in which we can function reliably, roughly 95 degrees F to 105 degrees F. Weather conditions that push us out of that window are life threatening and need to be considered in trip preparation. You need to know as much about the weather as you do about using your gear or planning a route.

The behavior of weather is unpredictable, but with a little knowledge, you can begin predicting it with more confidence. As your knowledge increases, your predictions will become more reliable, and you can use your knowledge to better prepare and to travel more safely in the wilderness.

THE ATMOSPHERE: WHERE WEATHER OCCURS

The earth's atmosphere consists of a mixture of gases we call air. Most of the air is composed of nitrogen, whose properties determine how the air heats and cools and gives air its blue color. Most of the air lies within 20 miles of the earth's surface; it is densest at sea level and rapidly thins with increasing elevation.

Virtually all of the weather takes place in the lowest part, called the *troposphere,* which is 5–6 miles (8–10 km) above the earth. Only in the troposphere does air move vertically, producing what we call weather. The temperature of the air within the troposphere decreases at a fairly constant rate. For backpacking purposes, you can plan on a decrease of 4 degrees F per 1000 feet; thus, if you are planning to climb from Whitney Portal to the top of the peak, your gain of 6000 feet would probably experience a drop of about 24 degrees F. Likewise, if you descend 6000 feet into the Grand Canyon from the North Rim, you would expect to see a rise of 24 degrees F.

Heat and Pressure Systems

The sun is the earth's primary source of heat. The surface of the earth and its atmosphere, however, do not heat and cool in a uniform fashion. The surface of the earth gets hotter where the sun is directly overhead. Since the earth has seasons, due to its axial tilt, the number of daylight hours varies with both the time of the year and latitude. For example, along our southern border with Mexico, we have fourteen hours of sunlight in the summer but only ten hours in the winter, whereas along our northern border with Canada, we have fifteen hours in the summer and only nine hours in the winter. That is the primary reason you get hotter in the summer than in the winter regardless of where you live in the United States.

This heat creates both local pockets and larger masses of heated air that expand and rise much like a hot air balloon. The hot air continues to rise and cool until its temperature equals the temperature of the air that surrounds it (air is cooler the farther from the earth's surface you go). Masses of rising air exert less pressure upon the earth's surface, and these *low-pressure centers* are called "lows." In turn, pockets or masses of cool air create areas where the air is heavier and descends. This denser air creates areas of *high-pressure centers* called "highs." Air from high-pressure centers (highs) flows toward low-pressure centers (lows) to replace the air that is being lifted. You experience the movement of this air as wind.

Prevailing Winds

Since the earth is hottest where the sun is directly overhead, the earth produces lows near the equator and highs near the poles. The earth rotates, so the ground slips from under the air, which produces prevailing winds. As the air heats up near the equator, it rises and starts to flow toward the poles. But at high altitude, the air dumps its heat into the blackness of space, grows colder and denser, and falls back to the ground—before it gets to the poles. In fact, it does this three times between the equator and the poles. The winds flow away from the descending pressure areas toward the low-pressure areas. The paths of the global prevailing winds get tilted because the earth doesn't rotate at the same speed at all latitudes. The prevailing winds for the United States come from the west; thus, our storms come from the Pacific.

Barometric Pressure

Air has weight, although it is small, and exerts pressure on the ground. Air pressure, also known as barometric pressure, is measured in inches of mercury. At sea level, the atmospheric pressure is normally close to 29.92 inches (sometimes reported as 1000 millibars). This figure is known as the *standard sea-level pressure* (it's an average).

Measurements above the standard sea-level pressure are designated as high pressures (highs). Measurements below the standard sea-level pressure are considered low pressures (lows)—the maximum difference

At higher elevations, clouds become an extension of the mountaintop landscape.
(Photo by Bob and Ira Spring)

is small and typically does not exceed 3 percent. Lows bring moist warm unstable weather conditions. Large billowing clouds form in these systems that can bring rain, sleet, or snow but are typically not violent storms. High-pressure centers (highs) normally bring stable, cooler, and drier conditions but can produce violent storms if they overtake and displace warm, moist air.

High and Low Pressure

Figure 8-1 is a typical example of a weather map of the United States and Canada that depicts *highs* and *lows* on a given date. The lines on the map are lines of equal barometric pressure *(isobars)*. The highest barometric pressure readings are found in the center of a high and lessen as you move away from their centers; the opposite occurs in lows.

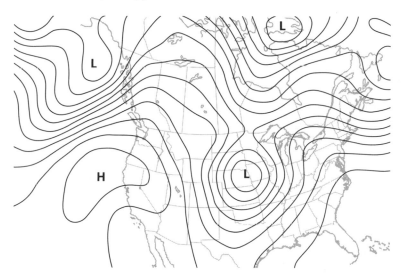

Figure 8-1. *Think of this weather map as a kind of topo map in which the contour lines (isobars) denote equal pressures across the surface of the earth. Generally, air moves from highs (H) to lows (L) across isobars, but the earth's rotation induces a clockwise circulation around a high and a counterclockwise circulation around a low. Just as on a topo map, the closer the contour lines, the steeper the pressure gradient. The steeper the gradient, the faster the winds.*

Strong winds occur where the isobars are crowded closely together; weak winds occur in areas where the isobars are spaced widely apart. In the northern hemisphere, the winds flow out from the center of a high in a clockwise rotation and flow into a low in a counterclockwise direction. The strongest winds occur where the high areas touch low areas. The centers of highs are normally clear, cool, and calm, while the centers of low areas tend to be mild but cloudy.

Because the earth rotates, the air does not flow directly from highs to lows. The earth rotates fastest at the equator and much slower near the poles, where inertia causes the air to be deflected, causing highs to circulate clockwise and counterclockwise in lows. Thus, if you stand with your back to the wind in the northern hemisphere you will have a low-pressure system on your left and a high-pressure system on your right—a good technique to remember if you are on a multiday trip without reliable weather information from an outside source.

Clouds and Precipitation

Water vapor, the gas form of water, is colorless and odorless. It enters the air through evaporation from oceans, lakes, moist soil, and plants. The amount of water vapor present in the air is highly variable by season and from one location to another, because warm air is capable of holding much more water vapor than cold air is.

When water vapor changes from a gas to a liquid state, it releases heat. When this occurs in the atmosphere, a visible cloud forms. This condensation can occur only when the temperature of the air cools down to the *dew point* when the air can no longer hold the water as a gas—at this point, we say the air is saturated and is at 100 percent relative humidity. If the air cools below the dew point, the tiny droplets form that we see as clouds, similar to how water droplets form on the outside of a drinking glass full of ice on a warm, humid day. If the air continues to rise, it may cool until it freezes and forms ice crystals.

Raindrops or snowflakes form when these tiny droplets and ice crystals collect around pollen and dust; once they grow too large to remain suspended, they fall to the earth. Rain, snow, sleet, and hail (commonly referred to as precipitation) occur when a mass of air is being lifted and cooled below its dew point. This lifting can occur through convection, because of mountains, or by weather fronts (see "Fronts and Storms" below).

Air rises when it expands by being heated by the sun and/or a surface below it that is hot. A hot surface creates an updraft. If the air rises and cools to a temperature below the dew point, a puffy cloud begins to form called *cumulus,* meaning "heaped" (see Figure 8-2). On nice days we often see small cumulus clouds that children like to imagine as animals and other shapes. The clouds show us where the air is rising; the blue sky between them is where it is descending. Most cumulus clouds have flat bottoms that form at the altitude where the temperature cools to the dew point. If the updraft is strong, a *cumulonimbus* cloud (a thunderhead) can develop. Thunderstorms, while violent, last only an hour or two. If there was a heavy

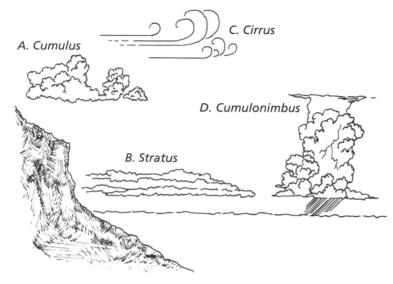

Figure 8-2. Cloud formations: A, *cumulus (lumpy, billowy) clouds are formed by vertical air currents; rain, hail, or snow can fall from these in heavy showers.* B, *stratus (layered) clouds are formed by gentle lifting of warm, moist air.* C, *cirrus (wispy) clouds are the high, gossamer-like formations of tiny ice crystals that often precede the passage of a storm front.* D, *cumulonimbus clouds are huge, towering clouds formed by strong updrafts. The friction from air movements within these clouds builds up the electrical charges that are released as lightning. These clouds can unleash great torrents of rain or hail, but they are short-lived.*

dew in the morning, expect lots of cumulus to form, with the possibility of thunderstorms forming in the afternoon—a good predictor for those frequent Sierra Nevada afternoon showers.

Fronts and Storms

A *front* is where two air masses collide, producing precipitation when the more humid air masses are uplifted. Recall that the centers of highs are normally areas of cool, heavy, clear, drier skies, while the centers of lows are normally areas filled with warm, moist air. When a cold high collides with a humid low, it's a sure recipe for precipitation.

Highs and lows alternate; they are carried along by the *jet stream.* In the northern hemisphere, three jet streams circle the world. One meanders in a broad, curving track over the United States and plays an important role in directing the path of storms. The mean latitude of the jet stream varies with the season. In the summer it stays up near the Canadian border, but in the winter it drops down to California, bringing winter rains in from the Pacific.

Low-pressure systems typically travel about 400 to 600 miles a day and are 500 to 1000 miles across. An approaching *warm front* creates the sequence of clouds shown in Figure 8-2. The high-altitude wispy *cirrus* clouds ("mares' tails") are made of ice crystals; they can sometimes be seen two to three days (1000 miles) ahead of a warm front and often produce halos around the sun and moon. Halos can give you a two-day warning of an advancing storm, especially if the winds shift to blow from the south and/or the east. The air in a humid warm front (Figure 8-3) forms low, flat, layered clouds called *stratus* that spread until they cover the sky. These typically produce a light to moderate steady rain or snow that may last for a couple of days.

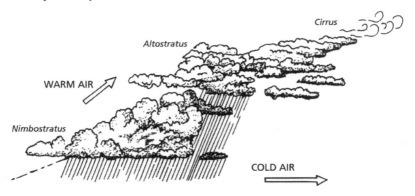

Figure 8-3. *Approaching warm front*

A *cold front* is heavier and remains in contact with the ground; being heavier, it wedges under the warmer, moist, light air found in a low-pressure area, forcing it to rise (see Figure 8-4). A fast-moving cold front can lift the warmer air, creating a line of violent thunderstorms (a *squall line*). Precipitation from an advancing cold front is usually brief but can be heavy, lasting only a day or two. After it passes, we get cold, crisp, clear skies with a few scattered fair-weather cumulus clouds following in the wake of the front. This crisp, cold air can become very hazardous for unprepared hikers, as subfreezing temperatures may prevail, especially at night.

A cold front does not typically give you a lot of advance warning, but you will probably notice a rapid increase in very dark cumulus clouds and many different cloud layers moving in different directions. When the storm breaks up, the winds will generally shift from the south and start flowing from the west. There may still be some precipitation associated with the front, but the end should be near.

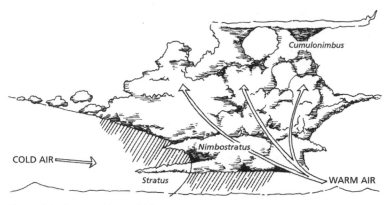

Figure 8-4. *Approaching cold front*

A cold front normally moves faster than a warm front. If a cold front overtakes a warm front, the warm air mass is lifted off the ground, forming an *occluded front.* The weather associated with an occluded front can be very violent, yielding the worst qualities of both warm and cold fronts.

A *stationary front* occurs when the surface position of a front fails to move. This occurs when the flow of air on both sides of the front is almost parallel to the front in opposite directions. The clouds and precipitation associated with a stationary front are very similar to the weather associated with a warm front. Being stationary, these fronts can last several days.

READING WEATHER MAPS

Figure 8-5 displays the various symbols used to display different types of fronts that can be found on weather maps. Cold fronts are shown on weather maps as a line with triangles on the advancing side. A warm front is shown on weather maps as a line with bumps (hemispheres) on the advancing side. A stationary front is shown on weather maps with triangles and bumps alternating on either side of the line. (Stationary fronts don't move because the winds on opposite sides cancel each other.) An occluded front is shown on weather maps as a line with alternating triangles and bumps on the same side of the line. (Occluded fronts occur when warm, moist air is violently forced up between two cold fronts.)

The weather map in Figure 8-5 shows two cold fronts with their triangle-shaped barbs; one is moving south across central Nebraska, while the second is moving southeast across central California. A warm front is shown moving northwest across northern Nevada, southern Idaho, and the western edge of Wyoming. An occluded front is shown extending from central Nevada to northern California. A stationary front is shown extending across central Arizona, New Mexico, and Colorado.

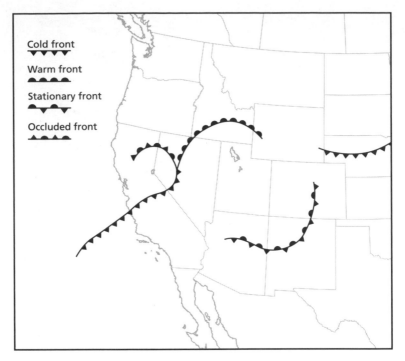

Figure 8-5. *Symbols used on weather maps for various types of fronts*

TOPOGRAPHY AND REGIONAL WEATHER

Previously, we've discussed global and continental North American weather systems. Weather can vary greatly depending on the local conditions and geography; you may find yourself in a microclimate. The latter often exist near mountains or large bodies of water, which affect the local weather.

Local Winds

Local winds are generated by mountains, valleys, and bodies of water rather than by the influence of large pressure systems. A sea breeze blows inland during the daytime because the land heats up at a faster rate than the ocean. The opposite occurs at night when the land cools faster, creating a breeze that flows toward the ocean (the wind stops at dusk and dawn). You will also note this when you are camped near large lakes. Mountain and valley winds work like land and sea breezes. Mountain winds are created when exposed rocky peaks heat up more rapidly than the grassy valleys. This causes the air to rise up the mountainsides to the summits; air from the valley flows upward to replace the rising air. During the evening the reverse occurs.

Downhill winds can occur as a result of gravity. The cold, dense air moves from an area of high elevation to a lower area. This typically occurs in winter when cold air accumulates on high plateaus and spills over the passes to lower elevations. These winds can be very strong and cold, especially in canyons. Since gravity pulls these cold winds to the lowest-lying points, set up your camp above and off to the side of the valley floor. Dry, warm mountain winds called *chinooks* can form when strong winds pass over a mountain range and are swept down the leeward rain-shadow slopes on the other side. As these winds lose altitude, they heat up rapidly and may cause snow to quickly melt, creating flash floods.

Santa Ana winds are caused by regional barometric pressure differences. In the late summer, a Pacific high lies north and west of California that causes the air to flow clockwise from the Pacific into the Four Corners area on the Colorado Plateau. A high develops that gets heated by hot desert ground. If a low-pressure system develops off of southern California, very dry winds from the interior flow toward the ocean. Since the Colorado Plateau is on average a mile high, the winds flow downhill and gain additional temperature by compression (adiabatic flow—like that from a tire pump) and can produce scorching-hot, high-speed winds and subsequent firestorms.

Mountains and Storms

When air is forced to rise over a mountain (called *orographic lifting*), it is cooled (see Figure 8-6). Once the air passes over the mountain and the cooled water vapor falls as rain, the air descends on the other side and gets warmer and drier, creating a rain shadow. The deserts of the American Southwest are an example of this rain-shadow effect.

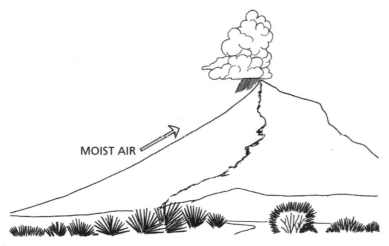

MOIST AIR

Figure 8-6. *Orographic lift*

Fog

Fog is a stratus cloud that lies close to the ground. While a nuisance, fog is not dangerous and often means that no violent weather is approaching.

Tule fog forms on cold, clear nights when there is little or no wind in low, marshy areas, typically in valleys, when the temperature of the air near the surface of the ground falls below the dew point. It can persist for days when conditions are stable and there is very little mixing of the air. It is normally not very thick, and a short climb can often put you above it.

Fog can also form when warm, moist air flows over a cold or snow-covered surface. This type of fog is common off the West Coast when warm, moist air flows across the Pacific's cold coastal currents, causing the water vapor to condense. This fog simply flows with the sea breeze onto shore.

Fog can also form when humid air gradually moves up a steep mountainside or a sloping plain. This type of fog can become very thick in the mountains, and it can make finding your way difficult when visibility is reduced to a few feet.

Fog can also form above lakes when cool air moves over the warmer water surface. Water vapor that previously evaporated from the water surface strikes the cool air and immediately condenses. This commonly occurs over lakes and rivers during fall and early winter, giving the body of water a steaming appearance.

WEATHER INFORMATION

Weather information can be found in newspapers, on television, and on the Internet. Information in newspapers becomes dated fairly quickly and may be several hours old by the time the newspaper is delivered. Television weather forecasts are more timely but lack details. The weather channel carried by cable television and the Internet are better and carry broadcasts continuously throughout the day. A number of websites can give you basic weather information, but the National Weather Service (see "Resources" at the back of this book) is the best official source. A helpful feature of this site is the ability to move the cursor anywhere on the map—for instance, to a distant mountain pass far from any population center—and get accurate forecasting for that location for a week in advance.

The National Oceanic and Atmospheric Administration (NOAA) maintains a network of weather radars and radio stations that broadcast weather conditions. Reports are updated every four hours; broadcasts are transmitted on the VHF FM band radios at eight frequencies between 162.40 and 162.55 megahertz. There are also backpackable NOAA-capable weather radios that are small and weigh only a few ounces (most sell for under $50). NOAA transmissions may be difficult to pick up in remote terrain, especially in canyons.

Before you leave on an extended backpack trip, you should study a satellite map of the weather approaching from the west. NOAA and the Naval Research Laboratory (NRL) publish these on the Internet (see "Resources" in the appendix). Many strong West Coast storms grow in the Pacific Northwest after leaving Siberia. These look like large commas in satellite images. Since they can move more than 500 miles a day, you can estimate when they will reach you. Recall that they will follow the jet stream—if the jet stream has large dips down to your latitude, these storms may reach you.

WEATHER HAZARDS

Weather can be dangerous. Every year someone outdoors is hurt or killed by lightning, windstorms, flash floods, blizzards, avalanches, hail, hypothermia, or heatstroke. Backpacking should be an enjoyable sport, so it's smarter to postpone a trek than to become a victim of dangerous weather. Here are a few safety tips to avoid becoming one of those victims:

- **Lightning storms:** don't seek shelter by lone trees or on high points; don't stand on wet granite or near water.
- **Windstorms:** Don't camp under trees that are dead or have dead limbs or huge cones.
- **Flash floods:** Don't camp in a wash or a gully.
- **Snowstorms:** Seek out or build a shelter; get out of the wind and stay warm!
- **Cold, wet weather:** Don't get soaking wet; if you do, change to drier clothes.
- **Hot weather:** Drink lots of water!

Cumulus clouds over Utah's Grand Staircase (Photo by Jerry Schad)

Thirteen Rules of Thumb for the Weather-Wise Backpacker

1. If the clouds are going in different directions (for example, one layer is going west while another layer is going north), bad weather is coming.
2. If you see growing billowy cloud towers (cumulonimbus clouds), expect thunder showers.
3. Mares' tails (cirrus clouds) high in the sky with long streamers can mean bad weather within the next thirty-six hours.
4. A cloud cover that looks like cottage cheese (mammatus clouds) is often indicative of a strong approaching storm.
5. "Mackerel" or "buttermilk skies" (altocumulus clouds) can mean bad weather within the next thirty-six hours. **Note:** When mackerel skies and mares' tails appear in the sky at the same time, rain is sure to follow the next day.
6. Cloud cover at night means you can expect a warmer night because the clouds prevent heat radiation that would lower the temperature on a clear night. If the stars twinkle furiously, expect a cold night and winds.
7. Check the grass for dew at sunrise. If it's a hot day and cumulonimbus towers are building, there is a good chance for afternoon thunderstorms.
8. A rainbow in the west at sunrise can mean rain is on its way. On the other hand, a rainbow in the east at sunset means that the rain is on its way out and you can look forward to sunny days.
9. Strong winds indicate high pressure differences and can be a sign of advancing storm fronts. If the wind shifts to the south or east, a storm is near.
10. Take a deep breath and smell the air. Scents are stronger in moist air associated with coming rainy weather. Also, many people can feel the humidity, especially in their hair.
11. Campfire smoke should rise steadily; smoke that swirls and descends is caused by low pressure, meaning rain may be on the way.
12. If there is a halo around the moon (or sun), expect rain or snow within thirty-six hours if the clouds get progressively lower.
13. At sunrise look east—a red sky at morning, take warning; a red sky in the west at sunset, expect good weather.

LEARN HOW TO PREDICT THE WEATHER

Create your own prediction methods. The methods provided in this chapter are based on a few key (but very general) principles:

- Major weather systems usually move from west to east.
- Advancing lows bring more humidity.
- Rapidly advancing highs can produce violent storms.

Predicting the weather is all about recognizing the signs of humidity and pressure changes. While prevailing systems may move from west to east, for example, individual storms in a particular region may not, due to local weather phenomena. On the average, tomorrow's weather will be much like today's (especially this evening's). Be alert when you see the clouds descend, the humidity rise, and the temperature fall. It's better to lay over another day in a good, safe campsite than to be caught on a high mountain, like Whitney, in a storm!

As your knowledge of weather increases, you'll become much more adept at predicting the weather, and you'll also be better at judging weather reports. If you can predict the weather with some confidence, you can manage your pack load accordingly. There is no sense carrying more than what's needed if it's going to be nice, but if it's going to be foul, then it's wise to be prepared.

Now Let's Get Out There!

Mike Fry, Robert L. Feuge, Nelson Copp,
Donald B. Stouder, and Carolyn Moser

The qualities of wilderness areas are preserved when travelers leave no trace of their passage. You can justify your visit only when you strive to leave no trace.

LEARNING NEW SKILLS

Being a novice in the backcountry means you need to, and get to, ask questions about anything you don't understand. Inexperienced hikers often don't ask questions or don't participate in making trip decisions because they may fear that their lack of experience will be obvious. Actually, being a novice means you need to ask questions about anything you don't understand. Ask other people what gear and techniques work for them. Don't hesitate to speak to the leader when a pace is too fast or when you need to stop to adjust your pack or clothing. Taking care of such needs immediately, rather than delaying, keeps you more comfortable and safe and increases your enjoyment.

Trailhead Tips

"The trail starts here." A trailhead is an access point to a trail, the place where your adventure begins! Here are some tips about trailheads:

- There may or may not be a sign with the trailhead name.
- There may or may not be parking; a parking pass may be required, and there may be restrictions on how long you can park there.

- There may or may not be bathrooms or potable water.
- There may or may not be cell phone reception, bear-proof storage boxes, bears that will break into your car (be smart and don't leave food in your car), or someone watching you hide your stuff in the trunk (don't leave valuables visible).
- There may or may not be informational signs about whether there are marmots or porcupines that will dine on your car's hoses and wiring (check with a ranger or online).
- There may or may not be a place to camp.

TRAIL WALKING

People rarely think twice about the act of walking in everyday life. When you're setting off on a long journey through uneven or hilly terrain, here are some things to consider:

- **Pace:** How fast or slow will you travel?
- **Trekking poles:** Will you want a backup for stability and propulsion?
- **Rest stops:** How often will you need a break?
- **Keeping your group together:** How will you keep from being separated from your hiking group?
- **Foot care:** How will you make sure your feet can carry you the whole way?
- **Maintaining energy:** How will you make sure you can get there and back?
- **Trail etiquette:** Do you know how to pass and be passed safely?
- **Crossing streams and rivers:** Do you know how to cross a stream on foot safely?

Pace

Finding your own pace or travel style on the trail can minimize fatigue and frustration. On your first few trips with a group, notice whether you prefer a fast, moderate, or slow and steady pace. You will know in the first fifteen minutes on the trail. If the group pace is too slow for you, you will feel antsy and want to go more quickly. If the pace is too fast, you will find yourself out of breath and struggling to keep up. Whether you have "piston legs" or amble, it is important to realize that even if you can't change the pace that is most natural for you, you can adjust it to hike with your companions. Equally important is realizing that once you find your pace and stick to it, you can reach any destination.

After about thirty minutes on the trail, it is a good time for the group to stop and adjust clothing, pack straps, and boots. A mixed group can use a "divided stop," suggesting that men go in one direction and women another for bathroom breaks. Never leave your pack on the trail as a signal to others that you have gone off for a break. You never want to be separated from your Ten Essentials—the items that will keep you alive. Chapter 5, "Gearing Up," will help you assemble these.

When walking up very steep slopes, you won't want to become so winded that you can't continue. One solution is to save energy by using the *rest step*. In this technique you pause briefly with your weight on your downhill leg, keeping it straight, before you begin a new step; as your weight passes over that leg, move that knee back so that it "locks" when it supports your weight. Then your leg muscles can relax for just a second. Do this on each step. This allows full circulation and keeps your legs much happier. Practice the rest step on stairs or a steep slope, and it will soon become second nature.

Trekking Poles

Many hikers are now using a pair of trekking poles or hiking sticks or a single pole or staff. The poles help you lower yourself (especially with a full pack) down steep trails that could otherwise damage your knees. They also allow you to use your arm and shoulder muscles to assist your quads when you're going uphill. Your poles or staff become part of the rhythm of your hiking pace. They add stability when you're crossing water and extend your reach to probe for deep water or mud.

Rest Stops

Throughout the day, stop at regular intervals of about an hour. The benefits of rest stops are not just resting; they are also times for eating, drinking, taking bathroom breaks, attending to feet and clothing, and applying more sunscreen. Make these rests brief. Five to ten minutes is good so you don't cool down too much. In unfamiliar areas, you should be keeping track of

Rest stops are important to adjust gear, hydrate, have a snack, and enjoy the view. (Photo by Sue Holloway)

your position, so rest periods are excellent times to update or confirm your location on a map.

If the weather is cool or cold, put on extra clothing immediately after you stop. The sensation of warmth you get from hiking uphill is your body shedding heat while it expends extra energy. Warm, sweaty skin can turn cold within minutes after you stop.

Slower hikers need as much time for breaks as faster hikers. It can be most frustrating to a slower hiker when he or she catches up to others taking a break, only to have them start up again. Feeling pressured to stick with the group, the slower hiker will not have enough time to recover, eat, and drink, thus increasing fatigue even more. Make sure that everyone in your group has time to take care of all their needs before you proceed.

Keeping Your Group Together

A hiking group can get spread apart along the trail—this is how hikers become lost. It is always good to stay together. If you do get separated, faster hikers should always wait at trail junctions, stream crossings, or any place that may be confusing. Leave clear directional signs or wait until your partner or group reaches you. Always stop when reaching the agreed-upon rendezvous point or time.

Foot Care

Foot blisters cannot be ignored. Heed *hot spots,* the first signs of friction. Don't wait for the next rest stop. Adjust your socks, put on moleskin, or do whatever it takes to relieve the pain and prevent further damage to the skin. (See "Blisters" in Chapter 13, "Ouch! First Aid in the Backcountry.")

Maintaining Energy

Two primary conditions contribute to maintaining your energy: your levels of hydration and blood glucose.

Hydration. When extra energy is needed, your body usually tells you right away. Dehydration is more insidious. When you're strenuously exercising, your body usually needs more fluids than thirst dictates. You will get increasingly dehydrated over the course of the day. In hot weather, it's difficult to drink fast enough. Even in cold weather, a surprising amount of moisture can be lost from breathing hard and from *insensible sweat.* Insensible sweat is your skin perspiring just to keep the air humid near your skin.

Drink water or sport drinks at frequent intervals, even though you may not feel thirsty. Drinking-tube systems (hydration reservoirs) allow you to drink frequently without having to take off your pack. If you don't feel the need to urinate every couple of hours or if your urine is bright yellow, you aren't drinking enough and your body will not be able to work at its peak performance.

Blood glucose. It is important to keep your blood sugar at the right level. If you deplete your muscle glycogen reserves, your blood sugar level will drop and you will run out of energy, or "hit the wall" (also called "bonking"). This can take four or five hours to happen but more than twenty-four hours from which to recover. Altitude may cause you to lose your appetite, and if you don't eat you will soon run out of energy.

Simple foods, high in complex carbohydrates, are good trail snacks. They don't have to be expensive nutrition bars or energy gels. Fresh or dried fruit, bread, and breakfast cereals are great snacks. Avoid processed candy. It is probably full of high fructose corn syrup and tropical oils that are not easily digested on the trail or at altitude. Fatty foods such as nuts and cheeses can also be hard to digest.

Trail Etiquette

Hiking etiquette and safety require that you yield the right-of-way to horses and other pack animals. The pack train leader, who knows his or her animals well, may ask you to move to a position where the animals can pass safely. You may be asked to remove your backpack. Gather your group to one side of the trail (not both sides), stand quietly, and don't do anything that may play upon the animals' skittish tendencies. If you are on a hill, the safest side of the trail is downhill, but take guidance from the rider or pack train leader. Talking in quiet tones to the packer may help put the animals at ease.

Crossing Streams and Rivers

Many trails have bridges of some sort across streams and rivers. Bridges might be elaborate structures or simply large logs. Bridges can wash out, or your intended stream or river might not have a bridge, and then you will have to know how to cross the stream on foot. If the water is not too deep and fast, fording on foot can be accomplished safely.

Choosing where and when to cross. First, you will need to choose the best spot to cross. Take the time to thoroughly investigate well above and below where you want to cross. If the stream is wide, more than knee deep, and very swift, consider turning back. Before wading in, try to estimate the stream's depth and toss a twig in to gauge the speed of the flow. A wide area with ripples on the surface shows you that it is shallow, and a still surface means it is deep. Use your trekking pole to check the depth.

Don't make any moves that you can't reverse, and remember that the weakest person in your group must be able to follow you. You can always make camp and try to cross in the morning when the snowmelt will be reduced. When the nights are cold enough to freeze, water volume is always higher in the afternoon than in the morning, and if you do get wet, you'll have the day to dry out.

Watching for rapids or waterfalls. Make certain there are no waterfalls or swift rapids downstream of your crossing spot in case you stumble. Every year, people are killed in the mountains by being swept over waterfalls.

Using a pole. Release your hip belt and sternum strap in case you fall in so that your pack won't hold you under. Use a hiking staff, trekking pole, or sturdy branch as a third leg securely planted upstream of yourself while crossing. Cross facing upstream and move sideways so that your two feet and your trekking pole form a sturdy triangle. If the current is swift, choose a path that takes you diagonally across and downstream so you won't have to fight the force of the water quite as much.

Using footwear. When fording fast-moving streams, always wear shoes to protect your feet from sharp rocks. Many people change into a pair of sneakers or river sandals, but wearing your boots, snugly laced to your feet, will protect your feet and give you better traction. Remove your socks before crossing, and dump the water out of your boots on the other side. The water won't hurt your boots, and you'll have dry socks on the other side. Don't carry your socks in your hands while you cross, as you can easily lose them. Don't hold anything but your trekking pole in your hands.

A tricky water crossing (Photo by Pauline Jimenez)

Crossing on rocks. If the water flows through a constricted area, as between boulders, you may be able to hop across. However, the water flows fastest in these areas, so they are the most dangerous places to fall into.

Using a rope. More technical methods of stream crossing involve rigging a rope across the stream to assist passage. Never tie yourself to the rope because if you fall, the rushing water could hold you under. Walk on the downstream side of the rope, holding onto the rope as you walk across the stream.

Remember: An alternate choice to a dangerous crossing is crossing elsewhere or *not crossing at all.*

CROSS-COUNTRY TRAVEL

Cross-country travel can be challenging and enjoyable. Cross-country travel can take a hiker or climber to remote peaks and other secluded destinations, but expect it to be slower and more strenuous than trail travel. Navigational difficulties increase as well. In some wilderness areas, off-trail travel might be restricted to small groups or might have restricted seasons because of wildlife. In Alaska and northern Canada, there are very few trails, and hikers routinely travel cross-country.

Using appropriate gear and techniques. Make sure your equipment and clothing are up to the task. Wear long pants and a long-sleeve shirt to protect your skin. Sturdy boots prevent ankle twists and stone bruises. Gaiters help keep debris out of your boots.

Gaiters can help keep all types of irritants out of your boots—rocks and debris, prickly plants, and ticks.
(Photo by Kristi Anderson)

Keep your group small and stay close together so you don't get separated, but don't let tree and shrub limbs that you have pushed aside snap back into the face of the person who follows you.

When traversing delicate ground or vegetation, single-file hikers can cut a deep furrow and hasten erosion. To minimize impact, spread out and, when possible, skirt around delicate areas such as wet meadows.

Choosing a route. Planning a cross-country route, either at home with maps on the table or in the wilderness itself, is intriguing and challenging. In most cases, you should try to follow the same route

Cross-country travel can be the most challenging and most enjoyable part of your trip. (Photo by Carol Murdock)

that a trail builder would use. Trail routes are chosen to avoid steep ascents and descents, steep terrain, and obstacles such as rock outcrops—even though hikers using trail routes will have to walk farther to get from point A to point B. When choosing a cross-country route, weigh the advantages of directly ascending or descending a steep hill against the advantages of a longer but more gradual route around the hill.

Take into account the nature of the terrain along each route. Try to avoid crossing steep gullies that could contain drop-offs or harbor snow late into the season. Consider the types of vegetation—thick brush, open forest, or perhaps a lack of vegetation (as on scree) that may be present on any of the alternate routes.

It may be more efficient to travel either along canyon bottoms or along ridges. The answer depends on the nature of the local topography and vegetation. Does the canyon bottom or stream meander excessively and is it choked with rocks or brush? Will there be frequent stream crossings to slow you down? Or is it clear for travel? Are the ridgelines spiked by rock outcrops? Or are they smooth and relatively free of impeding vegetation?

There are many trip reports posted on the Internet. Try searching for place names (mountains, lakes, etc.) on your route. You may find an excellent trip description and annotated maps.

Routefinding. In practice, routefinding over rough terrain is an exercise in improvisation. Despite your initial planning, you will find it necessary to change your intended course many times. Just keep your eyes open and your mind focused on the important milestones or destinations ahead on your intended route. When traveling cross-country, keep safety uppermost in your mind at all times. Cross-country travel is a mind game involving elements of intuition as well as navigational skills (see Chapter 7, "Finding Your Way: Wilderness Navigation"). Improvements in skill will come through experience.

TRAVELING AT NIGHT

Wilderness travelers should always try to arrive back at camp or at the car before nightfall. If late afternoon arrives and you're wondering how much time you have until sunset, there is an interesting technique you can use.

Gauging the amount of daylight. Hold your hand at arm's length with fingers parallel to the horizon, and count the number of fingers between the horizon and the sun (see Figure 9-1). Each finger represents about ten to twelve minutes. You can also determine how long the sun has been up in the morning using the same method. Since this technique depends upon your latitude, you may want to experiment first; check how long it takes the sun to traverse one finger-width.

If you're lost at night, it is always better to stay put and resume hiking in daylight. For a properly equipped hiker with the Ten Essentials (see Chapter 5, "Gearing Up"), an overnight bivouac (unplanned overnight stay) can be dealt with. Under special circumstances, it may be preferable to press on at night, assuming you're not lost and the route is safe.

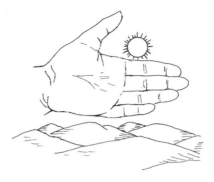

Figure 9-1. *Time until sunset is ten to twelve minutes for each finger above the horizon.*

Using available light. Travel at night requires that you see as well as possible. A full or nearly full moon in the sky is a lucky break. When traveling by moonlight, try hiking without a flashlight to preserve your night vision, if it is safe. Finding the trail is easier to a dark-adapted eye than to one dazzled by a glaring flashlight beam.

Using a flashlight. If you do use a flashlight, hold it low to pick out the shadows of obstacles on the route ahead. Headlamps worn on the head are of limited value for hiking because depth perception is greatly reduced. Either carry your headlamp in your hand, wear it on your waist or clip it to your belt, or use both your headlamp and a low held flashlight. Headlamps are great for use while cooking or in a tent. Just don't look someone straight in the eye and blind them!

PERMITS

Many hiking areas are now within the jurisdiction of official agencies. Each agency has its own management plan and permit system, so check online to find out what the permit policies are. Day hiking is often permit-free except in very popular areas, such as Mount Whitney in California. National forests and national parks often require a permit only for overnight use. Most rangers will check your permit in the backcountry, so you had better have one!

Most trailheads have daily quotas in the popular seasons, and some have quotas all year. If you don't have reservations you can take your chances on the unreserved portion of the trail quota at the ranger station. You may not get your first trail choice, but the available trail will be a whole new adventure.

Once you have your permit, make sure you know the local conditions such as where to park and whether any camping areas are closed. See Chapter 4, "Planning Your Adventure," to find out how to apply for your permit.

WILDERNESS CAMPING

When you choose a place to camp, plan for comfort and also take care of the environment. Observe Leave No Trace principles and clean up camping areas that have been abused by others. If we do not do this properly, we do more damage at campsites than in any other part of the wilderness (for the complete description of how to select a campsite, see Chapter 2, "Leave No Trace: Outdoor Ethics").

Campsites

When you're below timberline, restrict your campsites to forest duff (pine needles or dead leaves), sandy areas free of vegetation, or bare soil. Mountain meadows, especially just below timberline, are visually attractive as campsites but are not appropriate because they are fragile, plus too wet and bumpy for a good camp. Look along the edge of the meadow and find a good campsite there instead.

During mild weather, sleeping under the stars can be carefree and enjoyable. Cold, rain, or mosquitoes, however, may require you to use a tent.

You can eliminate the annoyance of mosquitoes by applying insect repellent, wearing a head net, or moving to a breezy spot where insects are blown away. Mosquitoes are less abundant on higher, drier, breezier ground, and you will have much better views as well. Since cold air flows downhill at night and collects in low-lying spots, a higher campsite will also be warmer than one in a low-lying area.

Consider also the position of the sun as it rises in the morning. Camping on an east-facing slope, with a low horizon, will make it brighter and warmer when you get up the next morning.

When camping in popular areas, be a considerate neighbor. Leave sound equipment, pets, and other reminders of the civilized world at home. Peace and quiet are two of the earth's most valuable resources. Listen to the soft music of the wilderness: wind, water, and birdsong.

Sanitation

Another challenge at the campsite is sanitation. The techniques of eliminating body wastes and maintaining privacy, especially when part of a group, are skills you can develop.

Urination is not a complicated issue, since urine is normally biologically sterile, although it can cause odor problems too close to camp (try to keep your toilet downwind from camp). Begin drinking fluids before you start dinner so you can urinate before you go to bed and perhaps not have to get up in the middle of the night. If nature calls in the middle of the night, elimination is simplest outside the tent, but you can also use a pee bottle inside the tent. This is common on mountaineering expeditions when weather conditions may not allow you to go outside. Women can use a pee bottle with a wide top or with a special funnel available from some backpacking shops and mail-order companies.

Make your pee bottle at home. Choose a leakproof one-quart plastic bottle. Mark the bottle so it won't be confused with your other drink bottles that might look just like it (also make sure you can identify it in the dark!). You can use spraypaint or duct tape, but leave part of the bottle unpainted so you can see how full it is.

Practice using your pee bottle at home first—the tent is not the place to learn. A one-quart bottle handles about two to four average "pees." Set up your private indoor bathroom before you go to sleep: have your pee bottle (and funnel), a small pack of tissues, a couple of premoistened towelettes, a self-sealing plastic bag, and your light (a headlamp works best) nearby. Always move your sleeping bag out of the way. After filling the pee bottle, screw the top back on immediately. Let the tissues catch any drips if you use a funnel, leave the funnel out to dry, and stash the tissues and towelettes in the resealable plastic bag. Next day, empty the bottle (scatter the urine and try to avoid hitting plants), rinse it if possible, and let it air dry.

Solid body waste. Always use a pit toilet or latrine when one is available. When it is not, to deposit solid waste, travel 200 feet or more from camp and any water source. Dig a cat hole 6–8 inches deep, squat down, and when you're finished, fill in the hole with soil and tamp it down. Mark your spot with a rock or stick. Pack out all toilet paper in a resealable plastic bag.

If you have lost your ability to squat, figure out the position at home. Your wilderness experience will be much easier if you have gained new leg strength and flexibility. Here are some suggestions:

- Hold on to a small tree or low branches of a large tree, and balance yourself over the cat hole.
- If you can find a small log or a rock in a private spot with soft soil beside it, use it as a kind of a toilet seat while extending your buttocks over the hole.
- Dig the cat hole near a log or rock that you can lean back into (although this is tricky), and put something soft between your lower back and the log or rock to prevent scrapes.
- Use your hiking stick for balance.

Many people report that half of their internal plumbing system refuses to function smoothly while on wilderness trips. Of course, no one ever dies from a few days of constipation. In some cases, constipation is due to dehydration or a change of diet. Some people are susceptible to "inhibition constipation," which is probably triggered by being uncomfortable about toileting in the outdoors. Inhibition constipation can be overcome by first understanding that you are not the only one who has experienced it.

Try drinking something warm. Take the time to find a pleasant spot far enough away from camp that affords absolute privacy. Allow yourself plenty of time to relax and let nature take its course. If you're on a trip with a tight schedule, then plan to wake up earlier if you need to so you'll have enough time. You can even prepare your latrine ahead of time. Be careful where you dig a hole, though. You don't want some unsuspecting member of your party tripping in it.

Feminine hygiene. For women, the decision of whether or not to travel in the wilderness during menstruation depends on experiences at home. If cramping and flow are normally no problem, you'll find your menstrual periods in the wilderness are only slightly inconvenient. Bring along resealable plastic bags for used sanitary products, extra tissues, and premoistened towelettes. Always pack in a full supply of sanitary products. Even women with menstrual cycles that usually run like clockwork may find that altitude, heavy exercise, or excitement can alter the normal pattern. If you don't end up using most of your supplies, there may be a less-prepared woman in the group who might be very grateful for your foresight.

In the event you run short of supplies, small clothing items or handkerchiefs can be used. Secure to underclothes with safety pins (make sure to bring some). When your improvised items need washing, wash them out at least 200 feet away from any water source, or bag them up in a resealable plastic bag and pack them out as you would with used sanitary products.

Don't burn used sanitary products, premoistened towelettes, or toilet paper. They usually won't burn completely away, since they're damp and made of nonflammable substances in addition to paper.

Bathing

How to live without the conveniences of a bathroom is a major concern for beginners, but life without a shower is simple to master. On shorter trips, you won't need to wash your whole body, your hair, or your clothes. For freshening up, use premoistened towelettes or baby wipes, but remember, for this type of convenience, you will be carrying in extra weight that you will also have to carry out.

On longer trips, bathing can be a welcome refresher. Often you can find a good swimming hole to rinse off the day's dust, but don't ever use any soap or shampoo! Fish can't swim in soap, and a person or an animal might be drinking the water just downstream.

Bathe a minimum of 200 feet from any water source. The simplest bathing facility is the largest cook pot you have brought along. (Lightweight plastic fold-up basins can serve as a minibathtub for washing feet and clothes, but this extra weight is probably justifiable only on longer trips.) Use only biodegradable soap, only if necessary, and use it sparingly. With a sunny site, you can wash with cold water. If you have enough fuel, heat some wash water or use any clean hot water left after washing dishes.

For full luxury, bring a portable plastic minishower bag, which, when filled with water and left on a sunny rock for a few hours, gives you an adequately warm shower. The bag is also useful for bringing water to camp or your shower location. A shower bag that holds one and a half gallons is fine for a two-person shower, including hair rinsing, if you are each conservative in your soap and water use. Remember to put your shower setup in a place where the runoff does not go within 200 feet of a water source. If possible, stand on a rock to keep your feet clean. Arrange your after-shower clothes for easy access. If there are other people around, rig a shower enclosure with your poncho, some rope, and a couple of trees.

Campfires

Many hikers look forward to the pleasure of a campfire. However, many wilderness areas prohibit campfires, especially in the summer. The short growing season of the alpine and timberline zones poses severe challenges to the survival of the unique plants and animals existing there. Campfires are rightfully prohibited in these areas. Leave dead wood to build soil or for someone to use in an emergency.

Actually, you rarely *need* a fire. Camp stoves are much more practical for cooking; a candle lantern or buddy burner will produce as much light; and your high-tech clothing will keep you warm. Also, a fire will advertise your location to every bear in the forest.

If you do have a fire, keep it small. Bonfires waste large amounts of wood and are difficult to extinguish. Besides, you'll enjoy the closer companionship of your friends as you crowd around the glowing embers of a small fire. Always use existing fire rings at sites where fires are permitted. Never build a campfire on duff, since duff burns and could start a wildfire.

Make sure your fire is completely out before you turn in. Empty your water bag on it, and stir the coals to make sure you've found all the hidden hot spots.

SAFETY CONCERNS

Poison oak, ivy, and sumac thrive in moist riparian (streamside) ravines and canyons, but they sometimes also grow on dry hillsides. They grow only below 6800 feet elevation. The maxim "leaves of three, let them be" is a good one, although poison sumac is a shrub with seven to thirteen paired leaves with red stems and berries of varying colors. Learn to recognize these plants and to distinguish them from other three-leaved plants (wild blackberries, for example) that are harmless.

These plants contain oil that is very irritating to the skin. Beware that the oil can get on your clothing, your dog, and your trekking poles and can stay until you wash it off. By wearing long pants and a long-sleeved shirt, you can keep skin contact to a minimum. In the fall, poison oak loses its leaves but still retains its irritating oil. Learn to recognize the stem color and structure of the plant before you do any cross-country hiking among the leafless plants.

All parts of the plant contain urushiol, a toxic oil. When absorbed into your skin, it sets off an allergic reaction of blisters and intense itching. Old remedies including calamine lotion and naphtha soap are far less effective than solvent-based lotions such as Tecnu or Zanfel. For effective treatment of exposure to these plants, see "Poision Oak, Ivy, or Sumac" in Chapter 13, "Ouch! First Aid in the Backcountry."

Ticks. When hiking along overgrown trails or bushwhacking (traveling cross-country in brushy terrain), check yourself frequently for ticks. These small blood-sucking parasites normally feed on wild and domestic animals. They lie in wait on the tips of grasses or shrub branches along hiking or game trails, dropping onto warm-blooded creatures (including you) that come along.

If you're in tick country, wear light-colored long pants and a long-sleeved shirt. Tuck the hems of your pants into your socks or gaiters for further protection. Wear a scarf around your neck, and wear a hat.

Scan your clothing and that of your hiking partners for ticks, and brush any off before they crawl out of sight. If a tick successfully hitches a ride on a human host, it usually crawls to some protected place underneath clothing before choosing a spot to attach itself. By visually checking yourself often, and by being aware of the slightest irritations on your body, you can intercept the tick before it digs in.

If it does bite, you will probably be aware of an itchy irritation or a sore spot. Ticks can be difficult to remove when attached. For instructions on removing ticks and treating their bites, see "Animal and Insect Exposure" in Chapter 13, "Ouch! First Aid in the Backcountry." Lyme disease and Rocky Mountain spotted fever are serious diseases that can be carried by ticks. If you see a red ring spreading outward from the bite, that may indicate Lyme disease, which can produce arthritis-like joint problems. See your doctor for tests and treatment.

Other safety issues involving larger critters are covered in Chapter 10, "Close Encounters of the Animal Kind."

Taking in expansive views over the McGee Creek area from a high point above Pioneer Basin in Inyo National Forest (Photo by Dan Girard)

GETTING UP HIGHER

Getting up into the higher elevations brings new experiences, exquisite views, and unique challenges.

Mountain Seasons: When to Go?

Most backpackers visit the mountains from late spring through early fall. In the *alpine* (high mountain) and *timberline* (upper limit of tree growth) zones, these warm seasons may be compressed into a period of just a few weeks, so you may have to time your visit carefully. A severe winter may have left high passes blocked by snow into August, and swollen streams at lower elevations may have knocked out bridges or rendered some streams impassable. Be sure to inquire with the local controlling agency (National Park or Forest Service, etc.) before your visit.

In the big mountain ranges of North America, such as a fairly typical range like the Sierra Nevada, the early summer months of June and July are the best time for flowers but also the time for rain and mosquitoes. In August and September, sunny weather usually prevails in the morning, but clouds building over the higher peaks signal that all prudent hikers should be ready to seek refuge from the rain, wind, and lightning that might start by early afternoon. Early autumn—anytime from mid-September through October—is the best time to enjoy the fall colors of aspens, cottonwoods, and maple trees. Mountain weather in the early autumn is usually calm and stable, but this is also when the season's first snowstorms can arrive.

Deer hunting season in the national forests and other public lands usually starts in mid-September. Check with your state fish and wildlife agency or local sporting goods stores for schedules and maps, and avoid the zones where most deer tags are sold. Lower elevations on a range's more populated side can be filled with deer and hunters. Alpine areas have few deer and fewer hunters. You should still be extra careful: wear bright colors and make your presence known. Better yet, visit state and national parks, where hunting is prohibited.

Altitude Effects

Air at higher altitudes is both thinner and drier. Both of these characteristics affect the local climate. Temperatures tend to be much cooler than in the lowlands, and they can swing from warm daytime highs to bone-chilling nighttime lows.

While trying to keep cool in the midday sunshine, you may be tempted to shed as much clothing as possible. Think twice. Ultraviolet radiation is intense at altitude. Bombardment comes from all directions as UV reflects off of snow, rocks, and water, even penetrating cloud cover.

Unprotected skin at high altitude burns quickly. Your face, arms, and backs of your hands are affected the most. Apply sunscreen frequently and liberally with a sun protection factor (SPF) of thirty or greater. Cover up with a long-sleeved shirt and a wide-brimmed hat. You might wear a bandana under your hat or visor to cover your ears and the back of your neck. Some hats have skirts for the same purpose. To protect your hands, wear lightweight cotton gloves during the day.

Wear sunglasses or glacier glasses (sunglasses with side shields) with a 100 percent UV absorption rating. Exposure to high-intensity sunshine and excess UV can cause snow blindness. Repeated episodes of UV overexposure may trigger serious vision problems like cataracts later in life. Chapter 12, "Winter Snow Travel," tells more.

How to Acclimate

Thin mountain air is refreshing once you get used to it, but that can take some time. If you live at sea level and have little experience at high altitude, you should plan a series of trips at increasing altitude to acclimate and acquaint yourself with it.

Don't expect to accomplish too much in the first days of your trip, and try to restrict your camp changes to an increase of 2000 feet of altitude per day, adding a day of rest when needed. You will be more comfortable sleeping low and hiking higher during the day. Your body is making changes that require you to drink a lot of water and learn to take much larger breaths, even while you're sleeping. Your appetite may suffer, and you may get mild headaches, but these are easily treated. Some people find that they acclimate faster on subsequent trips, though this is not proven. During altitude acclimation, while at rest or asleep, many people tend to fall into an alternating cycle of rapid breathing and very slow or stopped breathing known as apnea. This is not unusual and should lessen with time.

Anyone can be affected by high altitude symptoms. Some people are genetically unable to acclimate to high-altitudes, sometimes as low as 8000 feet. And anyone can develop a dangerous and life-threatening malady known as acute mountain sickness (AMS). See "Altitude Illness" in Chapter 13, "Ouch! First Aid in the Backcountry."

MOUNTAIN TRAVEL RISKS

Snow and lightning offer special challenges to the alpine traveler. Being aware of these challenges is the first step toward staying safe.

Snowfields and Ice

Sometimes snow can be helpful for travel on cross-country routes by covering brush, boulders, and downed logs on the less-steep terrain to make for smooth travel. Watch out for the holes around rocks, bushes, and trees that will try to capture your leg. Be especially careful when you cross snow bridges over streams, since these will eventually collapse as the temperature warms.

When trails are obscured by snow, you may have to follow blazes (ax marks in the trees) or other markers. Shallow trail depressions are often visible on the surface of the snow, and the cut ends of fallen logs or broken or trimmed branches on live trees mark the way. Where snow is present, a trail hike can often turn into a cross-country ramble, so keep your map handy, stay alert, and be prepared to use your navigational skills.

Ice-covered lakes pose another hazard. It can be all too tempting to venture out on what may appear to be thick ice. If the ice breaks, it's almost impossible to haul yourself out. Without a rope to toss or special equipment, a would-be rescuer can easily fall into the same trap. Walk around the lake instead of walking across it.

High passes may be choked with snow after a heavy winter. In the morning, and again late in the day, these slopes may be too icy to cross, especially if a slip and fall could result in a long and fatal slide. An ice ax, crampons, and the skills to use them may be essential for safe passage. Instead, bide your time and wait for the snow to soften enough to kick steps.

Sunscreen and sunglasses are particularly important at high altitudes, where UV exposure is strong. (Photo by Dan Girard)

Lightning

In many mountain areas, the pattern of crystal-clear mornings, afternoon thunderstorms, and clearing evenings repeats like clockwork for days on end. If you're planning to cross a high pass or climb a peak, the wise thing to do is get an alpine (early) start, and get off the peak well before the clouds move in.

Sometimes there's not much advance warning for these storms. First there's a billowing cloud above, then hail, then the first lightning strike somewhere nearby. As the charge builds, your hair may stand on end, and sparks (a corona discharge) may jump from eyeglasses, pack frames, or other metallic objects. If this happens, you're clearly in trouble, and a lightning strike is imminent. The types of lightning strikes that can cause injury are:

- **direct hit**
- **splash hit:** jumping from one object or person to another
- **step hit:** a series of strikes in rapid succession

- **pressure waves:** lightning's explosive force, which can result in blunt trauma

To determine the distance between yourself and a bolt of lightning, count the seconds between the visible flash of lightning and the audible crack of thunder: five seconds equals a mile. If lightning is imminent, immediately assume a position as low as you can. To avoid ground currents, crouch low on something insulating like your pack, but do not sit on it. After the strike, move quickly downhill. When you feel the charge building again, get into a low position as before. Ice axes, tent poles, and metal trekking poles should be carried horizontally or abandoned if lightning is a threat. Do not huddle in a group—spread out.

Any tall object reaching above its surroundings is a highly probable target for a lightning strike. Obviously, you do not want to be that object. Sharp-edged objects also have a tendency to attract lightning discharges. A good strategy, then, is to find a safe haven in a low spot close to but not directly under an object such as a tree that will attract a strike away from you. A 30-foot-tall tree offers some protection if you're 20 or 25 feet away from it.

When seeking a low spot, don't position yourself in a soggy basin, along a creek, along the base of a cliff, close to cracks in a rock, or at the entrance of a cave (the interior of a spacious dry cave is okay). These places are likely to conduct ground currents and are not safe. If you are down lower, avoid being struck by seeking shelter in low growth in the forest, in a ravine or valley, in a car with the windows rolled up, or in a shelter that has electricity (which will conduct a strike into the ground).

AS YOU PROGRESS

As you develop new skills and perspectives, remember that mastery requires time, patience, and experience. Remember to be patient with yourself and with others. Bring your powers of reasoning and judgment with you into this new environment. Take responsibility for yourself as well as for others, and enjoy your supreme outdoor adventures.

That was fun! Where to next?
(Photo by Pauline Jimenez)

Close Encounters of the Animal Kind

Robert L. Feuge

One of the greatest rewards of traveling through wilderness is the opportunity to see wildlife in their natural habitats. In the wild, you will see biological diversity that you won't ever see in urban settings. It is heartwarming to observe a mother bear cavorting with her cubs alongside a stream, to see a majestic elk in the forest, or to watch a mountain goat on a high rocky crag. As you hike along, keep in mind that the terrain you are passing through is the natural domain of wild animals and that you are intruding in their natural setting. As an intruder, you should do your best to avoid disturbing the inhabitants. As you hike, observe and be careful to leave little or no trace of your passage.

You will increase your chances for such sightings if you move quietly and observantly through the countryside. Sometimes, though, moving silently along a trail can lead to a sudden encounter with a wild animal. You may come around a bend in the trail and there in front of you is a bear. How you react during the first few seconds of that unexpected encounter may determine whether the meeting is enjoyable or turns into a dangerous one. This chapter contains information about how to manage such encounters with a variety of animals.

Elk in Yellowstone National Park, Wyoming (Photo by David M. Gottfredson)

SOME DOS AND DON'TS ABOUT ANIMAL ENCOUNTERS

Do Not Feed Wild Animals

No matter how cute, cuddly, or tame a wild animal appears, *never* give it food. (Some human foods are harmful to the digestive systems of animals.) When animals develop a taste for human food, such as the goodies you carry in your pack, they may come to eschew their natural food sources and develop a dependency on human food. Reliance on such unnatural, sporadic, and unpredictable food sources may reduce the animal's chances for survival in the wild. How often will a soft-hearted backpacker come by and freely offer food to an animal? Rarely! Or carelessly leave it by the trail? Hopefully not too often! If this happened, they might begin to look at humans as a source for their food. By coming to depend on such gratuitous and random sources of food, wild animals may lose their instinctive fear of people, one of their natural predators. This process of habituation can become destructive to the animal and dangerous to humans.

Though a marmot may look tame and friendly, you should never feed it or any other wild animal. (Photo by Blake Cournyer)

A classic example of habituated animals is the black bears of Yosemite National Park. They raid trash cans and campgrounds for food, undeterred by human presence. These animals become not only pests but a potential danger to humans. If it is hungry enough, even a black bear will attack you to get at food. Therefore, never get between a bear and what it perceives as food. When animals do become dangerous, they are either tranquilized and evacuated to remote areas or are destroyed. "A fed bear is a dead bear," states Stephen Herrero, a leading authority on bear ecology, behavior, and attacks. Dead animals should never be the result of wilderness travel.

Also, the very act of feeding a wild animal can also be dangerous. Some animals do "bite the hand that feeds." If bitten, you risk infection, rabies, or serious injury.

Never Harass Wild Animals

Even if it seems to you that the animal would suffer no harm, do not throw rocks, chase, provoke it, or invade its habitat, unless such actions are necessary for your self-defense. Photographers, in particular, are frequently guilty of unwittingly harassing animals to get better pictures. In doing so, they risk retaliation. A harassed mother bear can charge and even kill a person if she feels her young are under attack. It's better to remain quiet and observe or photograph animals from a safe distance. The objective in wilderness travel should be to witness animal behavior, nothing more.

Do Not Handle Wild Animals

The practice of handling wild animals, even if they appear tame and friendly, carries risks just as feeding or harassment does. Wild animals carry fleas and ticks that may spread Lyme disease, Rocky Mountain spotted fever, and other diseases. Further, handling wild animals also promotes harmful habituation and increases your risk of being bitten. Some wild animals may carry rabies. Handling may result in injury to the animal as well. Handling young animals (especially birds and eggs in nests) can result in parental abandonment.

Do Not Attempt to Help Wild Animals

In the wilderness, you may occasionally come upon an injured or abandoned animal. Being compassionate, you'll want to intervene and provide assistance. According to many naturalists, however, human intervention is not the best course of action. Animals have natural defensive abilities that may be thwarted by human actions or human scents, thus leaving them even more defenseless. A doe, for instance, may deliberately abandon its young fawn to lure a would-be attacker toward her and away from its offspring. In such situations, the fawn simply lies down and waits motionless for the doe to return and lead it away. A fawn has no odor, so if someone handles it and imparts a human scent to it, its mother might abandon it. Similarly, injured animals in the wilderness should be left to nature's course of action. As heartbreaking a thought as this is, it's best in the long run.

ENCOUNTERS WITH BEARS

Suddenly encountering a bear in the wilderness is very exciting but also potentially dangerous. At first, the hair on the back of your neck may stand up and your pulse will quicken. But don't panic! In that brief instance of first contact, it is extremely important for you to keep your wits about you and coolly assess the situation. Think before you act! Ask yourself, "What species of bear am I dealing with?"

Bear Identification Process

Okay, you've encountered a bear—is it a grizzly or a black bear? Knowing which type of bear you are dealing with is all-important in managing and surviving the encounter. Location, appearance, and behavior are all keys to identification.

Location. In that first instant of meeting, quickly recall where you are hiking. If you are hiking in California, you are automatically dealing with a black bear because there are no grizzlies left in California. However, if you are hiking in the Rockies, the Cascades, or in more northern climes such as the Canadian Rockies or Alaska, you may be dealing with either species of bear.

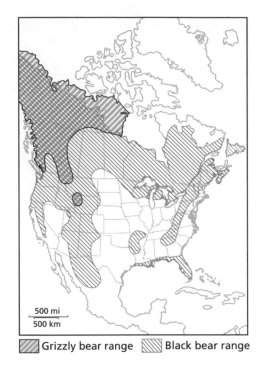

Grizzly bear range   Black bear range

Figure 10-1. *Comparative ranges of black and grizzly bears*

On the North American continent, the range of bears has shrunk to encompass only the larger mountain ranges of the West, a few mountainous areas in the East (see Figure 10-1), and several wild areas of the South. Black bears are found in all of those areas. The grizzly, however, has been hunted to near extinction in the United States and now exists mostly in the Rocky Mountains, particularly around Yellowstone and Glacier National Parks, plus the Cascades. A few grizzlies have been seen as far south as Washington's Mount St. Helens area, and they also exist in the provincial and national parks of western Canada and in Alaska. Alaska is a prime habitat for both black bears and grizzlies, as well as for the coastal variety of grizzly known as the Kodiak or the Alaskan brown bear. All grizzlies should be regarded as dangerous, though it has been estimated that there are now only about 50,000 grizzlies in North America. Northern Canada is home to polar bears, another dangerous bear species.

Appearance. Look specifically at the bear's nose, back, and paws, in that order. Figure 10-2 shows some of the anatomical differences between black bears and grizzly bears. Notice that a grizzly has an upturned snout, a noticeable hump on its back above its front legs, and very large claws. From a distance, the quickest way to classify the bear is, if there is a hump

No shoulder
hump

Straight
facial profile

Pronounced
shoulder hump

Concave
facial profile

Long
claws

A. Black bear   B. Grizzly bear

Figure 10-2. *Comparative physical characteristics of black and grizzly bears:* A, *black bears, despite their name, range in color from black to brown to cinnamon;* B, *grizzlies are generally brown in color and larger than black bears.*

on its back above the front legs, it is a grizzly. Secondarily, if the snout is dished (concave), you have confirming proof that you are dealing with a grizzly. Lastly, check the claws—though if you are close enough to gauge the size of the bear's claws, you may already be in trouble.

- **Color.** All grizzly bears are some shade of brown, ranging from tan to dark brown, but contrary to their name, all black bears are not black. Some may be brown but others may be tan, cinnamon, blond, gray-blue, or even white. Color of the bear's coat, therefore, is not very useful in categorizing bears. If the bear that confronts you is brown, treat it as either species, be wary, and consider other features.
- **Size.** Grizzlies are generally much larger (longer, taller, and bulkier) than their cousins the black bears. A male grizzly may weigh 600 pounds or more, whereas the average male black bear might weigh in around 400 pounds. If the bear is brown and very large, you are likely dealing with a grizzly, although grizzlies are relatively rare.

Behavior. There are behavioral differences between species of bears. Black bears are generally shy, preferring to avoid humans unless they are habituated or extremely hungry. If the bear sees you but does not seem to be concerned about you, it is likely a black bear. It will not act aggressively unless it is protecting its young or desperate for your food.

On the other hand, if the bear is a grizzly, it may immediately become volatile, territorial, and aggressive. It may face you, rear up on its hind legs, orient, and try to get a whiff of your scent as part of its threat assessment. Make no mistake, it is studying you and looking for a reaction. If the bear woofs at you and seems agitated, regard it as a potential threat. Try to slowly and quietly disengage from the scene. As you retreat, keep a wary eye on the bear lest it follow you, but do not stare at it. Staring may be interpreted as a hostile action. What seems threatening to a grizzly may not coincide with your idea of a threat. Grizzlies generally react badly to abrupt encounters and radical moves, so don't make any threatening moves or make bluff charges at it. This may trigger a grizzly to charge, maul, or even kill you.

Knowing Bears

Bears and their diets. All bears are omnivores and live mainly in forested areas. Between the two species, black bears are more herbivorous than grizzlies. Bears will eat almost anything, including nuts, berries, bark, insects, fish, and small animals. Black bears will leave forested areas to raid human food sources such as trash bins and dumping grounds. In addition to the above, grizzlies will also prey on large mammals, including deer, elk, caribou, and even its cousins, black bears. For that reason, smaller black bears will avoid areas inhabited by grizzlies.

A bear's diet will change with the seasons and the climate. Bears spend much of their waking hours foraging far and wide for food, moving mainly on established trails, along stream banks, or through wildlife tunnels in dense vegetation. A grizzly may range for hundreds of miles in search of food.

Bear capabilities. Much of the conflict that occurs between humans and bears stems from the human's underestimation of the bear's mental, sensory, and physical prowess. Bears are not far behind monkeys in order of intelligence and, of course, monkeys are just behind humans. Bears are extremely curious animals that tend to investigate whatever piques their curiosity. While humans rely primarily on visual sense, bears rely on a very keen sense of taste and smell, which is said to be about six times better than ours. Bears will readily investigate unusual odors, not necessarily those related to what you would call food. They'll check out sunscreen lotion, fuel, toothpaste, and lipstick, to name a few. Relative to humans, bears are superior in strength, probably poorer in vision, and probably equally endowed with regard to hearing. Despite their ponderous appearance, they're quite capable of outrunning humans, climbing trees, and swimming.

Endangerment of grizzly bears. Grizzly bears are listed as threatened on the Endangered Species list. Mostly because of habitat changes in the Northwest, bears have been restored to endangered status in the greater Yellowstone area.

Preventing Bear Attacks

Since 1980, there have been only sixteen unprovoked attacks by black bears. The best way of preventing a bear attack is to avoid confronting them, surprising them, or threatening them in any way. *Never, never, never* approach a bear or stalk one, trying to get a better photo.

Avoid a mother bear and her cubs. *Never* do anything to threaten cubs or get between a mother bear and her cubs. If you see cubs, back away from them. The mother bear is almost certainly nearby and more than willing to defend her cubs aggressively. If you do somehow provoke a mother bear with cubs, she may posture and charge at you. Do not run, but retreat as quickly and as unthreateningly as possible. Allow some time to pass. Once the mother bear perceives that you mean no harm, she will gather her cubs and retreat into the wilderness. That is your cue to go the other way.

Make noise. In grizzly country, it's wise to make noise (sing, talk loudly, ring bells) as you hike along the trail. This noise will alert the grizzly to your presence and eliminate chances for an abrupt and potentially dangerous meeting.

Look for bear signs. As you walk along, *stay alert!* Look about you for signs of grizzly presence, such as claw marks on trees, scat (feces), and large paw prints on the trail. Grizzly paw prints are astonishingly large and unmistakable with those large claw marks. If you do spot evidence of a grizzly, if you think you might know where the bear is, circle widely, staying downwind of where you think the bear might be, or simply abort the hike. With grizzlies, you have little or no control of the situation once you meet, so aborting the hike may be the wisest course of action. Live to hike another day.

Women and bears. Is it foolish for women who are menstruating to go into areas frequented by bears? Experiences vary. Plenty of menstruating women have visited bear country without incident. Female bear-keepers at zoos report that no additional precautions are taken around animals, nor have any been recommended, during their menstruation. There has been only one report of a menstruating woman being fatally mauled. A basic precaution is suggested in the book *Bear Attacks: Their Causes and Avoidance* (see "Resources" at the back of this book): Wear unscented tampons, not pads.

RESPONDING TO A BEAR ATTACK

Grizzlies. If a grizzly does attack, it is likely responding to what it considers a territorial dispute. You are the intruder, and it regards you as a threat! When it charges, you have only one option: *play dead!* (see Figure 10-3). By all means, *do not turn and run!* Sometimes a grizzly will make what is called a "bluff charge" and it does not really intend to maul you or kill you but merely intend to drive you away. When a bear charges at you, you have no way of knowing what its intent might be, so playing dead or remaining motionless may alter the animal's perception that you are an immediate threat. A passive response may result in some posturing and possibly some aggressive behavior, but generally the bear will not continue its attack once it has asserted its dominance.

Figure 10-3. *Positions for "playing dead" during a grizzly bear attack:* top, *hands behind neck, with arms protecting the face and side of the head;* bottom, *fetal position, lying on one's side*

Occasionally, grizzlies will view humans as food. If that is the case in your encounter, this is really bad news. If the bear begins to maul you, at that point, *change tactics* and do whatever is possible to save your life. Scream! Kick! Thrash! In the ensuing melee, try to keep your head covered but definitely *fight back!* Force the bear to reevaluate its strategy. Do anything, but don't charge at the bear—that will only confirm that you are indeed a threat and cause it to go for the kill with a vengeance.

If a tall tree is immediately available, you might try to break free and outclimb the bear, but since grizzlies are fast and decent climbers (for such large animals), that strategy may not work. If all else fails, stall for time with the hopes that the grizzly will lose interest in you or that help will arrive. *Keep fighting and continue to shout for help.* Your best strategy, of course, is to not get into that situation by being alert, detecting the bear first, and then avoiding it altogether.

Black bears are not prone to attack humans without provocation. Most of these attacks have been over ownership of food, particularly fish. Anglers are particularly vulnerable because fish smells are all about them and their equipment. A bear won't stop to distinguish between fish and human meat. A few of the rare black-bear attacks on humans have likely been predatory. That is, the bear may have perceived a child or a small adult as food. If such a rare event happens, don't be passive! Defend yourself or your child—kick, yell, throw rocks, or hit it with a sturdy limb. If you are successful in making yourself a threat, the black bear will usually relent and back down.

Don't climb a tree unless you are very athletic, since black bears can probably climb a high tree much faster than a human can. If you do choose to climb, go as high as you possibly can.

Pepper spray. Another tool to defend yourself is pepper spray. If a bear decides to take your food or attack you, using pepper spray may be the only effective way to ward off both species of bears. According to research by Stephen Herrero and Andrew Higgins, pepper sprays that contain cap-saicin, or extracts from the variety of tropical plants of the genus *Capsicum,* drive away bears if sprayed from a short distance directly into their faces and eyes. Pepper spray seems to be effective with both black bears and grizzly bears but less effective with a mother bear protecting her young.

The spray, however, does not prevent bears from returning later, nor is it a bear deterrent. You cannot keep bears away by spraying your clothing or camp equipment ahead of time. In fact, research has shown that bears seem to be attracted to red pepper sprayed on an object. Remember that bears will sample anything they smell that might be food, including water bottles and even fuel bottles. So *do not* spray your tent, clothing, or sleeping bag, and before you leave home, ensure that your spray canister actually works.

When in bear country, keep the spray canister handy, in a holster or clipped to your shoulder strap. If you see a bear, assess the situation and ready your spray canister if needed. If it behaves aggressively, position your-self so you don't spray into the wind (causing the spray to blow back into your face, disabling you instead of the bear), and when the bear is within ten to twenty feet, spray continuously and directly into its eyes, nose, and mouth. **Pepper spray is effective only when it is sprayed directly into a bear's face.** This action will probably halt the bear's progress but may not drive it away. Spray again and again until it leaves. If the bear is after your food, it will probably be back later.

The good news is that research has shown that pepper spray does not enrage bears or lead to an escalation of the encounter, so it is a good idea to use spray when necessary. If you are with a group of hikers, everyone should have a spray canister and know how to use it.

CAMPING TECHNIQUES IN BEAR COUNTRY

When selecting a campsite in bear country, it's best not to camp immediate-ly alongside a trail or a stream, because bears travel in those areas searching for food. Bears also like to investigate regularly used campsites, usually at night. They have likely found unprotected food there before. If you detect tracks, scat, or other signs of a bear (for instance, claw marks on trees) in the vicinity of your selected campsite, keep moving and pick another site.

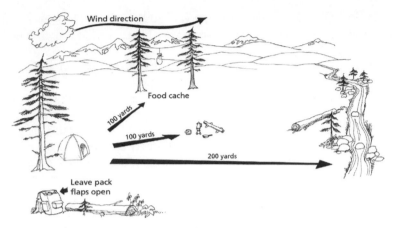

Figure 10-4. *An ideal campsite in grizzly bear country*

At the campsite, try to eliminate food odors that may attract bears (see Figure 10-4). Cook downwind and away from the main campsite, and pack out food residue. Bury fish remains as deep as the soil allows, well away from camp, and wash fish odors from hands and clothing. Strain dishwater, pack out any food particles, and scatter water 200 feet from camp and from water sources.

FOOD STORAGE IN BEAR COUNTRY

If you plan to backpack in bear country for an extended amount of time, you will need to carry a lot of food with you, so you will need a strategy to protect your food from bears and other animals. Take into account what food storage capabilities the Park Service or Forest Service may provide in the area where you intend to hike. You likely will also need specific gear in your backpack to protect food.

Bear-proof boxes. Many state and national parks provide bear-proof boxes at campsites to prevent bears from stealing food. If you are fortunate enough to camp at such a site, using a bear box is an easy and convenient way to protect your food. However, be aware that they are being phased out in some locales in preference to bear canisters. Before you depart, check with the appropriate wilderness authority about food protection.

Bear boxes are heavy metal boxes that are firmly anchored to the ground (see Figure 10-5). Each box has dual latches on a heavy, front-facing door. This system operates on the assumption that bears lack the manual dexterity, patience, or intelligence to open two separate latches simultaneously and allow the door to drop down. As I write, a mother bear somewhere in Yosemite is teaching her cubs how to open the boxes.

Where bear boxes exist, all campers in the area are expected to store their food in the same box, so it's best to keep your food well organized and marked in some manner (for example, in a stuff sack with your name on it) so that you can readily distinguish it from another hiker's food. All bear box users are expected to keep the box fully locked except when depositing or extracting food. Upon leaving the campsite, be sure to check the bear box and ensure that you have actually removed all of your food. Also, be certain that

Figure 10-5. *Bear-proof box with double latch and chain*

you are taking only your own food. If you take someone else's food, your next animal encounter may be an angry *Homo sapien!*

Bear-proof food canisters. When you are hiking outside of state or national parks, you may not find bear boxes or other bear-proof food storage methods at your campsites. One popular technique is to use portable bear-proof food canisters. They can be purchased for around $100, and many sporting goods retailers rent them or sell them used. Generally the lighter they are, the more they cost. They weigh between two and three pounds and come in different sizes so you don't have to carry a larger one than you need. Depending on the type of food you bring, a bear canister will likely carry a three- to seven-day supply for one person.

Cylindrical in form, the canisters fit readily within most backpacks but do take up a lot of space. Even so, make sure it fits into your pack, but if it doesn't, you can strap it securely onto the outside of your pack. Either way, make sure you work out the configuration well, and test it before you go.

In addition to food, you need to store toiletries, sunblock, and anything else with a scent in the canister. You can store clothing or other items in the canister to fully use the space in your pack. And, they are also useful to use as a stool to sit on while cooking or chatting around the campfire.

They are strong enough to withstand the onslaught of bears yet light enough to pack. Once in camp, you need not hang the canister but just leave it out near camp. The canisters are virtually indestructible and, most importantly, they maintain their structural integrity in the grasp of bears so that food inside is not harmed. Bears may fumble with the canisters for a while but eventually abandon them for easier pickings. For these reasons, do not leave it near a river, lakeshore, or steep dropoff. Canisters are highly recommended for those who plan to backpack in the wilderness.

Grizzly attacking a bear canister (Photo by Garcia Machine)

For the technically minded, the canisters are made of various types of plastic or carbon fiber, generally measuring approximately twelve inches long and nine inches in diameter, but they come in several sizes: smaller for overnight trips and larger for weeklong adventures. For some canisters, the latch system opens easily with a coin, and others require that you turn the lid in a way similar to opening a medicine bottle. Bears lack the manual dexterity to open these canisters. Though that same mother bear in Yosemite is now counseling her young cubs to carry a nickel with them at all times!

The National Park Service has done extensive testing with food canisters in bear country (Yosemite, Glacier, and Yellowstone National Parks) and has established that they are effective at keeping food from bears. As a result, bear-proof food canisters are now recommended, and in some parks required, as a means of preventing bears from stealing human food.

Bear-proof sacks. A bear-proof sack is basically a stuff sack made of a highly rugged fabric that is somewhat like the material used to make bullet-proof vests. Bear-proof sacks measure about eight inches by twelve inches and have sturdy draw cords used to close the sacks.

Unlike canisters, the sacks should be hung in trees where possible (much as you would use a bear bag), cached in rock crevices, or placed on the ground at least 300 feet from camp. While the sacks offer some security, they do not eliminate food odors, and bears will still be attracted to them.

If a bear succeeds in getting to the sack, it probably will not be able to penetrate the bag and take food. But in the process, the bear may crush some of the food inside the sack and/or leave saliva on it, making some of the foods inside unusable.

Bear-proof sacks do have some advantages over canisters in that they are lighter, more easily stored in packs, and cheaper than canisters, but they are not rigid enough to prevent bears from crushing the food they contain. You might consider using a bear-proof sack to protect food that can withstand being crushed (for instance, granola) and put the rest in a canister.

Is there an alternative to a bear canister or bear-proof sack? Yes! Before bear-proof containers were developed, hikers had to hang their food in trees. However, bear canisters have made hanging food a less-used option. Some hikers still hang their food in trees so as to keep their pack weight down, but many hikers find bear canisters more convenient. Techniques to hang your food require a lot of skill, dexterity, and practice to implement effectively. Unless you have practiced and learned a method to hang food to the point of mastery, we do not recommend that you employ it. An unsuccessful attempt can cause you to go hungry on a multiday trip or can even cause a bear to be euthanized if it becomes a nuisance. If you would like to save the weight in your pack, there are many resources that can instruct you on proper food-hanging techniques. *Backpacker Magazine* has videos that show you how to properly hang bear bags in trees (see "Resources" in the appendix).

A word of advice: Circumstances may change and, as a result, you may need to adapt to new conditions. By knowing several techniques and packing accordingly, you will be fully prepared for anything. A twist on the old Boy Scout motto goes "be prepared or be repaired."

In summary, when you plan to venture into bear country, prepare for an encounter ahead of time. Think about how you would manage such an encounter. Take appropriate gear with you to protect you as well as your food and be skilled at using it. In other words, practice before the big show!

ENCOUNTERS WITH MOUNTAIN LIONS

Also known as cougars or pumas, mountain lions are stealthy and elusive creatures. You may hike your whole life and never see a big cat in the wilderness. Hikers who have encountered mountain lions are impressed with their sleek beauty and graceful movement. But behind that calm facade lies a dangerous animal.

How to Recognize a Mountain Lion

Location. Mountain lions are generally located in mountainous regions west of the Mississippi River, but small groups of them have moved into states around the Great Lakes. One of the largest concentrations of mountain lions in the United States is in the mountainous regions of San Diego, Orange, and Imperial Counties in California, where they are a protected species. Cuyamaca State Park, in particular, has a relatively high density of big cats.

Appearance. Mountain lions are tawny in color and relatively large in size. In the members of the cat family found in North America, only the panther is larger. Mountain lions have unusually large tails. If you encounter a large cat that is tawny in color and has a long, thick tail, it is a mountain lion.

Diet. Mountain lions are carnivores and therefore are constantly on the hunt for deer, elk, mountain goats, bighorn sheep, and other animals that comprise its natural diet. They also prey on domestic animals such as cattle and sheep. They stalk their prey relentlessly and attack when the advantage is in their favor, usually from above and behind. For this reason, they are classified as ambush predators. They generally pounce from above on their prey, leaping from a limb, a ledge, or a large boulder. They dispatch their victim with a vicious bite to the neck.

Mountain lions are ambush predators.

Mountain lions generally regard humans as a threat, not a food source, and will therefore seek to avoid them whenever possible. Only in extreme cases (such as dire hunger, defense, or illness) will a mountain lion attack and kill humans. When this does happen, the offending cat is hunted down and killed by federal or state game wardens to prevent further attacks.

Behavior. Stealth is perhaps the best way to describe the behavior of a mountain lion. They are solitary, reclusive creatures that stay hidden much of the time, usually in dense brush. When they do stalk and attack, they move silently and rapidly to kill their prey. They hunt mainly at night but may occasionally move about during the day.

Mountain Lion Attacks

The likelihood of encountering a mountain lion on a hike is very, very small. Nonetheless, encounters do happen between mountain lions and humans. According to the US Fish and Wildlife Service, there have been fewer than a hundred dangerous encounters between mountain lions and humans in the past century. Of those encounters, there have been only a dozen or so fatalities, but the trend is upward due in part to governmental protection of mountain lions and new housing developments encroaching on lion territory.

Mountain lions are territorial but roam widely in search of food, mostly at night. Each mountain lion needs at least a hundred square miles of territory. Overpopulation in a mountain lion's domain can trigger territorial disputes among the big cats. Such conflicts force weaker ones into new territory, often land that is occupied by humans. When a cat invades another's territory, one or the other will be displaced. Often, the offending lion in an encounter with humans is a young male that has been pushed out of its territory by stronger lions and has become desperately hungry. These displaced lions then enter human-populated areas looking for food. Pets and livestock become targets in these circumstances, also increasing the risks for their owners who try to protect their property. Most encounters between humans and mountain lions result from such displacements, but some do occur when hikers are in mountain lion territory.

How to Behave in Lion Country

When hiking in lion country, it is best not to hike alone. A group of humans poses a much greater threat to a mountain lion than one person and therefore decreases the chances it will attack.

If you are hiking in mountain lion country, do not allow a hiker to straggle far behind the group. A mountain lion may zero in on that isolated hiker and ambush him.

Figure 10-6. *Mountain lion versus canine tracks—note the claws on canine prints.*

As you hike, look around and be aware of what is going on around you, taking the time to look over your shoulder occasionally. Look down the path that lies ahead, scanning large overhanging limbs and boulders where a lion might lie in ambush. While they are difficult to spot in foliage, they have a big tail that may tip off their presence.

Learn to recognize mountain lion tracks (see Figure 10-6) on the trail and distinguish them from canine tracks. Cats move with their claws retracted so you will not see claw marks at the ends of their toes as you would with a dog's or coyote's paw print. If you do see fresh mountain lion tracks, increase your vigilance and plan your next move carefully.

Camping in Mountain Lion Territory

Unlike camping in bear territory, no special precautions need be taken to protect your food in mountain lion country. A mountain lion is not interested in your granola or your celery sticks. They don't even like freeze-dried food! They want meat.

Managing an Encounter with a Mountain Lion

If you do cross paths with a mountain lion, assess the situation and take bold action. You must immediately convince the lion that you are a threat to it and not its prey: Stare intently at it and shout as loud as you can. Do not break eye contact and do not run! Its prey-chase instinct could kick in, and it might chase you down and attack you. Raise your arms above your head (use your trekking poles for added height) and make yourself appear as large and as menacing as possible. Do not appear meek—unlike with grizzlies and the need to play dead, timidity here is not the first approach.

During the encounter, however, try not to corner the animal. Cornered and threatened, it may attack! Give the lion a chance to break off the encounter and flee. To do so, edge away but maintain firm eye contact with the cat. Continue to face it, and back away, even if it appears to be disengaging. If you are hiking with a partner, slowly move away back to back so you can keep eye contact with the lion while your partner makes sure you have a clear path while retreating. Resist the temptation to run, as running changes you from being a threat to being prey.

Given the opportunity to escape, normal mountain lions will disengage after they have lost the element of surprise and after their initial attack has failed. Once the cat has left, slowly move away yourself, keeping a wary eye out for its return.

If the big cat does not disengage, keep it at bay and edge away from it in the direction of help. Use pepper spray if you have it. If you have a cell phone, try calling for help. Be certain to provide your location. Keep your guard up, abort the hike, and retreat toward your car or toward a populated area, if you can. Once safely back in civilization, report such encounters to authorities and provide as much information about the encounter as possible.

If a mountain lion does attack you, fight it with everything you've got. Arm yourself with a limb, rock, or some other weapon, if possible. Scream at it, use a weapon, and swing it at its head with authority. If it manages to get you on the ground, protect your neck with your arms because it will try to kill you by breaking your neck. If you have a hiking stick or limb, jam it into the lion's eyes or mouth and keep it there. Stall for time. The longer you keep the mountain lion busy, the better chance you have for survival. At some point, it will give up and go searching for easier prey.

Even though mountain lions are dangerous when a true attack happens, keep in mind that such encounters are extremely rare and should not deter you from hiking in the wilderness.

POISONOUS SNAKES

When you hike in the wilderness, you are highly likely to encounter snakes along the trail. Some of them are poisonous and therefore dangerous to humans, but most aren't. Although many people are put off by the sight of a snake, take time to observe it and determine whether the snake that confronts you is poisonous or not. Regardless of lethality, do not kill it—snakes do us a great service by eating rodents. Who gets bitten? Hikers who test a snake or engage it. You risk a painful, dangerous bite doing anything other than just staying away from it and leaving it to its own business.

Before you leave home, learn to identify the types of poisonous snakes in the areas in which you plan to hike. Remember that, like most other wild animals, a startled snake prefers to leave the area quickly if an escape route is available. Step rapidly away from the snake, and it will probably slither away in the opposite direction.

Types of Poisonous Snakes

There are four types of poisonous snakes in the United States:

- the coral snake
- the copperhead
- the water moccasin
- the rattlesnake

Perhaps the best known of the American poisonous snakes is the rattlesnake; it is prevalent in the Southwest. It has a distinctive rattle on the end of its tail that it uses to alert you to its presence. In an anthropomorphic sense, it is asking you not to step on it. You will be wise to heed that request.

The only venomous snake in California is the rattlesnake. It has eight subspecies, including the northern Pacific, western diamondback, sidewinder, Mojave, and red diamondback.

A coiled, alert rattlesnake (Photo by Dan Girard)

How to Recognize a Poisonous Snake

Location. All of the poisonous snakes in the United States thrive in a broad range of environments. Water moccasins and coral snakes can be found in swampy areas of the South, while copperheads occupy wooded areas in both eastern and some southern states as far west as Texas. Rattlesnakes are found in a wide range of environments, including forests, mountains, and grassy prairies. They are found from sea level to tree line in the mountains, inland prairies, and deserts. Rattlesnakes are generally found where rodents are plentiful. Rocky ledges and dead-fall logs are just two places where they are likely to be found.

Appearance. The four types of poisonous snakes differ in appearance. The **coral snake** has distinctive bands of red, yellow, and black around its body, but so do other snakes. The sequence of colors allows you to distinguish a coral snake from its impostors: "Red on yellow, kill a fellow—red on black, friend of Jack" is a phrase that has been developed as an aid to identification.

A **copperhead** is brown with a distinctive copper-colored head, as the name implies.

Water moccasins are generally black, but they may be brown or yellow with dark crossbands.

Rattlesnakes are distinguished by their rattle and other characteristics. In color, they range from a reddish tan to dark gray to black and even greenish (Mojave rattlers), plus they all have a pit viper head, which is triangular and different from other poisonous snakes. Diamondback rattlesnakes are so called because they have a repetitive diamond pattern down the length of their back.

Rattlesnake Behavior

You're most likely to see snakes, since they are cold-blooded critters, out and about when temperatures are in the 75- to 90-degree F range. Like other snakes, they hibernate in the winter when their food sources also hibernate. Of the poisonous snakes in the United States, rattlesnakes are the only ones that coil and strike.

Normally not aggressive, rattlesnakes usually issue an unmistakable buzz if you approach too close to them. A rattlesnake can strike only about a third to half its length, so you will be wise to give it more space than that.

As with other dangerous encounters, the best strategy is avoidance. When in snake country, scan the path ahead and never put your feet or hands in places where you cannot see. If you are crossing a rocky ledge or fallen log, probe ahead with a hiking stick, if possible. Since a snake in those places would likely strike you on the foot, ankle, or lower calf, wearing long pants and high-top boots will give you a little protection.

Managing Snake Encounters

It can cause quite an emotional start to hear the whirring sound of a rattle-snake near your feet. That distinctive sound stirs something deep in your DNA, and you are instantly put in the "fight or flight" syndrome. The ensuing adrenalin rush makes it difficult to think, but think you must.

If the snake is several feet from you and uncoiled, then step back and move away from it. It will not pursue you. However, if it is closer and coiled, stay motionless. It will likely continue to rattle at a nominal rate. Your inactivity will send a signal to the snake that you are not a threat to it, and the rattling may abate a bit. After a couple seconds, step back smartly and get out of its range. Leave it alone and retreat. Resume hiking and please do not kill the snake! In the larger scheme of things, it is beneficial.

Hikers are rarely bitten by poisonous snakes, but it is wise to educate yourself in the first-aid steps to care for someone who has just been bitten (see Chapter 13, "Ouch! First Aid in the Backcountry," for steps to handle a snakebite wound). If you are bitten, remember that not all strikes transmit venom. If the snake does inject venom, use a cell phone to call 9-1-1, and provide your location. Get to a hospital as soon as possible. There, emergency-room docs will begin treatment with antivenin.

Unfortunately, antivenin can be quite costly. A recent case of snakebite in Santa Fe, New Mexico, led to a $180,000 hospital bill because it took eighteen vials of antivenin to treat. Most emergency rooms do not stock that much antivenin. Transporting it from other sources to Santa Fe caused the high cost. Do not take the live snake with you to the hospital if you want prompt treatment (yes, some hikers have done it!). The emergency-room docs aren't appreciative nor will they be amused!

CLIMATE CHANGE AND ANIMAL BEHAVIOR IN THE WILD

It is widely accepted today that the climate of our planet is changing. What is causing that change and how permanent that change will be is open for debate, but it is an established fact that our environment has been getting warmer and dryer year by year for more than five decades. In 2012 nearly 60 percent of the United States suffered some degree of major drought, and that was particularly true in the American Midwest, the Southwest, and southerly portions of the Northwest.

These increasingly hot and dry conditions borne by droughts have directly affected the forests, rivers, and mountains that are home to wildlife. It has concurrently affected the behavior of animals in the wilderness, causing them to alter their behavior in pursuit of food and water. As an example of how drought conditions have affected wildlife, the area in and around Yellowstone National Park has suffered an infestation of beetles in the past decade that has resulted in the devastation of large tracts of white-bark pine trees. The seeds from that tree are a major food source for grizzly bears. At the same time, the drought has reduced the flow of rivers in the area and that has affected fish populations, also a major food source for bears. At lower elevations in Yellowstone, the drought has severely affected berry-producing plants on which bears also depend for seasonal food.

Those reductions in traditional food sources (berries, seeds, fish) have forced the bear population to expand their foraging range to survive. That wider range has put them in even more conflict with humans (especially ranchers), as well as other species in the area. The changing climate has had a ripple effect on other species as well. With forests dying off, birds have had to forsake their traditional wooded nesting areas and relocate. In the process of adaptation, many critters are dying and some species are again nearing extinction.

Another result of a hotter and drier climate, for example, is that hibernation periods for many species are being shortened. Species such as ground squirrels and other rodents are obligative hibernators. That is, something in their physiologic makeup compels them to retreat to their den when winter approaches and allows them to remain dormant for much of the winter. Critters that feed on the rodent population, such as snakes, are also forced to hibernate in the winter because their primary food is hidden in subterranean dens, covered by snow and unavailable to them. Bears also hibernate in the winter because their main food sources are covered by snow and ice or have hibernated. Those hibernation patterns will change as the climate warms. Already, some of these species seem to be delaying going into hibernation.

For hikers, climate change may make water less easy to find, and it will make animal behavior a little less predictable. Animal territories may be extended, and hibernation patterns may be altered. Find out, stay informed, stay current, and stay safe.

One of the greatest joys of hiking in the wilderness comes with encountering wild animals in their natural habitats. By recognizing threats ahead of time, you will be able to either avoid them or counter them effectively. Such knowledge will give you the confidence to venture into the wilderness and wander more freely.

chapter
11

The Quiet Beauty of the Desert

David M. Gottfredson, Hal Brody, and Mike Fry

The desert has a different spiritual quality than that found on the seashore, in the mountains, or along the rivers. There's an overriding sense of stillness, solitude, and space that is awe-inspiring, with isolation and quiet that are restful and seldom interrupted by other hikers. With its meager vegetation and clear, dry air, the desert is full of expansive perspectives. There's often not much to block the view, so even a slight elevation gain yields breathtaking broad vistas. Stand on a ridge, and you can see thousands of square miles of open desert landscape with little or no sign of human influence.

There are few established trails in most parts of a desert, so hiking is often cross-country, but going cross-country in the desert is relatively easy. Just pick a direction and start walking! However, sometimes it may not be as easy as that. Expect to find occasional dry "waterfalls" in canyons and patches of spiny vegetation in the bottoms of washes and stream courses. When camping, you needn't be concerned about bears getting into possessions and food, though rodents can be curious about your food supply.

As you travel through the desert, its geologic structure is laid bare, revealing millions of years of the earth's history in diverse shapes and colors.

One of the joys of desert travel is sighting rare bighorn sheep. Here, a bighorn ram peers down from a canyon in Anza-Borrego Desert State Park, California. (Photo by David M. Gottfredson)

But the desert is full of other surprises as well. It's a real thrill to come upon a bighorn sheep, a rare bird or cactus, a trickling spring, a hidden palm oasis, or an ancient Native American artifact.

NORTH AMERICAN DESERTS

The desert regions of North America have little and irregular rainfall, ten inches or less per year. The rain can come suddenly in the form of violent summer thunderstorms or with more gentle rain in the winter. Other common features are high summer daytime temperatures, low humidity, high evaporation rate, wide swings in temperature from day to night, predominant sunshine, and clear blue skies. The soil is low in humus and high in minerals, so the ground surface is easily eroded by wind and water. Under these severe conditions, plants and animals have had to employ unique—and sometimes bizarre—strategies in order to survive.

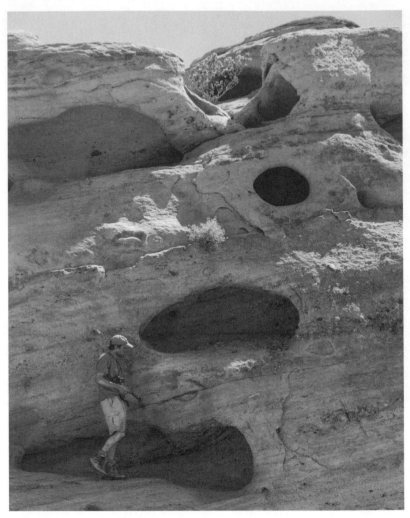

Wind and water carve fascinating cave formations near the Calcite Mine in Anza-Borrego Desert State Park, California. (Photo by Dan Girard)

The true North American Desert is divided into four regions based on distinct kinds of vegetation:

- the Great Basin Desert
- the Chihuahuan Desert
- the Sonoran Desert
- the Mojave Desert

There are also semi-arid areas in North America that are similar to true deserts. The Four Corners area of Utah, Colorado, New Mexico, and

Arizona is perhaps the best-known example. The Great Basin is another, stretching from southeastern Oregon through Nevada into western Utah.

The desert entices us with its mountains that rise from the desert floor, the storm-carved canyons and dry river courses (*washes*) that carry infrequent but sometimes violent runoff from these mountains, the enigmatic, salt-encrusted sinks that collect the runoff, and the fascinating badlands that are formed wherever water has forced its way through soft earth, often old fossil-bearing seabed sediments now exposed to view.

WHAT TO EXPECT IN THE DESERT

The desert's water availability, flora and fauna, and weather are unique facets of this area. Plan ahead and be aware so that you can make the most of a trip to the desert.

Scarce Natural Sources of Water

Availability, acceptability, and abundance of natural water sources in the desert are subject to the whims of nature. Although many natural water sources exist in the desert, you cannot trust maps that purport to show them. Springs dry up seasonally or permanently, and cartographers have a tough time keeping up with such changes. Check with rangers regarding water availability in the area you plan to visit.

More often than not, you'll be traveling in areas of the desert that have no reliable sources of water, so you *must* carry all the water you'll need for both drinking and cooking. *Carrying water is crucial for traveling in the desert.*

How much will you need? A rough guideline is one gallon per person per day, but this actually refers to sunny, mild weather conditions. Actual requirements could range from as little as two quarts per person per day on an overcast winter day in the high desert to more than two gallons per person per day on a 100-degree F day in the low desert.

How much can you carry? Water weighs 8 pounds 5 ounces per gallon, so the number of miles you plan to hike may need to be adjusted when you're carrying your entire water supply. Also, water is bulky; your carrying capacity might top out at three or four gallons. Don't run out of water before you run out of miles. Remember also that the heavier your pack, the more energy you exert and the more water you need, so carry enough.

How should you carry it? Divide up your water into several sturdy, leak-proof containers, so that if one of them is punctured, you still have water in the others. Overbag your hydration reservoir (also called a *bladder*) and water bottles with sturdy plastic bags, so if they leak, you can still drink the water. The best way to have your water available for immediate use is to drink from a hydration reservoir. Outdoor recreation stores sell a variety of hydration reservoirs as well as rigid plastic water bottles, but empty soda bottles from the grocery store are just fine too. Don't carry your water bottle in your hand. All water should be safely stowed in your pack.

Can you cache some? If you're planning a trip where you hike in and out the same way, consider stashing (also called *caching*) some of your water on the way in. This is a good strategy, but it also requires you to stash it in a spot with an evident landmark for finding it on the way back. Make a written note of compass bearings or a GPS reading on your map. As you leave your stash, turn around and look at it again. Everything looks different when you're traveling from the opposite direction. Do not ever abandon the cache, because even the soft plastic bottles take hundreds of years to degrade. Find out and follow the land agency's rule on caching.

Backpackers in Paria Canyon, Vermilion Cliffs Wilderness, Utah and Arizona
(Photo by Robert Burroughs)

Few Trails

Because it's possible to hike in almost any direction in the desert, it's very tempting to do so. If you're accustomed to staying on marked and maintained trails in the mountains, you may not realize how easy it is to become disoriented out in the open. Navigational skills are of paramount importance in the desert. You must constantly be aware of major landmarks around you.

Be sure to bring all appropriate maps and your compass, and use them! Don't rely solely on GPS receivers, as they don't work well in narrow canyons (there may be no clear view of the sky to acquire satellite reception) and batteries do die. Know where on the map you started and check your location often; landmarks have a way of changing appearance as you move along.

Don't allow yourself or others to become separated from the group. The desert's corrugated surface, just like a dense forest, can conceal a separated person in very little time.

Prickly Plants

The desert harbors a wonderful variety of beautiful yet troublesome cacti and shrubs. These remarkable plants survive heat, drought, and hungry animals through various strategies. Being sharp and thorny is one. If you're not watchful and careful of their sharply pointed defenses, then you deserve what you get!

Ocotillo branches contain long, sharp spikes. Wear a hat and sunglasses for eye protection, and look up often if you are hiking through an area that contains these plants; the branches have a tendency to hang over the trail just at head height.

The **catclaw acacia**, or Wait-a-Minute bush, or Gotcha, is another fun plant. A close look at the branches of this plant reveals sharp, curved thorns that resemble a cat's claw. These claws are great at ripping flesh and clothing, so learn to recognize its color and form from a distance and steer clear whenever possible. If you become entangled in catclaw, slowly back out the way you came in, individually detaching the claws that hold you.

The **cholla cactus** is easy to recognize and is one of the prickliest plants in the desert. One variety is nicknamed "teddy bear" cholla because the light through its needles gives it a soft, fuzzy appearance. This plant is anything but soft and fuzzy. Each stem is covered with thousands of barbed spikes like needles that pierce anything, and the barbs make the needles hard to pull out. Adding to the threat this plant presents is its unique strategy for propagation: from the end of its branches, it drops spine-laden balls that sprout to form new plants. Because of the barbed spines, these balls attach themselves to animals (including humans) to further their

Cholla cactus balls; a comb is useful for removing them.
(Photo by Charles R. Freeman)

distribution. Another common name given to the plant is "jumping" cholla. If you aren't watching where you step, you can pick up a ball on your boot and then jam it into your other leg. Or you could launch the ball from your foot to the person in front of you. Whether coming or going, the cholla ball appears to have jumped up from the ground.

If you do end up with a cholla ball attached to you, don't grab it with your fingers. The easiest way to get the ball off is to slide a pocket comb between your skin and the ball and then pull it off carefully. In a pinch a rock, stick, or trekking pole in each hand can work. Make sure that no one is standing in your line of fire or you will just expand the agony. Needle-nose pliers or strong tweezers are useful for removing any remaining spines.

Snakes

Some people are quite anxious about rattlesnakes in the desert, even though these snakes are far less common in the desert than in the mountains. Between late fall and early winter, most desert-dwelling snakes are in hibernation. When they're out and about in warmer times, they're not aggressive unless provoked. Most retreat if given the opportunity. Still, always avoid placing your hands and feet in places you can't see clearly (see "Poisonous Snakes" in Chapter 10, "Close Encounters of the Animal Kind"). Never harass or provoke a snake; just be polite and follow the practice of staying away from them.

Flash Floods

Desert washes are particularly prone to flash flooding, especially during the summer thunderstorm season. Remember that runoff can be funneled into places far from where the rain falls, resulting in a wall of moving water packing enormous force. People have been killed on hot, sunny days because of heavy rains 30 miles from where they were hiking. If a flash flood is coming, there's usually some forewarning in the form of a low roar or quickly rising, muddy water, but often it is not enough time to allow you to get to higher ground. Before your trip, keep a close check on the weather report for the region where you will be hiking (see "Weather Information" in Chapter 8, "How's the Weather?"). During the hike, keep a watchful eye on the clouds, wind, and sky for signs of rain. You need to know what is happening far upstream. Never sleep in a wash in flash-flood country.

Weather Extremes

Except for summer (late May through September), the weather in the desert is often quite mild; expect daytime highs in the 60s to 80s with warm nights. Winter nights, however, can get downright frigid: low 30s in the lower deserts, 20s in the Mojave, and even colder in the higher elevations of the Great Basin. Even the driest parts of the desert can get occasional heavy rainfall, while snow dusts the upper-elevation Mojave and Great Basin Deserts regularly. Hypothermia can be an unexpected threat.

In desert areas, shade may exist only in caves. (Photo by Robert Burroughs)

Springtime weather in the desert can be erratic and changeable, ranging from high winds with mild temperatures to a dead calm with ovenlike heat. If the weather service says a warming trend is building, with predicted temperatures in the 90s or higher, you should consider either canceling your trip or scaling back the miles you expect to cover.

In late May through September, the temperature can easily exceed 100 degrees F, which for most people is too hot for strenuous activity in the desert. You should also be wary of early May, when the daylight hours are long and the sun's high angle at midday steals away the shade. Shade can be very hard to come by in the desert. Early October can also continue to bring high temperatures. Again, check the weather before you depart on your trip, and plan accordingly.

WHAT TO BRING FOR DESERT TRAVEL

As with any trip, the appropriate clothing and gear make for a more enjoyable, safer trip to the desert.

Clothing

Footwear. The desert can be extremely tough on your boots and feet. The spiny vegetation, rocky terrain, and soft sand present unusual challenges. Boots with leather uppers provide excellent protection from cactus spines, rocks, and the intense heat of the ground, as well as providing good support. When walking over rocks of all shapes and sizes, your feet and ankles need as much support as possible, especially if you're carrying the weight of a full backpack. Before wearing boots made of lighter material, consider that a cactus spine can easily penetrate nylon fabric.

A low gaiter will keep out the abrasive sand and small, sharp rocks that can work their way over the top of your footgear.

Pants and shirts. Wear long-sleeved and long-legged garments, especially if you're fair-skinned. In a high-temperature environment, head-to-foot clothing offers protection from the radiant heat of the sun and from high winds that might evaporate perspiration too quickly. Also, comfortable, loose-fitting long pants protect you from bruises and scrapes from clambering over rocks or from the perils of spiny plants. For the same reasons that cotton clothing is discouraged for most hiking situations (doesn't dry, is cold when wet, etc.), white, loose-fitting cotton clothing performs well for hot, dry days in the desert.

Headgear. A sun hat with a large brim is a necessity not only to prevent sunburn but to keep from overheating your brain. Gray matter is very sensitive to heat and can be the first part of your body to malfunction when overheated, leaving you disoriented when you need to be alert. Without a hat you risk sunburn, headache, nausea, dizziness, or worse, so bring your own shade.

Equipment

Sun protection. When the sun's up, wear sunglasses that block ultraviolet rays. Don't forget to apply sunscreen with an SPF of at least 30 on all exposed parts of your body. After sweating, reapply sunscreen to continue the protection.

Trekking poles help with balance and propulsion in deep sand and areas of loose rocks.

Cold-weather gear. Depending on what part of the desert you are traveling in and what season, you may need to be prepared for cold temperatures and even snow. Take along the appropriate clothing and sleeping bag (see Chapter 5, "Gearing Up"). Carry a lightweight tent if you'll be camping away from the car.

Raingear. If you travel in the desert when rain might be expected, bring raingear. One word of caution regarding raingear in the desert: any clothing that is baggy or subject to billowing won't miss a chance to snag on the many thorny plants in the desert. If you use a poncho, in no time those plants will have shredded it. Ditto for garbage bags and other forms of makeshift raingear. A standard rain suit is the best choice for desert travel, but remember that rock and catclaw will shred anything.

DESERT SURVIVAL

Surviving in the desert requires careful planning and preparation. Be sure that you have (or bring) enough water, are ready to deal with the high temperatures, and are prepared for the possibly poor conditions of access roads.

Never Trust the Desert to Have Water

Do not have water emergencies in the desert in summer. Carry all your water unless you have rock-solid, current knowledge that there is drinkable water where you are going. Estimate how much water you will need, keep track of what you drink, and when you have used up half of your supply, head back from whence you came. Do some solid planning, and don't abandon a wise turnaround plan.

If you are critically low on water, think and plan. Rest in the shade during the hottest part of the day, then go directly back to your car (or other point of safety) in the cool of the evening or early morning. Drink your remaining water as your thirst dictates rather than rationing your water too strictly, since saving your water is not the best solution—water left in your bottle does you no good. Eat your food sparingly, especially anything salty. Don't waste time on schemes to extract water from cacti. Contrary to some popular (Hollywood-inspired) myths, lopping off the top of a barrel cactus does not reveal a piña colada or a reservoir of water but, instead, a bitter, pulpy mass.

If you just want to go out exploring and seeking water for fun, survey the desert landscape, looking for a line of trees or bushes that may indicate water at or near the surface. Palm trees are an indicator of surface or near-surface water, as are clumps of grass or sedges. Flocks of birds can sometimes be seen circling over waterholes, especially during mornings and evenings. But remember: *Carry all the water you will need.*

If you discover water on your travels, mark it on your map with the date. Build a valuable history of water sources in your favorite areas. Take note of the types of vegetation around a source of water. If perennial grasses or cattails aren't present, then the source probably dries up during the summer.

If you do find water, unless it is a stream, it might not be water as you know it. It may look like coffee, but it probably isn't. . . . A few areas of the desert contain springs with unpalatable (salty or alkaline) or even poisonous water. Beware of water sources close to mine tailings (spoils). If the water has a normal amount of algae and crawling or wiggling critters, it's probably not poisonous, but beware of stagnant water with nothing alive in it. Tracks of animals around the water source are another positive sign, unless there are a lot of skeletal remains in the area. If in doubt about the water quality, avoid it, and if you choose to drink it, purify or filter it.

High-Temperature Strategies

For most people, it makes good sense to stay out of the desert during the summer months, yet it can be frustrating to be locked out of your favorite desert areas for three or four months each year. Below are some strategies that make summer desert backpacking not only feasible but actually enjoyable. These strategies are also quite applicable to the hot and dry conditions often found elsewhere in the arid West. Remember, however, that the hazards of summer desert travel are severe and should never be taken lightly or without proper training and preparation.

If you'd like to try high-temperature hiking or camping, then work up to it slowly. Start in the spring with short trips in the 90-degree F range. Try camping near your car and experiment with hikes that take you only a short distance away. Never let yourself become isolated from a source of water. You should carry a supply that is adequate for anything, including emergencies, as discussed above.

Heat conditioning. Good aerobic conditioning is a prerequisite for any kind of high-temperature exercise. Always consult with your doctor before beginning a new exercise regimen, particularly one that involves high-temperature training. For three weeks before a trip, practice heat conditioning in conjunction with normal exercise. Evidence of proper heat conditioning is profuse sweating. If the weather won't cooperate, then wear sweat clothes or other heat-retaining clothing while exercising to induce heavy perspiration. This practice trains the body's sweat glands to dilate quickly in response to overheating and the blood to circulate near the skin so as to liberate the body's internal heat, and it accustoms the body to fluctuating electrolyte levels (see "Electrolyte maintenance" below).

Psychological acclimation to heat is another benefit of heat conditioning. You become more comfortable with the feeling of simply being very warm. Forty-five minutes per session, three or four days per week is adequate. Never withhold fluids while exercising or afterward; ignoring thirst is a dangerous practice. If you begin to feel dizzy or nauseated, stop immediately, cool down, and drink something. Watch for signs of heat exhaustion or heatstroke (see "Exposure to the Elements" in Chapter 13, "Ouch! First Aid in the Backcountry").

Clothing and equipment. In a high-temperature environment, head-to-foot white, loose-fitting cotton clothing and a white, broad-brimmed hat perform well. In the absence of wind, some air circulation is needed to

White clothing helps keep desert hikers cooler. (Photo by Hal Brody)

evaporate moisture from the skin and thereby cool it, so cut slits or holes in your clothing where the sun doesn't shine—from armpits to elbows, from crotch to knees. Holes in the hat also help, but be sure to avoid sunburn on the top of your head. Shirts that can be easily opened in the front when walking with the sun at your back are a real advantage. Skirts solve the air-circulation problem too, though they're awkward when you're climbing or scrambling and can get caught on all of the spiny bushes. Also try garments made of performance fabrics that have designed-in sun protection and ventilation features.

You can also carry a small misting bottle full of water. A few sprays now and then on the face, neck, wrists, and other body parts can go a long way in helping to keep the body cool.

Electrolyte maintenance. The body must have a proper balance of electrolytes to function at peak efficiency. Electrolytes are the salts in the blood that make it electrically conductive. Without them, you are a device with a flat battery. The electrolytes to be most concerned with are potassium, sodium, magnesium, and calcium. When you perspire, these salts are lost because they are moved outward and deposited on your skin. Normally you replace any losses by eating a normal diet, but high-temperature activity causes perspiration fluid loss of up to two gallons per day and, consequently, an extreme loss of electrolytes. Fatigue, muscle weakness, muscle cramps, confusion, and nausea are the typical signs of electrolyte depletion.

Drinking water without supplementing electrolytes will solve the water problem but not the electrolyte problem and can create a condition called hyponatremia (low salt), which can be serious or even fatal.

Replenish electrolytes with commercial sport drinks or "thirst quenchers." Endurolytes by Hammer Nutrition are electrolytes in a capsule. Products such as Vitalyte and Cytomax are sold in ready-to-mix powder with glucose (sugar) that gives a boost of energy and an isotonic (same salt and sugar concentration as the body) mix that ensures quick absorption by the body. Avoid sport drinks that are overly sweet with high fructose corn syrup or other sweeteners or that have too much sodium.

Heat exhaustion measures. Even if you do everything right, you can still overheat. Watch each other closely for signs of heat exhaustion. A victim is often the last to notice the adverse effects of an overheated body and brain. Early signs are unclear thinking, slurred or incoherent speech, faintness, fatigue, loss of balance, stumbling, nausea, and pale, moist skin.

Treatment is to get the person cool and hydrated—quickly! Steer him or her to a shady spot, making shade from a lightweight emergency blanket or space blanket if necessary. Insulate the person from the hot ground by placing him or her on insulating sleeping or sitting pads and immerse, douse, sprinkle, or mist the person with water. Fan him or her vigorously with sit pads or other items to encourage cooling. Meanwhile, have the person drink water supplemented with electrolytes. Never try to give fluids to an unconscious person (see "Heat Exhaustion" in Chapter 13, "Ouch! First Aid in the Backcountry").

On the Road

Automobiles are essential tools for reaching the edge of the desert wilderness, but keep in mind that the farther you drive into the backcountry, the farther you are from help. Unpaved desert roads can be in very poor condition, especially after severe weather, and it's better to turn back when in doubt than to push your vehicle past its limits. The following suggestions are meant to help you with the reliability of your transportation.

When traveling the back roads of the desert, it's better to have two or more vehicles rather than one, so that if one breaks down, the other can be used to go for help. In hot weather, monitor your temperature gauge or warning light as you're driving.

Any vehicle used in the desert must be in good mechanical condition, so if it's been a while since your car's last tune up, it may be a good idea to have your mechanic inspect it. Make sure your cooling system is in good working order, and if you're driving in hot weather, your radiator should be filled with a mixture consisting of water and a coolant designed to withstand higher-than-normal temperatures. Check the condition and tightness of the hoses and fan belts, but also carry spares and the necessary tools to install and tighten them. It's also wise to carry an extra five gallons of water in case you lose your radiator water through a ruptured hose. Carry clean water in case you need to drink some of it.

If you intend to carry extra gasoline, do so in an approved container. Legally these containers must be carried securely attached to the outside of the vehicle rather than packed inside. This is for obvious safety reasons. Extra motor oil and jumper cables should be carried.

Protecting the car's underside. It's easy to rupture your gas tank while bouncing over rocky roads, especially if you yield to the temptation to cover those endless desert miles too quickly. So use caution even if you are driving an SUV that has a skid plate. Often the stock skid plates are thin and offer only limited protection. If you will be driving off-road often, consider installing upgraded skid plates.

When driving through rocky areas, be particularly aware of the parts of your car that hang down the lowest. Take a look underneath and memorize whether the lowest parts are at the center, right side, and/or left side, and steer around rocks to avoid hitting the car's low points. If you do hit one of these components, you could crack the engine case or oil pan, causing it to lose all of its lubricant, and there is no repair in the field for this.

Sometimes it's better to drive by placing the car tires directly on rocks rather than trying to straddle them. If you do straddle a rock, make sure it won't hit the car's low parts.

Changing tires. Hone your tire-changing skills, and make sure the jack is operational and the spare tire is pressurized. The jack is a powerful tool for getting your vehicle off a big rock or anything else that the vehicle might hang up on. However, the jack that came with your vehicle was made for lifting on smooth, level surfaces, and it may not work in the soft, uneven terrain of the backcountry. Become familiar with its operation and limitations. A 12-inch-square piece of plywood can act as a base for your jack and allows it to lift more efficiently in soft sand. If you travel the back roads frequently, consider purchasing a high-lift jack.

Getting unstuck. Stash a tow rope and shovel in the vehicle and know how to use them. Getting stuck in the sand happens to almost every desert adventurer sooner or later. Strips of old carpet or hardware cloth (wire mesh) placed under the tires can help you escape problem sandy spots. When you start to drive out of the soft spot, keep the front wheels straight and apply power slowly. Don't spin the wheels, as this digs the tires in deeper. Soft, sandy roads can be more easily negotiated by deflating the tires to about 15 pounds per square inch (psi). Carry a lightweight 12-volt tire inflator as part of your equipment, and pump the tires back up to recommended pressure when you are back on paved roads.

However, if you get stuck in sand in the middle of nowhere, let some air out of the tires even if you don't have a tire pump. Reducing the air pressure increases the footprint of the tire, giving you better traction. Once you're out of the sand, even at 15 psi you can drive short distances on the highway at slow speeds (less than 35 miles per hour, slower on winding roads). Keep in mind, however, that driving on the highway with reduced tire pressures can be dangerous, should be done only in an emergency, and should never be done at high speeds. Repressurize the tires to the appropriate level at the first opportunity. Don't wait until you get home.

Surviving a breakdown. If your vehicle breaks down irreparably, stay with it unless it's obvious you can reach help on foot. Consider both your capabilities and the weather conditions. There are many stories of people stuck in the desert in which one person goes for help, leaving the other with the vehicle, and the rescuers find the person with the vehicle safe and sound while the partner is found dead a few miles away.

Use your head. It is much easier to spot something the size of a vehicle than it is to spot a person. In an emergency, call attention to yourself by using the vehicle's horn, lights, and mirrors, but don't run the battery down. If you spot a rescue plane flying overhead, lie flat on the ground and make yourself big by spreading your arms and legs; don't jump around. Signal the plane by using a mirror to reflect the sun. As a last resort, remove the spare tire and drag it well away from the vehicle. Deflate it, douse it with gasoline, ignite it, and let it burn with copious black smoke (be careful not to set the desert on fire).

If you need shelter from the sun, dig out enough room under your vehicle to comfortably lie on your insulated sleeping pad. Store water in your body, not in your water bottles. Don't drink radiator water—antifreeze is poisonous.

See Chapter 14, "Getting Lost and Dealing with It," for more information.

PRESERVING THE DESERT

More so in the desert than almost any other place, Leave No Trace principles apply (see Chapter 2, "Leave No Trace: Outdoor Ethics"). It's important to pack out all trash. This includes paper items such as toilet tissue and sanitary supplies. Everything decomposes very slowly in the absence of water. If buried around a campsite, paper can be unearthed by winds, animals, or an unfortunate hiker. Don't burn your toilet paper. As strange as it may sound, numerous fires have been started in the desert through this simple act. Even orange peels stay exactly where they are for a long time, polluting the desert for the next visitor to see. The simple rule is: If you pack it in, pack it out.

When you break camp in the desert, return the site to its natural appearance. The sand and rocks are a big part of the natural landscape, so scatter or remove campfire rings or blackened rocks and sand, and never build a fire under or next to a rock overhang because the smoke will blacken the rocks. Many state and national parks allow ground fires only if they are contained in a metal pan and the ashes are packed out. Consider doing this even if it isn't required, to reduce the impact on the land.

A **buddy burner** is often all you really need at night. To make one, cut a strip of cardboard as wide as the height of a small, shallow can such as an empty tuna-fish can, spiral the cardboard inside the can, and then fill the can nearly to the top with melted paraffin (don't completely cover the top of the cardboard). To use the buddy burner, light the cardboard, which acts as a wick. Ideally, use a can with a metal lid so you can replace the lid to extinguish the burner, and it's ready to go the next evening. A buddy burner of this size burns for about two hours, even in a strong wind, and has a flame sufficient for light and a substitute campfire for a group of fifteen. It does not create much heat but enough warm light to chat by. A larger-diameter can yields a larger flame, and a deeper one burns longer. Bigger, however, means heavier—an important consideration when backpacking.

The toughness of the desert is, in a way, just a facade. The desert ecosystem is actually quite fragile. Desert plants grow very slowly and are

A small buddy burner provides a surprising amount of heat and light.
(Photo by Carol Brody)

always struggling for survival. Any damage inflicted can scar the land for decades, and in some areas of the desert you can still see tank tracks left by US military training efforts during World War II. In other areas, grazing cattle have displaced the native wildlife and trampled the vegetation. One insensitive person with an off-road vehicle can do a tremendous amount of destruction in only a few minutes. Even hikers can do damage.

Tanks, or *tinajas* (naturally formed water-filled depressions in rock), often hold the only water available for desert animals. If the water supply is low, don't draw water from them unless you have to, as they should be left for the native wildlife. Large tanks holding thousands of gallons are better sources, though the water probably needs filtration or chemical purification. Spring-fed pools should be used only for drinking. Never do any washing (clothing, dishes, self) in any natural water source; always carry the water at least 200 feet from the stream, and wash with a very small amount of biodegradable soap only when necessary. Swimming in pools of the larger streams is a real treat in hot weather!

Cryptobiotic crust is a little-known life-form that needs protection. It is a brittle layer of soil at the top made up of lichens, mosses, algae, and fungi. This crust appears as a lumpy ground cover about an inch thick that is black, green, or white, depending on the organisms it contains.

Cryptobiotic crust is an important link in the desert ecosystem. It stabilizes and builds fertile soil by preventing erosion and fixing nitrogen, making this nutrient available for other plants. Spongy and resilient when wet, it becomes vulnerable when dry, which is most of the time. Crunched to a powder when stepped on, it can blow away with the next breeze. Research has shown that it can take from 50 to 200 years for cryptobiotic crust to regenerate. Hikers needing to cross areas covered by cryptobiotic crust can minimize impact by using a single set of footprints while walking single file. Please avoid cryptobiotic areas whenever possible, particularly when selecting a campsite. Restrict your route of travel to durable surfaces such as washes or over rocks to avoid crushing this delicate desert resource.

If you find something of interest in the desert, your grandchildren and their grandchildren will probably find it fascinating too. Leave it there for

A blooming beavertail cactus adds a splash of color to the desert.
(Photo by Bobby Haruno)

Anasazi potsherds near Hovenweep National Monument, Utah
(Photo by David M. Gottfredson)

others to see and enjoy. Artifacts of past human habitation, such as potsherds or arrowheads, are still found in relative abundance. In the desert they provide an almost magical reminder of past civilizations and their spiritual heritage. In many desert areas it's illegal to remove anything at all. So should it be for all wilderness areas. Native American pictographs and petroglyphs (rock art) are particularly vulnerable. Do not touch them or build a campfire too close to the rocks. Please do your part to protect the land's cultural heritage by taking your souvenirs home in your camera, not in your backpack. See Chapter 2, "Leave No Trace: Outdoor Ethics," for more information.

In *Desert Solitaire,* Edward Abbey offers us a powerful insight into the nature of the desert wilderness: "Despite its clarity and simplicity . . . the desert wears at the same time, paradoxically, a veil of mystery. Motionless and silent it evokes in us an elusive hint of something unknown, unknowable, about to be revealed. Since the desert does not act it seems to be waiting—but waiting for what?"

Searching for that "unknowable" is what keeps us going back to the desert again and again.

Winter Snow Travel

Mike Fry, Dave Ussell, and Robert L. Feuge

An outing in the snow is enhanced by breathtaking scenery and is both an invitation to enjoy one of nature's most beautiful spectacles and a warning to be more wary and respectful than usual of the dangers that await the unprepared. Most high peaks in northern climates had glaciers during the ice ages, so winter gives us a view through time and suggests to us how the mountains might have looked back then. Traveling in the mountains in winter, the fourth season, reveals a unique stillness and tranquility.

CLOTHING AND WINTER EQUIPMENT

Winter travel places stringent demands on clothing and equipment. Except for cotton fabrics, you can use the same clothing in winter that you use in summer. You will also need extra insulation layers for cold and more insulation for your hands. You may need a larger pack for extra clothing and other winter gear.

Winter Clothing

Clothes keep you warm by trapping air next to your skin. If you are exercising, you also perspire, so winter clothing must both insulate and ventilate. The layering system discussed in Chapter 5, "Gearing Up," becomes critically important. These layers should be light in weight, compact, and low in cost.

Keep adjusting your clothing all day. When you warm up, you will perspire into your layers, they will get wet, and you will be colder later on. Take off some layers when you feel warm, and they will be dry and ready for you when you feel cold again.

Cover your head. When you get cold, cover and insulate your head. More than 30 percent of heat loss is from your head alone, and you need to keep your brain warm, so use the layering system for your head. A ski mask, or balaclava, is a good first layer; the second layer is a ski hat; your jacket should have a generous hood that can be cinched tight for the third layer. If you have an additional hood on another layer, use it for a fourth layer.

Breathe through fabric. You lose a lot of body heat and moisture when you breathe. If you breathe out through a scarf or ski mask, the fabric warms up and water vapor condenses. Then when you breathe in, the fabric warms up the cold incoming air and raises the humidity. It is very effective, and very convenient, to add this layer by pulling the lower part of your ski mask over your mouth. It takes only a second, and you don't have to take off your pack.

Cover your hands. Gloves and mittens keep your hands warm. Gloves allow you to use your fingers, but mittens do a better job of keeping your fingers warm. Use the layering system for your hands—mittens over gloves is much warmer, and waterproof overmitts complete the system. Expensive expedition overmitt systems are quite good, but get a system that has removable liners. The liner will dry much faster when removed. Wool resists crushing better than fleece, so wool-blend gloves or mitts will be warmer than fleece against the handles of your ski poles.

Warm your hands and feet. In cold, windy conditions, even expedition overmitts might not be enough. Chemical heat packs are the answer. They are small bags filled with powdered iron and a catalyst. When removed from their sealed bags, they start to oxidize and generate heat. One bag in each glove or boot can keep your hands or feet warm for eight hours. Don't let them get wet, as it reduces their heat output. Buy fresh ones plus one extra, and open the extra one at home to make sure the batch is still active. The powder should not have hardened. When the iron powder turns into a hard lump, the bag is no good.

Boots

Boots used for snow travel should keep your feet dry and warm. Be careful not to put on too many layers of socks. If you restrict the blood circulation in your feet, it will only make them colder.

Trekking poles can be indispensable when climbing steep areas.
(Photo by Skip Forsht)

Conventional leather boots should be thoroughly waterproofed. Even properly sealed boots can become soaked on long trips. It may be due to perspiration from your feet or from leakage from outside. Change your socks during the day, and always have any wet pair drying.

To keep your boots from freezing solid at night, keep them in your tent next to your sleeping bag. Keep them in a plastic bag inside your sleeping bag if you have room. Be sure to completely loosen the laces and pull the tongue out to make as large an opening as possible for your foot in the morning. You won't be going anywhere the next morning until your boots are on your feet.

Plastic mountaineering and ski boots with removable inner boots are an excellent choice for the fourth season. They're rugged, warm, and waterproof, and they easily accept crampons, gaiters, skis (if they are ski boots), and snowshoes. The inner boots can be worn alone in the tent.

On the negative side, they're fairly stiff, heavy, and expensive. Stiffness in a boot can be an asset in many situations. Even when you are walking on flat terrain, the snow gives a little, which compensates for the lack of flexing in stiff boots. Plastic telemark backcountry ski boots flex at the ball of your foot and thus are more comfortable for walking.

Gaiters are necessary to keep snow out of your boots. Even short gaiters do a good job, but knee-high, waterproof gaiters will also help keep your legs warm.

Packs and Sleds

A stable summer backpack is probably also a good winter backpack. An unstable summer backpack is probably a terrible winter pack. Pack balance is much more important with heavier winter loads and more unstable footing. The pack should hug your back and not shift around.

The gear inside should be packed so that heavy items are low and close to your back. If you will be snowshoeing or skiing, your pack must not be too wide at your waist. You need to be able to swing your ski poles close to your sides, and you don't want to keep hitting your pack. An external-frame pack could work well in the snow, but most do not. Most internal-frame packs are good winter packs, but some are not. Make your best guess and rent one to try it out.

Walking in deep, soft snow with a pack is an exhausting process. With each step you sink in, and forward progress is excruciatingly slow. This is called postholing. The solution: wear either snowshoes or skis, which keep you from sinking in.

It's possible to lighten or eliminate any load on your back by placing your gear in a lightweight sled specially designed to be towed by a skier or snowshoer. Rigid harness sleds are effective for hauling gear. The rigid harness keeps the sled from slamming into you when you are going down-hill and allows you to start up smoothly without jerking and falling down. If you try to pull a cheap plastic sled with a rope, you will soon discover what a bad idea that is.

Sleeping Equipment

Sleeping equipment for winter mountaineering should be maximized for warmth, and the layering system works here too.

The first layer is your clothing (not ideally, but all of it, if you're cold). If you wear everything to bed, it is much easier to get up in the morning or for the call of nature during the night. Hopefully, the clothes you sleep in are dry or will be soon. Put on your extra pair of thick socks or down booties.

The second layer is your sleeping pad and sleeping bag. A summer-weight sleeping pad is not insulative enough for snow camping. You need twice the thickness, so a good combination is a full-length summer-weight self-inflating pad and a full-length closed-cell foam pad (the closed cell pad is both insulation and insurance in case the self-inflating pad leaks). You can also use a closed-cell pad of double (deluxe) thickness. Sleeping pads may be too bulky to fit inside your pack, but they are light enough to tie securely on the outside of your pack. See the sleeping pad discussion in Chapter 5, "Gearing Up," and while you're at it, review the section on sleeping bags.

It's not likely that your summer sleeping bag will be warm enough for all four seasons of the year. For your winter bag, pay even more attention to getting a bag that is rated for the lowest temperature that you expect to encounter, and don't cut it too close just to save weight or money. You want a warm, comfortable bag because you're going to be spending a lot of time in it. If you push the comfort limit with your winter bag, you won't just be colder, you'll be colder for longer nights.

Two summer-weight bags could be used together if you have them: one inside the other as a double bag. As with any gear, test it for fit and function before you rely on it. The temperature rating won't be known, but you will soon find out.

Many couples like to zip together two sleeping bags, which provides extra warmth and space for the pair, and during cold weather, this arrangement is especially attractive if one person sleeps cold. Having an additional heat source can make the difference between a cold sleeper being able to camp in cold conditions or being limited to seasons having moderate night-time temperatures. Be aware that two people tossing and turning can mean more air movement in and out of the bag. Like any piece of gear, test it in mild conditions before you rely on it. You may find it more practical to just sleep close beside your partner, each in your own sleeping bag.

Extra layers. A thin closed-cell foam pad can be slid into your bag for an extra layer. It works best when it is between you and the top layer of the bag. It keeps warm air next to you and is very effective.

Don't put a poncho or other waterproof, impermeable vapor barrier fabric over the outside of your sleeping bag. You will get condensation on top of and inside your sleeping bag, and it will be quite wet in the morning. Sleeping in your raingear is a better idea if you are cold. If your bag does not get an occasional chance to dry out during the day, any water vapor trapped in it can make it successively colder each night.

Special Equipment

A snow shovel speeds up the tasks of building snow kitchens and snow trenches, and it may be needed for avalanche rescue. If you are in avalanche country, you will have your lightweight snow shovel with you.

A snow saw is needed only if you intend to cut snow blocks to build an igloo or snow shelter (see "Shelter" later in this chapter).

Altimeters can be used to keep track of barometric pressure and changes in the weather. They can also be crucial if it's necessary to navigate in whiteout or poor-visibility conditions, as can a GPS device.

Eye protection. Most sunglasses are not adequate for snow travel in bright sunlight. In addition to a pair of sunglasses for use in shady conditions or on overcast days, you should carry glacier glasses, which feature extra-dark lenses and panels on the sides to keep out glare. Ski goggles are necessary if you must travel during a snowstorm. You will also need to treat your glasses to prevent condensation (fogging up).

Repair supplies are needed to keep all that equipment working: lightweight tools (pliers, knife, screwdriver), ⅛-inch nylon line to lash things together, a small coil of baling wire, cable ties, duct tape, and a hose clamp and tent stake for ski or tent pole repair.

SNOW TRAVEL GEAR

You have many choices for your winter travel gear, depending on your chosen activity.

Snowshoes

Snowshoe selection is based on the weight of the user, plus gear, in addition to the type of snow and terrain to be covered. Your local outfitter is the best source for advice about appropriate snowshoe sizes and types of bindings. Flat and open terrain allows larger snowshoes to be used, while smaller snowshoes are better for steep, rough, or brushy terrain. Snowshoes are now made from lightweight, high-tech materials. They have convenient bindings, toothed grips for climbing slopes without slipping, and side rails

Snowshoes allow you to travel to areas boots can't take you to during the winter.
(Photo by Dan Girard)

for better traversing (sidehilling). Some manufacturers offer molded plastic snowshoes with tail extensions that can be added for increased flotation when carrying the extra weight of backpacking equipment.

Cross-Country Ski Gear

Cross-country skis, unlike snowshoes, require special boots and bindings. When shopping for skis, you're really looking for a system of skis, boots, and bindings. A full service cross-country (XC) ski shop can help you sort through the many options and help you choose the right system.

XC boots for backcountry touring should be durable and warm and have good side-to-side stiffness. Backcountry ski boots are usually all plastic and resemble downhill ski boots. There are two types: telemark and alpine touring (AT); the latter is also called randonée. Both telemark and AT have a lot in common.

Telemark boots flex at the ball of your foot and are more comfortable for walking. The boot is connected to the ski only at the toe, and the heel is free to lift. Telemark skiing is cross-country skiing in the mountains.

Alpine touring boots have a rigid sole and are not comfortable for hiking. AT bindings allow heel lift for touring and heel lockdown for turns. AT skiing is very much like downhill skiing without chairlifts.

Light leather touring ski boots are used with narrow skis on groomed tracks. Light touring gear is not appropriate for winter backpacking.

Cross-country skis are designed to grip the snow when your full weight is applied to one ski and to slide smoothly on the snow when your weight is shared by both skis. This allows you to kick and glide forward on the snow. The "kick zone" of the ski is pressed into contact with the snow during the kick and springs back up off the snow during the glide. Most XC skis use a grip pattern molded into the bottom of the ski to keep it from sliding backward.

Backcountry touring skis are used for ski travel in mountainous terrain. These are wider than light touring skis, and they have a narrow waist (side cut) that gives them better turning performance, plus metal edges to hold on steep, icy slopes. They are used with plastic telemark boots and rugged bindings. Backcountry skis usually have a grip pattern (waxless skis), but smooth-bottomed skis are also common. Waxing is complicated and requires experience and an intricate wax kit, so start out with waxless skis. "Waxless" is a bit of a misnomer, since all skis require the application of glide wax to prevent snow from sticking to the base.

Climbing skins are an optional but very useful tool in the backcountry. They provide a more powerful grip on icy snow than waxless (grip pattern) skis do. Today they're made from nylon fibers. One side has short hairs that all face toward the tail of the ski, and the other side is coated with a reusable adhesive. When the sticky side is applied to the bottom of the skis, the hairs that all point backward grip the snow. This keeps the ski from sliding backward and allows you to climb up steep hills. Skins are removed for a fast descent or left on for a slow descent.

Ski poles are essential to maintain balance and to assist with forward motion. Aluminum alloy poles, preferably a high-grade aircraft type, are best. If bent, they can usually be straightened in the field. Fiberglass poles should be avoided, as they can shred into a break that is difficult to repair. Carbon fiber poles are lightweight and very strong. Adjustable poles can be shortened for making downhill turns and lengthened for turning. For touring, XC ski poles should fit just under your armpits when the tips are touching the floor. Elbow length is better for downhill turns. You can also use larger snow baskets on your poles for better balance.

Cross-country skiing is counterintuitive, so you will make lots of mistakes and develop bad habits if you try to teach yourself. The best way to learn how to ski is to take lessons. Group lessons, which are inexpensive, can teach you proper form and allow you to progress more quickly. Telemark turn ski lessons, which are held at downhill ski resorts, take a lot more instruction, with several seasons of practice and lessons needed to reach the intermediate level.

Ice Axes and Crampons

For winter mountaineering, an ice ax and a pair of crampons are absolutely necessary. If you fall on a steep, icy slope, an ice ax may be the only piece of equipment that can save your life.

Mountaineering: Freedom of the Hills has a full discussion of ice ax selection and use (see "Resources" at the back of this book). Some climbing clubs still teach the ice ax self-arrest technique, but accredited mountain guides are the best teachers. See the information on the American Mountain Guides Association in "Resources."

SHELTER

Shelters in the winter wilderness can range from lightweight tents to semi-permanent igloos, snow trenches, and emergency snow caves. **Note:** If snow falls during the night, it could conceal all your gear. Stand up your skis, snowshoes, and poles so you can find them, and they can also act as markers for any other gear left outside.

Tents

Four-season winter tents are expensive and heavy to carry, but they do provide safety and comfort. They can be either single- or double-walled. Compared to three-season tents, they usually have the following:

- Weather-resistant tunnel entrance
- Larger vestibule for cooking and storing gear
- Structural design (including that of larger poles) that withstands severe winds and resists collapse even when weighed down by snow
- Full double-walled construction for insulation and reducing condensation
- Less ventilation mesh
- More guy (tie-in) points for stabilizing the tent in the wind

Some lightweight single-walled expedition tents have omitted the sewn-in floor, which allows ski poles to be used as tent poles and allows (very careful) cooking in the tent. The lower edges of this type of tent should be buried in the snow to keep out the wind. Best of all, you never have to sweep out the snow.

Deadman anchors. Small tent stakes used for summer camping are practically useless in the snow. Use wide, strong, lightweight aluminum stakes, or improvise in the field and make your own *deadman* tent stakes. Secure deadman anchors can be difficult to remove, so try to use natural materials that can be left in place. Here's how:

Tie a 30-inch section of ⅛-inch or thinner rope to each corner or tie-down point on the tent, and loop the other ends of the ropes around 6-inch or longer pieces of rigid material (finger-thickness tree or shrub branches

Warm inside, cold outside—snowy morning view from inside the tent
(Photo by Michelle Renaud)

will do). Never break off live branches for this; always use fallen wood. Dig a shallow trench in the snow for each deadman anchor, and bury it with rope looped once around it, making a U shape around the branch, not an O shape. By stomping the snow above and around each deadman, you can create secure anchors. To remove, pull the tent end of the rope straight up, and the rope should slide out, leaving the tree branch buried in the snow. Skis and ski poles can be used as very long and very secure tent stakes (don't bury them).

Winter tent sites. When choosing a tent site, avoid spots beneath trees that can dump large amounts of snow or broken branches on your tent. A clump of small trees provide good wind protection, and you can tie the tent to the trees. A large rock is deceptively poor wind protection, because the wind moves faster when it is forced to blow around the rock. Select a site with an unobstructed eastern exposure, and the warmth of the rising sun will welcome you in the morning.

Igloos

Igloos are luxury accommodations that a winter traveler can fashion in the snow. A well-built igloo with warm bodies inside can maintain a temperature well above freezing, regardless of the weather outside. It can make a wonderful base camp for longer trips. Construction of an igloo takes too much time if you are traveling each day; a group may require three to four hours to build an igloo. But building an igloo for one night would make for a fun weekend outing. For safety and to follow leave no trace principles, break down any snow structures before you leave.

First, select a flat site as a quarry. This will become your snow kitchen (see "Cooking" later in this chapter). Stomp on the quarry site to compress the snow. Wait thirty minutes to let the snow consolidate, and don't walk on it. Build the igloo on the edge of the quarry so the entrance tunnel can connect to the quarry site.

Cut blocks of snow from the quarry using a snow saw (lightweight 18-inch steel pruning saws are excellent). The blocks should be cut about 30 inches wide, 8 inches thick (this dimension is the thickness of the wall), and 18 inches tall. With a little foresight, you can cut blocks from the quarry so as to leave a snow kitchen when the igloo is complete. Carry the blocks over to the igloo site and place them in an ascending circular pattern.

The igloo team consists of block cutters, block carriers, and chinkers (think cementing between masonry blocks) on the outside, plus a block

First layer done, second layer next for an igloo! (Photo by Megan Meduna)

placer, a block steadier, and a chinker inside the igloo. The three inside crew members need to wear raingear, and everyone needs to adjust their layers to avoid sweating or freezing.

Mark the center of the igloo with a ski pole, and mark a starting circle 6 feet in diameter (larger if the people sleeping inside are tall!). Place the first layer of blocks on the perimeter of the circle. Each block you place must face the center mark and must lean inward. Each new layer must lean farther than the last. If you don't lean the blocks inward enough, you will build a snow silo rather than an igloo, and you won't be able to close the top. When you complete the first layer, slice two of the blocks across the diagonal to start a ramp to the next layer. The igloo is constructed as a spiral.

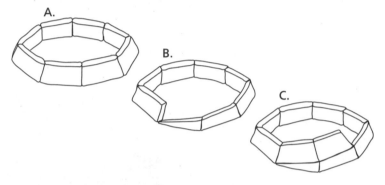

Figure 12-1. A. The first circle of blocks for an igloo; B. and C. Then establish a spiral by tapering two or three blocks.

The blocks must be trimmed to fit their place on the circle. Three corners of each new block must touch two corners of the previous block and the wall below. The two contacting surfaces must be shaped with a small saw so that only the corners touch. This is the secret that supports a block when it is leaning in past 45 degrees. When the block and wall fit together, a gentle but firm shove will cement the block in place. Once the block is set, carefully chink the gaps with loose snow. The block steadier inside the igloo can hold the block, just in case.

The last block is the easiest. The block carrier slides the last block up to the very top of the igloo and pushes it over the opening. The block placer inside reaches up with the trimming saw and cuts around the edge of the opening until the block sinks in. A perfect fit! Saw a 3-inch-diameter hole in the top of the roof for ventilation.

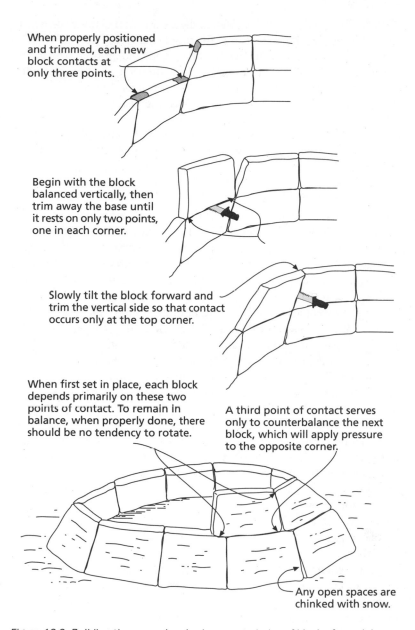

When properly positioned and trimmed, each new block contacts at only three points.

Begin with the block balanced vertically, then trim away the base until it rests on only two points, one in each corner.

Slowly tilt the block forward and trim the vertical side so that contact occurs only at the top corner.

When first set in place, each block depends primarily on these two points of contact. To remain in balance, when properly done, there should be no tendency to rotate.

A third point of contact serves only to counterbalance the next block, which will apply pressure to the opposite corner.

Any open spaces are chinked with snow.

Figure 12-2. Building the second and subsequent circles of blocks for an igloo

When the igloo dome is completed, dig a short tunnel under its wall to your snow kitchen. Keep the top of the tunnel below the floor level of the igloo. This prevents warm air from escaping and cold air from blowing in. At night a single candle provides all the light you need, and several candles really warm up the igloo. From the outside, an igloo has a magical glow when lit up by candles or a buddy burner on the inside!

Cooking inside an igloo is not a good idea. Too much stove heat can melt the igloo, and a stove explosion could be fatal. For websites with pictures and further instructions on how to build an igloo, see "Resources" in the appendix.

Emergency Shelters

If you are caught unexpectedly by nightfall in the winter wilderness, shelter is your first priority, and with your Ten Essentials you can create an emergency shelter fairly quickly. That large trash bag or commercial tube-shaped (not flat) space blanket or shelter that you always carry can be used as an emergency bivy sack; you will be cold, but it is an insulation layer that could save your life.

Your Ten Essentials kit contains firestarting supplies. Start a safe ground fire with whatever materials are available, and keep that fire going all night. Make the biggest fire you can. A fallen log is the best. If you have been reported missing, the smoke will help the search and rescue team find you.

Look for a cave or a dense grove of trees with branches down to the snow to further shelter you from the elements. Under the skirt of a pine tree with branches touching the snow, you can dig out snow close to the tree trunk and make a cave to shield yourself from the wind. While bivouacking, you'll be warmer if you curl up, and always put something insulative between you and the snow: pine boughs, bark from a fallen log, your pack, etc. Open a heat pack, loosen your boots, and do the best you can with your clothing layers. Put your feet in your pack if you're not sitting on it, and wait for sunrise.

If you are able, build a more protective emergency shelter rather than bivouacking. Practice making these shelters before you need one in an emergency.

Snow trenches are quick to construct, much quicker than building an igloo or a snow cave. A snow trench is little more than a narrow, rectangular pit dug in the snow. Dig to a sufficient depth and length to accommodate your body and your gear. You can use your potty trowel, cook pot, or snowshoe if you have them to dig. Lie on top of your gear, your skis, or anything you can find. If you have the tools, cut snow blocks to form an inverted V for the roof. Gaps should be chinked, and a ventilation hole must be made near your head. Ideally, you would dig a tunnel with an entrance lower than the sleeping enclosure to keep out cold-air drafts. If that isn't possible, a horizontal entry with a wind block can be fashioned.

Snow caves are good shelters, but they take a very long time to dig because a lot of snow needs to be moved through a small opening, and you will end up wet and exhausted. There are some tricks to make a modified cave that is easier and faster to build.

Select a place that is safe from avalanche danger where a thick blanket of consolidated snow lies against a slope. Dig straight in about 4 feet and hollow out an open sleeping platform about 8 feet wide and 4 feet tall. Make sure you fit inside. Now start making blocks with your shovel, and close up the wide opening. Leave a low opening by your feet, and when the cave is finished, poke a hole in the roof near your head for ventilation.

COOKING

Once your tent is pitched and your clothing layers are adjusted, your group can have fun building a snow kitchen for cooking and eating. Use a snow shovel to dig a two-tier trench to be used as a seat with a back, with the undisturbed snow in front being used as a low dining table. For a larger group, you can construct a circular trench with an island in the middle. You are going to spend a lot of time in your snow kitchen melting snow, so it should be a comfortable spot. Consider also building a snow privy . . . away and downwind.

You burn a lot of calories while snow camping, and cooking is more difficult and takes more fuel and time than in warmer weather or at lower altitude. You need a high-output stove and isobutene-propane or white gas fuel that will work in the cold (see Chapter 5, "Gearing Up"). Don't forget to bring your insulated stove pad and windscreen. In a storm, you may be forced to stay inside your tent and reach outside into your vestibule to use your stove.

Keep your meals as simple as possible. There are plenty of foods or freeze-dried meals that require only boiling water (see Chapter 6, "'Eating Out' in the Wilderness").

You may enjoy a little nip of alcohol in the summer, but it is not a good idea in the cold. The red flush of your face from a drink is caused by your skin capillaries opening up. That will cause your body to lose heat much faster.

In the winter, it may be impossible to locate a source of flowing water, so you will have to collect and melt snow—a tedious process. On clear, sunny days, fill water bottles (dark-colored bottles work best) with snow and let the sun melt it. Melting snow with a stove is much faster but uses considerable fuel. Snow itself is hard to melt, so always start by heating some water (not snow) in your pot and adding snow as the warm water is able to melt it. Otherwise, because snow is an insulator, the bottom of the pot will just burn, leaving the snow still sitting there. When planning fuel needs, consider both the extra demands of cooking in the winter environment and the need to melt snow for water.

On subfreezing nights, your water bottles will freeze unless you take precautions. You can keep a full bottle of hot water placed in a sock inside your sleeping bag, which will keep you warm for hours. Bring your other bottles into the tent to insulate them from the cold, and turn them upside down so the threaded end won't freeze. You can bury water bottles or cook pots filled with water in the snow. Below the surface, the snow is usually close to 32 degrees F, and that isn't cold enough to freeze your water overnight. Make sure you can find and dig out the bottles in the morning!

TIPS FOR STAYING WARM AT NIGHT

It is crucial to stay warm at night after a day on the snow. These tips will help you spend winter nights more comfortably and enjoyably.

1. After you return to camp, take off any wet layers, and put on your warmest clothing and your raingear. Make sure your feet are dry.
2. Don't allow yourself to even *begin* to get cold! If you shiver, that is a sign that your body is cooling down and you should have put on more layers sooner, so add more clothing now, move around a bit, and start up heat packs for your hands and/or feet. If that is not enough, get into your sleeping bag with a bottle of hot water until you feel warm, and then reemerge into camp life.
3. While in camp, sit on a closed-cell foam pad, not on snow. A pad under your feet, keeping them off the snow, helps as well. Find a wind-sheltered spot, or orient yourself so that your back is toward the wind. Wear dry gloves and a warm hat to prevent heat loss from your extremities.
4. Eat a big, hot dinner with plenty of carbohydrates.
5. After dinner, snack on high-calorie foods. Fat calories can provide energy to keep you warm, but they are difficult to digest at high altitudes (above 8000 feet). Keep snacks in your tent for later at night.
6. Exercise. If you feel cold, get up and stretch or shovel some snow. Work for ten minutes before getting into your sleeping bag. The exercise will increase body heat. Dress so that you capture that extra body heat. When in your sleeping bag, do isometric exercises (muscle contractions) if you begin to chill.
7. Drink warm fluids, and through the night, continue to drink warm fluids. This will increase the likelihood that you will have to urinate during the night, so be sure to urinate just before you crawl into the tent.

8. Use a pee bottle (clearly marked!) to urinate into while in your tent. This bottle will save you from getting up in the middle of the night, getting dressed, and losing the heat in your tent and bag as you go out in the cold. Instructions to make a pee bottle are given in Chapter 9, "Now Let's Get Out There!"

9. Just before you turn in for the night, make an extra bottle of hot water, ensure that the bottle does not leak, put it into a spare sock, and then put the bottle into your sleeping bag. This will be something you can snuggle with during the night to keep you or your feet warm; it will prevent the water from freezing and will provide "warm" (or at least not frozen) water to start morning coffee.

10. Share your tent or shelter with others to add body heat.

AVOIDING WINTER HAZARDS AND INJURY

When you are traveling in the winter, be aware of the season's special hazards and prepare carefully for the possibility of injury.

Hypothermia

Once called exposure, hypothermia is the decrease of core body temperature to a level at which normal muscular and cerebral functions are impaired (generally 95 degrees F). Mere temperature readings are not always a reliable indicator of the severity of the cold environment. The windchill index (see Table 12-1) provides a better guide for cold, windy conditions. When wetness is a factor, the effective temperatures are even lower.

Wind Speed (in mph)	Actual Temperature (in degrees F)							
Calm	40	30	20	10	0	-10	-20	-30
	Equivalent Windchill Temperature (in degrees F)							
5	35	25	15	5	-5	-15	-25	-35
10	30	15	5	-10	-20	-35	-45	-60
15	25	10	-5	-20	-30	-45	-60	-70
20	20	5	-10	-25	-35	-50	-65	-80
25	15	0	-15	-30	-45	-60	-75	-90
30	10	0	-20	-30	-50	-65	-80	-95
35	20	-5	-20	-35	-50	-65	-80	-100
40	10	-5	-20	-35	-55	-70	-85	-100

TABLE 12-1. WINDCHILL

It's important to recognize the signs of hypothermia, both in yourself and in companions, so that remedial actions may be taken immediately. The symptoms and treatment for hypothermia are discussed in Chapter 13, "Ouch! First Aid in the Backcountry."

Frostbite

Unlike hypothermia, frostbite is a localized injury, readily affecting extremities such as fingers, toes, face, and ears. When exposed to cold air, wind, or snow, the tissue freezes, causing injury by ice crystals forming in the frozen area. The victim might not be aware of the problem until someone indicates that there is something unusual about his or her skin color.

Frostbite can occur in any very cold winter environment, but it is usually associated with the conditions causing hypothermia: inadequate clothing, inadequate food consumption, exhaustion, inactivity, or a combination of these factors. A good preventive measure is to keep all your extremities covered. For more about frostbite causes, signs, and treatment, see Chapter 13, "Ouch! First Aid in the Backcountry."

Dehydration

Though it may seem unlikely, you can easily become dehydrated during winter conditions, particularly at higher altitudes. Cold air contains very little water vapor and is as dry as the desert, so every time you inhale, moisture is picked up by that incoming dry air, and with each exhalation, you lose that moisture to the outside environment.

Since the sensation of thirst may not be strong in the cold, you need to make a conscious effort to consume enough liquid. Hot drinks are best, but cold water is fine as well. Don't eat snow unless you are more than warm enough. It requires a great deal of energy (body heat) to transform snow into water.

If you are consuming enough fluid, you should feel the need to urinate at least every few hours, and more often is better. If you're not properly hydrated, you'll experience the symptoms of dehydration: headache, fatigue, dizziness, muscle cramping, and a feeling of faintness.

Sunburn

The winter environment presents some unique challenges for your skin. Clean, dry, thin air allows ultraviolet (UV) energy to pass through the atmosphere more easily than at low elevation. Snow and ice reflect UV light like a mirror, so you can be burned from above or below on any uncovered areas, especially cheeks, ears, nose, lips, underneath your chin, and even the inside of the nostrils. Keep this in mind when applying sunscreen, and keep your skin covered up.

Glacier Travel

Glacier travel is an integral part of wilderness travel in the northwestern United States, western Canada, and Alaska. Because it is more dangerous than it seems, considerable planning and training is required for a safe outing. Ropes should always be used, regardless of how simple the crossing appears. All members of the team should be trained and have ice axes, crampons, helmets, climbing harnesses, and crevasse rescue gear. If you're a novice, get training on glacier travel and then travel with experienced mountaineers. Additional information on glacier travel is available in *Mountaineering: The Freedom of the Hills* (see "Resources" in the appendix).

Avalanche

Avalanche is a significant danger in the winter wilderness. When the snowpack is unstable, anything or anybody can start it sliding—a snowmobiler, a traveler walking or skiing across a slope, or the slightest mechanical force—even the sound pressure of a sonic boom, thunder, or gunfire. The most important part of avalanche safety is to learn to recognize when the danger level is high (take an avalanche class before your trip), then be smart and have the resolve to turn back when it's unsafe.

Forecasts. Most wilderness areas are served by regional avalanche forecast offices, and their information is published online. They are avalanche experts, and they also publish reports and photos by other backcountry travelers. See "Resources" to find the closest office to your snow travel location. You can greatly reduce the risk of avalanches simply by checking with the local avalanche office. They have been following the snowpack conditions all winter and can tell you what the next storm might cause. If there has been a warm spell followed by a freeze, there will be an ice layer in the snow, and a new storm will almost certainly cause avalanches. If there are no avalanche offices in your area, the local mountain community may have Internet user groups that will report snow conditions. You can report your observations, too.

Courses. The local avalanche offices also have avalanche safety course schedules, and that is the best way to become educated. Most of the classes are taught by the American Mountain Guides Association (AMGA) guides. Some classes are given by professional avalanche experts from ski resorts. The classes start with snow science. You learn how the snow crystals change after they reach the ground and how temperature and weather can increase the danger. Then you leave the classroom and study the local snow. The second part of the course is how to search for and find buried victims. The Level 1 course takes two days and is designed for recreational users. Level 2 takes four days and is for guides, ski patrol, etc. If you want to travel in the mountain wilderness in winter, you need to take the Level 1 course or always travel with a guide trained in avalanche safety.

Equipment. Avalanche safety also requires special equipment. In addition to your shovel (each member of the group must carry one), each person also needs an avalanche transceiver (beacon) and an avalanche probe pole. The avalanche beacons use multiple antennas and digital signal processing to indicate distance and direction to the victim. The probe pole (which looks like a collapsible tent pole) is used to locate a victim in the last few feet of a search. You still need instruction and practice, especially because of the panic and terror of an actual avalanche.

Avalanche equipment is necessary, but it won't prevent avalanches, and it won't prevent the trauma and injuries of being caught in an avalanche. Don't let avalanche training and equipment lead to overconfidence and too much risk taking. It is best to err on the side of caution and turn back when you need to, even when the risk appears to be small. If you always dismiss the warning signs, your number will soon come up.

If your companions have avalanche gear and training, your chances of being rescued are good. If you are not found in the first thirty minutes, chances of survival drop quickly.

There are many books and videos on avalanche science. There are far too many details to describe here. Find a Level 1 course and take it. You will have a new awareness of the mountains, and it can save your, or someone else's, life. Winter snow travel is a beautiful (and can be a dangerous) experience. While it requires more preparation than most summer trips, the enjoyment it provides is well worth it.

chapter
13

Ouch! First Aid in the Backcountry

Laura A. Wolfgang

Leaving the lights, sounds, smells, and conveniences of the city and venturing out into the wilderness can be invigorating. However, with this transition you are also leaving the security of rapid professional medical response and moving into the realm of uncertain and, likely, basic first aid. Even the most decked-out gearhead may have all of the latest gadgets to make his trek easier, but if he doesn't have the knowledge of basic first aid, a seemingly minor incident may become life-threatening.

Being in the wilderness can expose you to medical circumstances that are unique only to the great outdoors. Therefore, it is highly recommended that wilderness enthusiasts arm themselves with an American Red Cross first-aid course, a Basic Wilderness Life Support class, or, minimally, either the American Red Cross or American Heart Association cardiopulmonary resuscitation (CPR) course. The more remote and sketchy the journey, the more important it is to have at least one member of the group with more advanced training specifically related to wilderness first aid.

BEFORE YOU GO

Preparation not only includes gathering your gear and a map but also making sure you are at your optimal health to decrease the chances of preventable illness and injury.

Vaccinations

Checking your vaccination status is a good start to pretrip preparation for optimal health.

The tetanus vaccine is good for ten years. When was your last tetanus vaccine? Tetanus is a nerve ailment caused by the introduction of common bacterial spores through an open wound. The bacterium lives in soil, house dust, and the colon. If this bacterium enters the body through a cut or bite, it can be taken up by the nervous system, leading to tetany (in about three to twenty-one days). Tetany is a sustained contraction of the muscles that may block the ability to breathe.

The hepatitis A vaccine would be another vaccine to consider. Hepatitis A is a liver disease caused by the consumption of contaminated food and water. The illness is hallmarked by severe abdominal pain, diarrhea, jaundice, fever, and muscle aches. This disease will not kill you, but you will feel as if you are dying for approximately three weeks.

Other vaccines should be considered if you are traveling internationally to your trekking destination. Consult your primary care provider or a travel medicine expert if this applies to you.

Preexisting Conditions

Any preexisting conditions that you may have must be stable prior to your venturing out into the wilderness. Be sure to pack any special first-aid items you may need, and if you are on any medications, be sure to bring enough for your full trip plus a few extra days.

Many disastrous outcomes of backpacking are due to participants overestimating their personal capabilities and taking on too big an adventure for their conditioning. This endangers not only the participant but those in the group that will then have to care for and be responsible for evacuating the victim.

BASIC FIRST-AID KIT

Creating a complete first-aid kit that is light enough to carry but filled with essential supplies can be a daunting task even for a seasoned backpacker. Kit size and contents will vary depending upon the number of days on expedition, the type of terrain covered, availability and timing of potential evacuation, preexisting medical conditions, and the environment visited. Although you can create a kit based on the numbers of persons in the party, having personal kits with basic supply items and any medications for preexisting medical conditions is ideal to ensure there are enough supplies for everyone. A list of medications should be kept in your wallet if you have a medical condition, and this information should be shared with the group leader in case of an adverse event. The specialized items in the victim's backpack or wallet can provide an important clue to what may have "downed" someone or help rescuers be more aware of potential complications.

The more days involved and the more treacherous the terrain, the more will be needed for the kits. Often kits are sacrificed for weight allowances; this is a critical mistake, similar to leaving water behind when there is no water en route. A worthy first-aid kit is one of the Ten Essentials. Table 13-1 lists items to consider for a one- to three-day trip with a basic kit. Empty your first-aid kit annually to check for expired medications and deteriorated bandaging supplies that need replacing.

Prepackaged first-aid kits are available for purchase but will likely need some customization (see Figure 13-1). Optimally you will want a lightweight, sealed, waterproof container with separate compartments to organize your items. Or you can organize your items by purpose into individual resealable plastic bags for easy access and identification. All kits should include nitrile or vinyl gloves to protect the caregiver and the victim. Latex gloves should never be used due to the high incidence of latex allergy.

While rendering first aid you will want to identify any allergies the victim may have, especially if you are offering any medications or using any topical agents. Make sure the recipient is not allergic to any drug you want to administer. Ideally, personal kits will not include items the victim is allergic to, reducing the risk of a severe allergic reaction. Identification

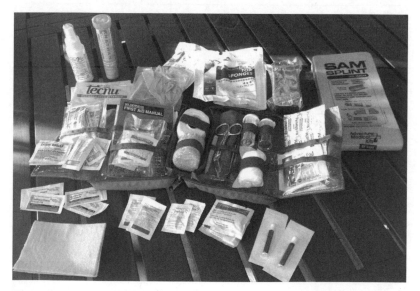

Figure 13-1. *Wilderness first-aid kit* (Photo by Laura A. Wolfgang)

TABLE 13-1. WILDERNESS FIRST-AID KIT

Recommended Items	Quantity	Use
Nitrile or vinyl gloves	1–2/day	Protection for victim and rescuer
Adhesive bandages, ½ in. or ¾ in.	5–10	Treat cuts and abrasions
Cloth tape, 1-in. roll	1 roll	Secure splints
Gauze wrap, 2-in. and 4-in. rolls	1 each	Secure dressings
Gauze pads, 4-in. size	4–8	Cover abrasions—Telfa also works well
Moleskin or molefoam, 6-in. square	2	Prevent and treat blisters
Triangular bandage, 36 in.	1	Sling; multiple uses
Elastic wrap, 4 in.	1	Support sprains, splints, and dressings
Aspirin, 5 gr (325 mg tablets)	4 per day	Treat pain and fever; also good for someone having a heart attack
Antibiotic ointment, 15 mg tube	1	Treat skin infections
Antihistamine, 10 mg loratadine (Claritin)	1 per day	Treat allergic reactions
Antihistamine, 25 mg diphen-hydramine (Benadryl)	4 per day	Treat allergic reactions
Decongestant, 30 mg pseudo-ephedrine (Sudafed)	12–24	Treat runny or stuffy nose
Antidiarrheal, 2 mg loperamide (Imodium)	16 mg/person per day	Treat diarrhea—if no blood in stool or fever
Burn gel dressing	1–2 packets	Treat minor burns
Anti-inflammatory, 200 mg ibuprofen (Advil)	8/day or more	Treat pain, inflammation, or fever
Benzalkonium solution or wipes	6–10 wipes	Clean wounds
Corticosteroid cream (Cortaid) 1% (15 mg tube)	2	Treat rashes, swelling, and itching from plant contact
Thermometer	1	Measure temperature
Lip balm with sunscreen	1 tube	Prevent sun damage to lips
Insect repellent (1-oz. tube)	1	Discourage insect bites

Wire mesh or SAM splint	1	Cervical collar or splint
Small scissors	1	
Paper and pencil	1	
Tweezers (fine)	1	
Safety pins	4	
Suggested Rx Items*	**Quantity**	**Use**
Rx. 125 mg acetazolamide (Diamox)	14	Prevention of acute mountain sickness
Rx. promethazine (Phenergan), 25 mg suppository	4	Treat nausea and vomiting
Rx. 500 mg Ciprofloxacin	6	Treat refractory diarrhea or diarrhea with fever or blood in the stool
¼ in. Steri strips and Benzoin	1 pkg and 2 vials	Treat laceration needing closure
Zanfel or Tecnu	1 tube	Cleanse oils from poison ivy, oak, or sumac contact
Additional Items	**Quantity**	**Use**
Magnifying glass (plastic)	1	To see small splinters
Electrolyte replacement drink	Varies	Treat dehydration
Sanitary napkins	2–3	Absorb bleeding from cuts

* Rx. indicates prescription from physician required. Discuss possible side effects with your physician.

Note: First drug name is generic, with brand name in parentheses.

bracelets should be worn for those with allergies or chronic illness as another means to help identify potential problems early.

Special considerations for women on longer treks are vaginal suppositories or creams to treat potential yeast infections and antibiotics for urinary tract infections. The antibiotics will need to be prescribed by your primary care provider.

FIRST AID IN THE BACKCOUNTRY

1. **Assess the scene.** First aid in the backcountry when an incident has occurred will always begin with assessing the scene for safety before assessing the victim. Never rush to the victim until it is fairly certain no further harm will come to the victim, yourself, or other members of the group.

2. **Ask for permission to help.** Always try to approach the victim from the side so he or she can see you without strain or increased anxiety. If the victim is conscious, identify yourself and ask permission to assist the person, then ask what happened. If the victim is unconscious, permission is implied. Do not assist a victim who is refusing your help, as this can be construed as battery, unless, of course, the person has an altered mental status and does not know better.

3. **Check for massive bleeding.** After assessing the scene and the victim's level of consciousness, look for massive hemorrhaging or spinal injury. These will have to be very quickly managed if the patient needs to be moved to a safer area.

4. **Check for spinal injury and airway obstruction.** Always assume a spinal injury if the victim was found unconscious or sustained trauma such as from a fall. If this is the case, whether the victim is conscious or not, the spine will need to be supported and managed until rescue can be achieved.

5. **Check circulation.** Once these initial worries have been addressed, airway, breathing, and circulation (the ABCs) must be assessed and addressed if abnormal. This is where a basic course in cardiopulmonary resuscitation (CPR) is important. The old form of CPR assumed A-B-C were checked, but the new form of CPR is circulation, airway, then breathing (CAB) or, if there is no experience in CPR available, "hands only" chest compressions are performed at approximately 100 beats per minute. This is at the rate of singing the song "Staying Alive" by the Bee Gees.

   At least one person in the group should have completed a CPR class. For drowning, lightning, or hypothermic victims, CPR may need to be continued for a very extended period of time. All other victims will likely require CPR until he or she has recovered, the rescuers become exhausted and cannot continue, or medical help arrives. Ideally, CPR should be practiced in a controlled setting prior to using it in a real situation.

6. **Shelter the victim.** Are you calm? Have you provided any reassurance and comfort? Do not forget to stay aware of the environment; is the victim cold, warm, in the rain, wet? These are all factors that can quickly worsen an already bad situation. If you are cold, the victim will be colder; if you are warm, the victim is likely warmer.

   Also, the need for immediate evacuation and how this will be done must be determined, and if someone, ideally two people, needs to be sent for help, now is the time to go. Unfortunately, most backcountry regions do not have good cell phone or radio reception.

Figure 13-2. *Proper positioning of an unconscious person*
(Photo by Carol Murdock)

Try not to send someone out with no information—at least have the person go with basic information such as what happened: is the victim bleeding, does the victim have a spinal injury, is the victim conscious, and, especially, where the victim is! (For more information on rescue steps, see Chapter 14, "Getting Lost and Dealing with It").

7. **Check head to toe.** Once all of the initial assessments are made, hemorrhaging is managed, and airway and circulation are stable, the secondary physical exam can be completed. This is when focus can be placed on a complete head-to-toe look and feel of the victim to be sure no other injuries have been missed or need to be managed, such as splinting or wound care. Start from the head and look and gently touch everything—check the scalp, look at the pupils, look at the ears (fluid or blood is a very bad sign) and in the mouth, feel the neck and back (if there is no chance of spinal injury), check the chest and abdomen, check each limb. Is the victim able to move the extremities, is sensation intact?

8. **Ask for a medical history.** Also, if the victim is conscious or has a family member familiar with his or her medical history, this can be obtained. This is when allergies, medications, chronic conditions, toxins ingested, or psychiatric conditions may be discovered that were not in the initial assessment.

9. **Plan the evacuation.** If the victim needs to be carried out, how is this going to be done? As a group it is good to have some knowledge or idea of how to make a litter in the case of an emergency evacuation. All of these things should be discussed or thought about prior to heading out.

10. **Record time and treatments.** Record the time of original injury and what treatments or care you have provided in the interim.

Summary

No one is comfortable dealing with backcountry illness or injury, but everyone should be prepared. Hopefully this section's information amplifies the importance of being prepared. Here is a summary of steps to take in backcountry first aid:

1. Assess the scene for safety and approach the victim cautiously. Does the victim need to be moved? Start thinking how this can be done safely.
2. Identify yourself, ask for consent to help, and ask what happened.
3. Is there massive hemorrhaging? Take care of this now!
4. Check for spinal injury and airway obstruction—this could simply be positioning. Maintaining an airway for someone with a spinal injury is different than if there is not one—a good CPR class will review proper techniques for different situations.
5. How is the circulation? This includes pulses to all extremities—especially those that are bleeding. If the victim is bleeding and there is no pulse, this could mean a major artery has been cut or obstructed. This increases the priority for evacuation.
6. Does the victim need to be sheltered, warmed up, or cooled down?
7. Check the victim from head to toe and manage injuries from the worst to the minor.
8. Find out more about allergies, medical history, last meal eaten, and any toxins such as alcohol or drugs.
9. Have you called for help or can you move on? When sending someone for help, be sure to provide written information to take—basic victim information (name, age, gender), summary of incident, what injuries were sustained or the victim's medical condition, what care has been rendered, and exact location of victim.
10. Keep a running log of time and treatments until help arrives.

GASTROINTESTINAL ISSUES

Many nicknames have been given to the abdominal woes that people can experience. Having the "trots," being "plugged up" or having a "bellyache" out in the wilderness can be fuel for a good teasing. However, if left unchecked, these symptoms can escalate and put a quick end to an adventure.

Diarrhea

Symptoms. The most common medical problem in the backcountry is diarrhea. The diarrhea experienced can be very watery, high volume, and nonbloody (nondysenteric) or lower volume, bloody, and mucus-filled (dysentery), with or without fever. Causes can be viral, bacterial, parasitic, or amoebic and affect only one of the trekkers in the group or potentially the entire group. Spread generally occurs from the fecal-oral route (dirty hands) or through contaminated food and water. Nondysenteric diarrhea will typically run its course in a few days with resolution in about three to four days.

Treatment. Diarrhea is not life-threatening if treated effectively. Treatment usually consists of hydration and replacement of lost electrolytes. Mixing a sport drink such as Vitalyte or Gatorade with water half and half is good for rehydration, or other oral rehydration solutions can also be used. Urine color can be used to monitor hydration status; urine should be clear, and hydration should continue with clear urine as the goal. If the diarrhea is nondysenteric, loperamide (Imodium) can be used to help reduce the diarrhea and cramping.

Evacuation for diarrhea is usually not necessary, and once the victim is rehydrated the excursion can continue. However, if the victim is unable to tolerate rehydration, exhibits signs of severe dehydration, or has copious amounts of bloody stool, evacuation is immediately necessary. Dysentery will likely need to be evaluated further when medical help is available and will potentially require antibiotics or other treatment.

Prevention starts with washing hands well and often (or using an antibacterial gel), especially when handling foods. Water sources need to be appropriately disinfected and food sources should be reliable. If the excursion is out of the country, the causes for diarrhea greatly increase and vaccinations or preventive medications should be considered.

Constipation

Symptoms. Constipation is a common affliction in the backcountry. Causes include dehydration, change of diet, low fiber, changes in routine, and the fact that many trekkers are uncomfortable taking a "nature poo." Symptoms are fairly obvious: potentially days between bowel evacuation, hardened stools, and straining. Some victims will have "gas cramps" and bloating, with a notable hard lump that can be felt in their left lower abdomen. This is generally not an emergency, but if impaction occurs, then things can be more serious and seeking medical help will be called for.

Treatment is simply to increase fluid intake along with some fiber. Caffeine can also work as a stimulant. For those who know they have issues with constipation, taking some Miralax, a powder that is added to drinks, can help to move the bowels.

Prevention is to stay well hydrated and be sure to have fiber in your diet daily. Another preventive can be the use of tablet-form probiotics such as Align or Culturelle. If these are started the week prior to the excursion and continued daily while out, bowel function may continue to be fairly normal.

Abdominal Pain

Symptoms. Abdominal pain in the clinical setting is difficult to unravel; out in the backcountry, underestimating abdominal pain can be tragic. It is true that usually a case of severe abdominal pain can be caused by something as simple as "gas cramps" but, on the other hand, can be as severe as an abdominal aneurysm. Any abdominal pain that is accompanied with fever, loss of appetite, nausea, and frequent or projectile vomiting needs to be evaluated as soon as possible by a medical professional. Some of the common causes of abdominal pain that require urgent attention are appendicitis, bleeding ulcers, bowel obstructions, ruptured ectopic pregnancy, and urinary tract or pelvic infections. While out in the field, any abdominal pain lasting four or more hours needs to be seriously evaluated.

Treatment. If the decision is made to evacuate a victim, allow only sipping of small amounts of water every fifteen minutes to help with hydration, but do not allow eating. This may prevent symptoms from worsening and allow for immediate surgery, if necessary, after rescue.

Prevention. As stated earlier in this chapter, using probiotics can be helpful, but the most beneficial preventive measure of all is simply to stay hydrated. Urine color is always a clue; always hydrate enough to keep urine clear!

EXPOSURE TO THE ELEMENTS

We all hope for perfect weather and conditions when we plan our outward-bound expeditions. We may expect heat in the desert and snow and ice in the upper elevations and do our best to acclimate to these extremes. But what about those unseasonal extremes? And what about those "weekend warriors" who are exploring a new destination? The unprepared trekker may have underestimated his or her tolerance of the destination's conditions, or seasoned trekkers may find themselves in conditions or situations that challenge their survival skills beyond the unexpected. Mother nature does not always play nicely.

Sunburn

Symptoms. Sunburn can be classified as a superficial burn when redness and pain are the primary symptoms. However, a partial-thickness or more severe burn can cause blistering, low-grade fever, chills, nausea, vomiting, and diarrhea.

Treatment in the field is usually limited to cool-water soaks and analgesics such as ibuprofen or aspirin. Hydrocortisone cream can also be applied sparingly to unbroken skin to help in the healing process. Reexposure to UV needs to be limited to prevent further damage.

Prevention. Overexposure to UV light causes sunburn. This hazard is intensified during the middle of the day and at altitude. UV rays can also reflect off soil, rocks, water, and snow. Protect yourself prior to exposure with a good sunscreen with a sun protection factor (SPF) of at least 30 or more that blocks both UVA and UVB rays. Reapplication every few hours is also a must.

When using sunscreen concurrently with the insect repellent DEET (N,N-diethyl-3-methylbenzamied), the effectiveness of the sunscreen will be approximately 30 percent less, and therefore a higher SPF should be used. There is still debate whether applying the DEET before the sunscreen or vice versa is more beneficial. What is known is that either application should be dry before applying the next.

Clothing is also necessary to cover as much body surface area as possible; the tighter the weave of the fabric, the more protective it is. Some newer fabrics have built-in UVA- and UVB-blocking agents. And don't forget your hat.

Heat Cramps

Symptoms. Spasmodic muscle cramps of usually the legs after prolonged strenuous activity in warm weather is caused by the loss of electrolytes (sodium, potassium, calcium, and magnesium) in the body. Manipulating by massaging or continuing to use the muscles can cause recurrent cramps.

Treatment is simply to replace the electrolytes lost and allow the victim to rest in a cool place. A commercially prepared electrolyte solution such as Vitalyte or Gatorade is helpful in this instance but should be watered down 50 percent to prevent the stomach from not digesting properly and poor fluid absorption. If the fluid is less than 6 percent carbohydrate, it can be taken at full strength. Another option is to drink ¼–½ teaspoon of table salt in a quart of water.

If the victim recovers and does not continue to have repeated cramps, the excursion can continue. However, if frequent and severe cramping continues, evacuation should be initiated.

Prevention. Avoidance is by simply adding an electrolyte solution to your drinking water and consuming salty foods whenever trekking in the heat or for long periods. Fluid intake should be gauged by urine color rather than fluid ounces. Urine should remain clear!

Heat Exhaustion

Symptoms. Heat exhaustion is thought to be the same phenomenon as heatstroke but of a lesser severity. Heat exhaustion occurs from exposure to high temperatures when water intake has not been sufficient and electrolytes have been depleted, thereby inhibiting the body's ability to dissipate heat. Signs and symptoms can include fatigue, headache, weakness, nausea, lightheadedness, and, possibly, vomiting. The skin will likely be pale and moist. Body core temperature will be above 100.4 degrees F but no more than 104.0 degrees F. It is not likely that a thermometer is available when out in the field, so paying special attention to physical symptoms and any changes in these symptoms is foremost in recognizing just how dangerous the situation is. Fortunately, with heat exhaustion the heart rate (normal range is 60–100 beats per minute) and respiration (normal is around 12–16 breaths per minute) remain normal.

Treatment. To prevent advancement to heatstroke, treatment needs to be immediate. Remove the victim to a cooler environment and allow him or her to rest. Cool the victim down with tepid wet cloths or ambient-temperature wet cloths applied to the neck, armpits, chest, and groin and fan vigorously. This is known as *evaporative cooling,* the most efficient and effective cooling method. Avoid using cold water, as shivering creates energy that will again increase the core temperature. Provide electrolyte replacement, if available, or plain water. When the victim is cooled down and rested, and fluids and electrolytes are replenished, activity can resume.

Prevention. Avoidance measures are the same as for heat cramps (explained above). Recognition of early signs is paramount to a more positive outcome.

Heatstroke

Symptoms. Heatstroke is a true medical emergency that can develop rapidly and dangerously. The transition from heat exhaustion to heatstroke will usually start with mental confusion or loss of coordination and can advance to unconsciousness. The skin becomes hot and dry, with the body temperature rising to greater than 104 degrees F. Rapid heart rate, rapid breathing, and low blood pressure are also present and may be accompanied by shortness of breath and diarrhea. The victim may or may not be able to produce sweat. Seizures and coma can ensue if not treated immediately.

Treatment. All activity must be stopped at once; it is critical to place the victim in a cool environment. If no shade is available in the immediate environment, make your own shade with whatever you have in your pack—a tarp, a tent footprint, clothing, etc. If shade can be provided, remove most of the victim's clothing and wet him or her down with cool water or compresses to the neck, armpits, chest, and groin and fan vigorously. Immerse in cool water, if available. Cooling is critical, and the faster it can be accomplished, the lower the chance of progression to a bad outcome. Do not give fluids if the victim is unconscious. If you have a thermometer, check and recheck the temperature (orally or rectally) every fifteen to thirty minutes. Evacuate the victim immediately and continue the cooling process, during transport if necessary, until the temperature is 102.2 degrees F. At this point, stop the cooling process, as the victim's body should now be able to cool itself. Be careful not to overcool and cause hypothermia instead!

Prevention. Avoidance measures are the same as for heat cramps (see above). Recognition of early signs is paramount to a more positive outcome.

Snow Blindness

Symptoms. Snow blindness, or UV keratitis, is sunburn of the cornea, usually occurring from reflected ultraviolet light that strikes the surface of the unprotected or poorly protected eye. Expected symptoms may include severe light sensitivity, pain and redness of the eye, excessive tearing, swelling of the lids, decreased vision, and headache. These symptoms will typically occur approximately six to ten hours after exposure.

Treatment is to apply cold compresses over the eyes and to rest the eyes from further exposure. If available, ophthalmic antibiotic drops or ointments are also found to be helpful.

Prevention is always key and is best achieved with UV-protected lenses that either wrap deeply around the eyes or have side shields.

Trench Foot

Symptoms. Trench foot is also known as immersion foot, since it is caused by exposure to nonfreezing cold and wet for several days. Skin, nerves, blood vessels, and sometimes even muscle tissue are damaged, although there has not been any freezing. In addition to the feet, the legs up to the buttocks can also be affected. Early symptoms are numbness and a painful "pins-and-needles" sensation accompanied by increasing redness and swelling, eventually becoming red and/or blue mottled. If the legs are involved, cramps can develop. As days go by, blistering, ulceration, and further swelling ensue, with increased pain.

Treatment is to keep the area dry. Elevate the affected limb when the victim is not active. Change socks frequently (two to three times daily if necessary) to limit sweat accumulation, stay active to keep blood flow to the feet, and keep warm. The warming most likely will be painful.

Prevention. Keep your feet dry and warm and change your socks daily. Ideally, have a change a shoes.

Frostbite

Symptoms. Frostbite is the freezing of skin from exposure to cold or wind or immersion in snow or water. Frostbite is divided into degrees and thickness. First- and second-degree frostbite is considered superficial and will likely heal well, whereas third- and fourth-degree frostbite is considered deep and likely to produce significant tissue damage. See Table 13-2 for

TABLE 13-2. STAGES AND SYMPTOMS OF FROSTBITE

Degree	Depth	Symptoms
1	superficial	Most-superficial skin layers affected—aka "frost-nip": Person affected may not notice! Skin pale and white to white-yellow while frozen. Numb to touch; diminished "pliability" of skin. Pain and redness to affected area with rewarming. Swollen and red for hours after rewarming.
2	superficial	**In addition to above:** Skin pale and white while frozen. Numb; worsening skin pliability. Deeper tissue involvement. Blisters filled with clear or milky fluid.
3	deep	Skin and deep tissue completely frozen. Skin pale and white, with a "waxy" appearance. "Frozen steak" consistency. Pain, redness, and swelling with rewarming. Swollen and red for hours to days post-rewarming. Blisters filled with dark fluid (hemorrhagic).
4	deep	**In addition to above:** Skin, deep tissue affected, including tendons, muscle, and bone. Skin pale and white; may be gray-blue mottled. May have deep, dry, and black crusting lesions. "Wooden limb" consistency.

the stages and symptoms of frostbite. The final stages of damage cannot be determined for days to weeks after the freezing—what appears to be mild may, in fact, be severe frostbite. The head (face and ears) and extremities tend to be most affected; however, covered central areas of the skin cannot be overlooked.

Treatment. The cornerstone of care for any level of frostbite is immediate rewarming and should be performed only if there is no chance of refreezing. Walking out of the wilderness on frozen limbs does less damage to the tissues than inappropriate warming (thawing and refreezing).

First- and second-degree frostbite can typically be treated with immediate, gentle warming by skin-to-skin contact such as with warm hands, under armpits, or by other body contact. Ideally, third- and fourth-degree frostbitten limbs should be warmed in circulating water of 104 degrees F to 108 degrees F. Out in the field this is not typically available and evacuation should be initiated as soon as possible.

Always treat hypothermia (core body temperature too low) prior to managing frostbite, or treat concurrently (see next section). Remove any wet clothing and replace with warm, dry clothes, blankets, sleeping bags, or space blankets. Anticipate swelling and remember to remove any jewelry that can constrict fingers, toes, and limbs. Encourage active motion if possible but do not manipulate the limbs—be as gentle as possible to avoid further tissue damage. Do not rub the skin, as this can be extremely damaging to the tissue. Do not rewarm with dry heat such as from a campfire or chemical warmers, as this can promote burning and conteract what is being attempted.

The thawing process is extremely painful and if not performed as stated above can cause a serious inflammatory cascade to occur. Ibuprofen, if available (and the victim is not allergic), is ideal as it helps decrease the inflammatory process. Give 400 mg (two 200 mg tablets) every twelve hours with food if the victim can eat and swallow without difficulty. Make the victim as comfortable as possible, provide pain medication and reassurance, elevate the affected area, and pad and protect the affected areas with loose-fitting soft gauze. Do not put heavy blankets and covers directly on frostbitten limbs, as this can also damage tissue. Simply tent any coverings over the limbs using whatever is available to keep the tenting stable.

Prevention. Have the right gear and clothing to keep warm. Do not stay cold and wet; take the time to change into dry clothes or add clothing for warmth.

Hypothermia

Symptoms. Hypothermia is the result of excessive heat loss, decreased heat production, or the body's inability to regulate its temperature. We lose heat by four processes:

1. **Radiation**—heat loss from a warm body to cooler environment
2. **Conduction**—heat loss from direct contact with a cold surface (rocks, ground, ice)
3. **Convection**—heat loss from air circulation (wind)
4. **Evaporation**—heat loss through sweating or water drying on the skin

The definition of hypothermia is a core body temperature of less than 95 degrees F. There are three stages of hypothermia: (1) mild, (2) moderate, and (3) severe. Most thermometers do not register below 95 degrees F, making them useless in helping to differentiate between the stages of hypothermia. However, there are special thermometers specifically for use with cold environments that should be considered if you are doing a trek in extremely cold conditions.

In the backcountry, the most common cause of hypothermia is from immersion in cold water or simply cold and/or wet weather conditions. Improper preparedness, with inadequate clothing or shelter from wind and rain, can turn an anticipated vacation into a surprising misadventure.

Mild hypothermia occurs when the victim has a core temperature of less than 95 degrees F but higher than 90 degrees F. Initially the victim will feel cold and have uncontrollable maximal shivering. As the temperature continues to drop, clumsiness, slurred speech, forgetfulness, moodiness, and poor judgment can be seen. The pulse and breathing rate will increase. This is an important distinguishing sign for mild hypothermia.

Treatment. Get the victim out of the wind, rain, or cold environment, and remove any wet clothing. Protect the victim from further heat loss, especially from the head and neck. Give warm food and warm, sugary drinks to more effectively increase the core temperature by fueling energy stores. A common myth is that alcoholic beverages are warming; this is a myth and, in fact, may cause further hypothermia. The goal is to warm from the core out and retain the body's ability to shiver. If warm packs are applied to the groin, armpits, and neck, the body will not be able to warm correctly; it will think it is warm and stop shivering when actually the core may still be cold. If the victim recovers and has the clothing and gear to prevent another episode, trek on.

Moderate hypothermia occurs when the victim has a core temperature of less than 90 degrees F but higher than 83 degrees F. At this point, there is no shivering as the body has lost its ability and energy to shiver. Another distinguishing sign of advancing hypothermia is that the heart rate and respiratory rate are now decreasing. Stupor, possibly unconsciousness, or severe irritability can occur. The pupils may dilate. If the victim is conscious, he or she may start undressing. This is called "paradoxical undressing." This is not a good sign! This means the outer blood vessels are now open wide, allowing a rush of blood to the surface, making the victim feel very warm. Our perception of warmth comes from our outer temperature, not our internal temperature, causing a disconnect in how we think we feel. The result is a rapid decrease in the core temperature and worsening symptoms.

Treatment. Get the victim under shelter and out of the elements. Insulate the victim literally from the ground up. Be sure the clothing and coverings are dry. Do not try to give fluids or foods by mouth, as aspiration will just make matters worse. Steam for inhalation can be helpful if you are careful not to cause burns. Now is the time to provide insulated heat packs to the armpits, groin, and around the neck—why? Because the body has already lost its ability to shiver, and the victim is unable to consume warm products to help warm the core. Putting the victim in a sleeping bag with another warm person can be helpful. Do not massage or vigorously rub the skin. Unorganized heart rhythms are a danger, so do not overly jar or manipulate the victim; keep him or her horizontal and as immobile as possible. Evacuate as soon as possible.

Severe or profound hypothermia is extreme, with a core temperature of less than 83 degrees F. The victim will be lethargic and weak or most likely in a coma. The heart rate and breathing rate will be greatly decreased, potentially less than half the normal rate. The pupils will be dilated, and the victim may even appear dead. Most important, do not attempt CPR on the victim until you are absolutely sure there is no breathing or heartbeat. Feel for a pulse in the neck (carotid artery) and look for the humidity of a breath. You can place a smooth metal object or mirror near the mouth to see if it "fogs" from a breath. Always check for one or two minutes before initiating CPR. Again, the heart will be extremely irritable, and every effort not to jar the victim should be made. Make all of the efforts as in moderate hypothermia to warm the victim. Keep in the back of your mind that the victim is not considered "cold and dead" until he or she has been proven to be "warm and dead." Obviously, evacuation is essential for survival.

Prevention. For all forms of hypothermia, get under shelter and out of the elements. Remove any wet and cold clothing, and rewrap in warm replacements.

ENVIRONMENTAL HAZARDS

Lions and tigers and bears . . . possible, but not likely. However, there are still dangers of bites and poisons by some obvious and not-so-obvious creatures and plants. Prevention tips aren't included in this section when it's simply a matter of avoiding a hazard.

Poison Oak, Ivy, or Sumac

Symptoms. "Leaves of three, let them be" is a good adage to remember when thinking of poison oak and ivy. Poison oak, ivy, and sumac are plants in the *Toxicodendron* (meaning "poison tree") genus that secrete a resin known as *urushiol* (pronounced "you-ROO-she-ole"), a skin irritant that can cause a red, itchy, swollen rash with small *vesicles* (blisters) within one hour to two to three days after exposure. Poison oak and poison ivy can be either an ivy or a shrub, usually with the classic three leaves of various colors. Poison sumac is a shrub that can have seven to thirteen paired leaves, usually with red stems and berries of various colors, depending on the region and the season. Poison sumac prefers flooded areas in the eastern states. Poison ivy also tends to be more indigenous to the East Coast. Poison oak is more prevalent in the western states. Rash development can continue up to about ten days due to varying concentrations of urushiol on the skin. The rash itself can last one to three weeks and in extreme cases even up to six weeks.

Treatment will depend on the intensity of the rash. Washing off the resin is the first and most important step. To minimize the rash after

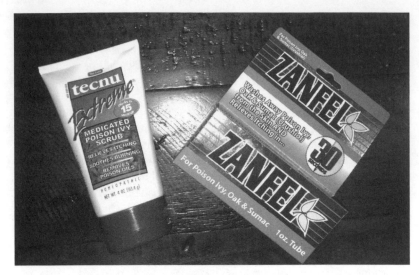

Figure 13-3. *Tecnu and Zanfel* (Photo by Laura A. Wolfgang)

exposure, wash the exposed area within sixty minutes of exposure with soap and water or with a commercial product such as Tecnu or Zanfel (see Figure 13-3). If washing is delayed no more than two hours, the reaction can be decreased by nearly 50 percent. No medications or topical treatments will be effective if they are applied over a noncleansed exposure site. Ideally, antihistamines should be taken as soon after exposure as possible. Steroid creams such as hydrocortisone or triamcinolone can be helpful for symptomatic relief but should be avoided on the face and genitals and should not be used for a long period of time due to potential side effects such as skin thinning or adrenal suppression. Colloidal oatmeal formulation (Aveeno Bath) or aluminum acetate (Domeboro or Burow's solution) purchased over the counter can also be calming once the affected trekker gets home. Some rashes are so severe they will require prescription oral steroids for relief.

Prevention. All trekkers should be familiar with how each plant looks in their region and how to avoid any contact. Wearing long pants and long-sleeved shirts can help keep skin from being exposed. Remove contaminated clothing inside-out and package separately from other clothing to prevent spread from repeated exposure to the resin. Avoid brushing against clothing, gear, or an exposed pet's fur to avoid spreading the resin. Also be sure to wipe down gear and your pets to prevent further exposure. Avoid scratching an exposed area prior to washing, which can spread the resin, therefore spreading the rash. Once the resin has been washed off of the exposed area, it can no longer be spread.

Lightning

Symptoms. Victims of lightning strikes who appear dead are likely the ones that need the most immediate care. Other injuries include superficial and partial-thickness burns, fractures, bruises, chest and abdominal injuries, seizures, confusion, temporary paralysis, and ear drum rupture.

Treatment of victims who appear dead is usually CPR or rescue breathing, which helps the heart "reboot" after the lightning has caused a disruption of the normal heartbeat. Treat other injuries as stated in the appropriate sections in this chapter.

Prevention. To learn more about how to avoid being struck by lightning, see "Lightning" in Chapter 9, "Now Let's Get Out There!"

ANIMAL AND INSECT EXPOSURE

Stings, bites, and envenomation can really ruin a trip very quickly! All need immediate attention and can range from a simple nuisance to an urgent life-threatening event.

Insects such as mosquitoes and ticks cause more death and illness than animal bites internationally, but here in the United States we have fewer deadly vector-borne diseases (a vector is an insect or animal that transmits an infectious agent). Mosquito, tick, and flea bites in foreign countries can be life threatening or disabling; they can transmit malaria, dengue fever, chikungunya, leishmaniasis, and more. If you are traveling abroad for outdoor adventures, always check with a travel clinic or with the Centers for Disease Control and Prevention (CDC) for what your exposure potential may be.

Mosquitoes

Symptoms. West Nile Virus (WNV) is an illness that occurs from being bitten by an infected mosquito. The mosquito was infected by biting an infected bird. WNV is most prevalent during summer and into fall, when the mosquito load is highest. Most people who are infected with WNV never have symptoms. Symptoms, if they arise, generally appear in three to fourteen days. Most common symptoms experienced are fever, headache, body aches, nausea, vomiting, and possibly a rash or swollen lymph nodes. These symptoms can last from a few days to a few weeks. More severe symptoms can be alarming and potentially permanent. These symptoms can include a very high fever, headache, muscle weakness, neck stiffness, confusion, disorientation, vision loss, numbness, and even paralysis.

Treatment is simply treating the common symptoms. Severe WNV will need hospitalization.

Prevention is protecting yourself with insect repellent (such as DEET), applying it to all exposed skin. You can also avoid mosquito-infested areas, such as standing water, and try to be in mosquito-proof shelter at dusk and dawn, when mosquitoes are most active. Also, do not handle any dead birds.

Ticks

Symptoms. Ticks sit in wait on brush, shrubs, weeds, and grasses for a warm-blooded passerby to latch onto. There are several tick-borne diseases, including Lyme disease, Rocky Mountain spotted fever, and tularemia, to name a few. The longer the tick (see Figure 13-4) stays attached, the more likely disease can be passed on. Symptoms commonly include body aches, fevers, and possibly other nonspecific flulike symptoms.

Treatment. If a tick is found, it must be removed correctly. What is the correct way? Using thin-tipped tweezers, which should be in all first-aid kits, grasp the tick as close as possible to your skin and gently and evenly pull outward. *Do not* burn the tick or apply Vaseline, gasoline, fingernail polish, or any other substance to "smother" the tick. Wash the area and your hands with soap and water.

Prevention. Wear long pants and long-sleeved shirts. Perform frequent tick checks.

Bees, Wasps, and Hornets

Symptoms. Bees, wasps, and hornets can cause a severe allergic reaction for some called *anaphylactic shock*. The usual reaction is redness, swelling, and itching that develops very quickly. Without treatment, a severe allergic reaction can develop into breathing difficulties and shock. Those with known allergies should always carry two EpiPens and let others in the group know of their allergy.

Treatment. If an allergic person is stung, the goal is to get the stinger out as quickly as possible and also avoid squeezing the stinger while removing it. The quicker the stinger can be removed, the less venom will be inserted into the victim. Use whatever is available to quickly scrape the stinger away—this may mean removing an entire insect. Immediately apply a cool compress or water to the site. To prevent a worsening reaction, give an antihistamine such as Claritin or Allegra along with an H2 blocker such as Zantac. If available, diphenhydramine (Benadryl) can also be given but will likely cause drowsiness. If the victim is allergic, hopefully he or she will have two EpiPens, as generally two will be needed approximately one hour apart for best results. Always check for allergies to medications before giving medications to a victim.

Prevention. Wear long pants and long-sleeved shirts, and avoid lingering in areas where bees or wasps are active.

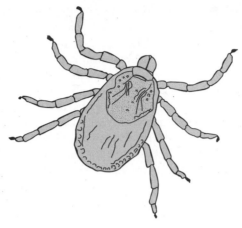

Figure 13-4. *Tick*

Arachnids

Two well-known dangerous spiders in the United States are the black widow and the brown recluse. Both spiders can give a nasty bite with a varying degree of local tissue reaction. There are two other venomous spiders in the United States that backpackers are as likely to encounter. These include the funnel spider (hobo spider) and the tarantula.

Symptoms. The **black widow** can cause a burning or stinglike bite that will usually cause some redness to the site. The reaction can remain minor, with some minimal redness or a "blanching" appearance an inch or two in diameter surrounding the bite. Other victims, however, may suffer severe muscle spasm and/or cramps, become restless and/or anxious, or complain of sweating and muscle weakness. Children and the elderly are more likely to be affected more severely. Anyone exhibiting symptoms, especially out in the wilderness, should be taken for medical care. There is an antivenin available for black widow spider bites, but it tends to cause allergic reactions.

The **brown recluse spider** will usually bite only when it is pressed, such as when you are putting on a pair of shoes with a spider in the shoes or if it is pressed between bedcovers. Most often, victims do not realize they have been bitten until they develop a red blister surrounded by the characteristic "bull's-eye" ring of pale bluish discoloration. Common symptoms experienced can include headache, nausea and/or vomiting, fever and chills, or an itchy rash. Skin breakdown, or *necrosis,* may eventually appear weeks to months after the bite and require medical attention.

Tarantulas (see Figure 13-5) can give a painful bite, but those in North America are not aggressive and their bite is harmless. They are found in rocky terrain and do migrate in the spring to mate. Most bites are from putting hands or feet in a nest. The bite is similar to a wasp sting.

Scorpions are found mostly in the southern parts of the United States. Scorpion venom has a fearsome reputation, but only one scorpion here, the bark scorpion (see Figure 13-6), can cause death in a healthy person. A sting will cause sharp pain and swelling at the sting site.

Treatment. No matter what the type of spider bite, all should be iced to decrease the amount of swelling that may occur, and all restrictive jewelry needs to be removed. Treat with antihistamines such as diphenhydramine (Benadryl) and ice. For scorpion stings, first aid is primarily symptomatic, with cold wet compresses and acetaminophen or ibuprofen to reduce the pain and swelling. Seek medical aid for severe pain or if the sting is to a child.

Prevention. When in the wilderness, roll up your sleeping bag when it's not in use and cover the opening to your boots or shoes with a sock to prevent unwelcome critters (spiders, scorpions, centipedes, etc.) from inhabiting these warm, dark, premade "dens." Avoid putting your hands in cracks and crevices in the rocks, tree bark, or holes in the ground. Obviously, do not attempt to handle any of these arachnids.

Snakes

The United States has two native types of venomous snakes: the pit vipers, which include rattlesnakes, copperheads, and cottonmouths (water moccasins); and coral snakes. Several new species of snakes are quickly inhabiting some of the states due to the importation of exotic snakes for pets that have been released into the environment. Travel outside of the United States may increase the chance of exposure to other, more deadly venomous snakes, and research prior to backpacking or trekking in a foreign country for risk is optimal.

Most victims of snakebites survive, but a bite must always be considered a medical emergency, as some reactions may be delayed. The severity of the bite depends on several factors, such as type and age of the snake, how much venom was injected (approximately 25 percent of bites are "dry"), the area of the body attacked, and the condition of the victim. Identification of the snake is helpful, but a snake should not be pursued for capture as this can cause another bite or a new victim.

Symptoms that can manifest can range from burning pain and swelling at the site to nausea, vomiting, numbness, and tingling around the mouth, a metallic taste in the mouth, increased heart and breathing rates, shock, etc.

Treatment in the field is generally supportive (care for the victim) with frequent checks on his or her status until evacuation is complete. All

Figure 13-5. *Tarantula* (Photo by Walter Konopka)

Figure 13-6. *Arizona bark scorpion* (Photo by Aamir Yunus)

tight-fitting clothes and jewelry in the area of the bite should be removed immediately to prevent restriction and a "tourniquet" effect that can be more traumatic to the injury. Limit physical activity for the victim, who may need to be carried out to the evacuation site. *Do not* apply a tourniquet. Mark the size of the swelling with a pen every fifteen minutes; this can help rescuers identify how serious the envenomation is. *Do not* use a Sawyer extractor (a device sold for snakebites), cut and suck on the bite site, apply ice, or apply a pressure immobilizer—immobilization is good but not with pressure directly on the bite. Also, it is very important *not* to give aspirin or a nonsteroidal anti-inflammatory drug (NSAID) such as ibuprofen or naproxen, which can worsen bleeding. *Do* keep the bitten limb lower than heart level to try to decrease the speed the venom travels to the heart. Evacuate as soon as possible.

Prevention. See Chapter 10, "Close Encounters of the Animal Kind."

Hantavirus

Symptoms. Hantavirus is a severe viral respiratory illness caused by exposure to, contact with, or inhalation of contaminated airborne dust from infected rodent saliva, urine, or feces. The usual suspects are deer mice, brush mice, western chipmunks, and, more recently, some squirrels. Early symptoms will be flulike with fever, body aches, cough, and mild shortness of breath. These symptoms can quickly worsen to include headache, chills, abdominal pain, nausea, vomiting, and possible hemorrhage. Deterioration to respiratory failure and hypotension (low blood pressure) is also possible.

Treatment is based on symptoms and is typically supportive.

Prevention. In the field, keep your food and water covered, get rid of garbage, and keep your campsite and cooking area clean. Do not pitch your tent or place sleeping bags near animal burrows, dens, or wood piles or breathe the airborne dust from the ground.

Animal Bites

Symptoms. Of course, any animal encountered on an excursion has the potential to bite. Bears and cougars can cause significant blunt trauma and crushing and tearing injuries to a victim (see "Trauma" below).

Treatment. All victims will likely need to be immediately evacuated. First aid will focus on stopping any bleeding and supporting the victim until evacuation is possible.

Prevention. The best way to prevent an animal bite is avoidance and awareness. All backpackers need to be aware of the animal life they may encounter when out on an excursion. Animal habits need to be understood when you are in bear or cougar country. Avoid the time of day or year you are likely to have possible contact. It is optimal to avoid animal encounters as much as possible (see Chapter 10, "Close Encounters of the Animal Kind").

Rabies

Symptoms. Rabies virus infection in humans is uncommon here in the United States, but if left untreated it will end in death. The animals most commonly affected in the United States include raccoons, bats, skunks, foxes, and coyotes. Bears have not been known to carry rabies. When traveling abroad, dogs become more of a threat, especially to "kind-hearted" Americans or those traveling rurally by bicycle. The virus is transmitted by saliva either through a bite, a lick to an open wound, or even breathing the virus in bat-infested caves.

The virus causes no symptoms until it reaches the brain, with a usual incubation period of two to sixteen weeks, but it can incubate for longer than a year. Once the virus reaches the brain, death is imminent. Nonspecific early symptoms can include fatigue, anxiety, insomnia, irritability, fever, headache, nausea, vomiting, and more. Neurologic symptoms can include hyperactivity, seizures, aggression, biting, and hallucinations.

Treatment. Rigorous cleansing and irrigation of the wound with benzalkonium chloride (BZK) or soap and water is necessary with any animal encounter. Wound closure is still controversial, so do not close the wound unless necessary to stop it from bleeding. Apply a gauze dressing, packing the wound if necessary. If the animal can be captured without risking another victim or another bite, the animal can be tested for the virus. Most importantly, medical care must be sought to determine what treatment needs to be administered.

Prevention. If you are planning an excursion that includes caving, cycling in rural areas overseas, or backpacking in known rabies-infected regions, consider vaccination for rabies. Even if you have been vaccinated, postexposure treatment will still be necessary.

TRAUMA

We all know the obvious dangers when trekking on rocky terrain, cliffs, or icy slopes—we use our greatest specialized gear and try to keep our wits about us. It's not always the obvious that can cause injury, however; the wrong shoes, exhaustion, wear and rubbing of gear, poor physical conditioning, and existing medical conditions can all be catalysts to injury. Again, no prevention tips are included if they consist simply of avoiding the hazard or being careful.

Blisters

Symptoms. Blisters are raised, fluid-filled bubbles of skin that form due to friction, most commonly from ill-fitting shoes. Left untreated, blisters may break and leave a painful, open area prone to infection.

Treatment. The best treatment for blisters is prevention. If the blister is small and still intact, avoid draining it and instead apply a donut of moleskin to protect it. You may have to place a few layers of the moleskin to prevent rubbing. Other products to consider are Compeed or other hydrocolloid (protective gel that absorbs water) dressings, especially if the blister has opened.

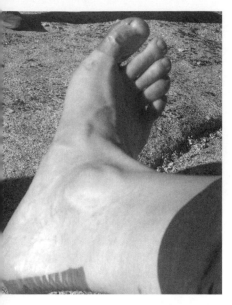

Figure 13-7. *Use duct-tape to repair your feet.*
(Photo by Kristi Anderson)

There is a trick to using hydrocolloid dressings correctly: you should warm them first (under your armpits or in your pocket), as this makes them more pliable. They must be applied to skin that is very dry where the adhesion of the dressing takes place. What is great about hydrocolloids is that they are waterproof and can remain in place for up to seven days. You must thoroughly clean the wound before applying.

If the blister is large, carefully drain it by puncturing it with a sterile needle or pin at the base of the blister and press out the fluid. Do not puncture the top of the blister. If the blister is deroofed (the skin covering has come partially or all the way off), you will want to apply a hydrocolloid dressing or, minimally, some antibiotic ointment covered with a nonadherent dressing or gauze pad—again, take steps to prevent further rubbing. Monitor daily for signs of infection: increasing redness, pain, swelling, or cloudy fluid drainage. With infection, the dressing will need to be removed to allow for drainage and, if not managed well, will require medical attention.

Prevention. The first sign of a blister is a hot spot, a red, irritated, and tender area of the skin. If you know where you get hot spots or feel one developing, cover them early with moleskin or molefoam to prevent blisters from having a chance to develop. Moleskin will stick better if you first apply some benzoin to the skin and securely tape the moleskin down. If you don't have moleskin, you can apply tape over the hot spot—duct tape works great! (see Figure 13-7).

Foreign Body in the Eye

Symptoms. Excessive tearing or pain when the eye is moved, with or without the eyelid closed, may indicate a foreign object in the eye.

Treatment. A nonembedded foreign body in the eye can usually be removed by rinsing the eye with clean water, from the nose to the outside of the eye. If this doesn't work, a cotton tip applicator (such as a Q-tip) or the corner of a moistened gauze pad may be helpful. The victim may feel a "sandy" sensation in the eye for a couple of days after the item is removed. If available, eye ointment can be helpful and relieving. Encourage the victim not to rub the eye, which further irritates it. Cool compresses to the eyes and using sunglasses or resting the eyes can relieve the symptoms. Do not attempt to remove an imbedded object. Instead, cover the eye and get to a medical facility.

Prevention. Using sunglasses or goggles while climbing, bouldering, or in the wind can help prevent foreign bodies from getting in the eyes. Also, avoid touching the eyes.

Burns

Symptoms. Heat, radiation, and chemicals can damage skin, causing a burn. Burn severity is determined by the size, depth, and part of the body that is affected. A superficial burn (formerly known as first degree) will cause the skin to appear red and can be painful. A common superficial burn is mild sunburn. Superficial partial-thickness or deep partial-thickness (formerly known as second-degree) burns will also have redness, but this will be accompanied by swelling, clear-fluid blisters, and pain. Full-thickness (formerly known as third degree) burns are severe and affect several layers of tissue to include the nerves, blood vessels, and muscle. Due to the extent of the damage the victim will not be in pain, unless the surrounding tissues have superficial or partial-thickness burns. The burn will appear leathery, charred, firm, and dry.

Treatment or the need for evacuation is indicated by severity or the burn size in proportion to the body. Out in the field, the best way to determine total body surface area (TBSA) affected is with the *Rule of Palms*. An individual's palm is roughly 1 percent of the body surface area and can be used to measure the burn size. Most burns of less than 5 percent of TBSA can be treated out in the field; however, this excludes any partial-thickness (blistering) or greater (skin destroyed) burns of the face, genitals, hands, or feet or a burn encircling an extremity. These will require immediate evacuation. Be sure to cut away any burned clothing (unless embedded in skin), and remove any constrictive clothing or jewelry.

Treatment for both superficial and partial-thickness burns involves cool, wet compresses or gentle water flushing to help stop the burning and provide relief. Application of an aloe vera gel or, in the case of second-degree burns, a thin layer of antibiotic ointment can be helpful. Also, ibuprofen (Motrin or Aleve) can help to relieve pain and influence healing if taken three times daily with food. Leave small blisters alone, but if there are large (greater than 1 inch in diameter), thin-skinned blisters, these can be drained with a sterilized pin to the side of the blister, but keep it intact and cover with a nonadherent dressing. Change the dressing daily. Any victim with a partial-thickness burn greater than 5 percent TBSA needs to be evacuated, as shock can occur from the loss of fluids.

Treat a full-thickness burn the same as you would a partial-thickness burn, but additionally be wary of shock, as large amounts of fluid will be lost with this burn. If the victim is conscious and not vomiting, encourage frequent sips of an electrolyte-based beverage such as Vitalyte or Gatorade. Any victim of full-thickness burns of any size must be evacuated as soon as possible. Any victim with a full-thickness burn of greater than 5 percent TBSA or affecting hands, feet, face, or groin or encircling a limb *must* be more urgently evacuated. If a facial burn is present, also check for singed hair in the nose, coughing black, sooty mucus, hoarseness, or wheezing—a victim with these symptoms also must be evacuated and the airway needs to be monitored closely. This can be an ominous sign that the victim's airway or lungs have been compromised.

Prevention. Always apply and reapply sunscreen to avoid sunburns. Avoid handling heat sources unnecessarily, and use caution when around heat sources.

Scratches, Scrapes, and Lacerations

Symptoms. Lacerations are a common injury in the wilderness and are likely caused by shear (tearing, crushing, or splitting) forces or punctures. The skin will be broken and most likely bleeding.

Treatment. The basis of care for minor open wounds is a good cleaning and prevention of infection. Irrigate the wound with clean water and, if available, soap or a disinfectant wipe such as benzalkonium chloride (BZK). Remove any debris with tweezers if necessary. For small (less than a half-inch long) or very superficial, uncomplicated lacerations, commercial skin glue (cyanoacrylates, such as superglue) can be used. Best not to use this near the eyes! Just apply to the wound and hold the edges together until dried. Do not apply any ointments to the wound if using skin glue, as the ointment will dissolve the glue.

Closing larger wounds with skin glue or sutures should be avoided, but butterfly taping (using steri-strips and benzoin) can be applied after cleaning. Apply an antibiotic ointment or cream such as Bacitracin or Mupirocin and cover with an occlusive (doesn't allow air in or out) dressing or nonadherent dressing. Occlusive dressings will not allow air in or out but will allow the wound to drain and prevent an abscess from forming. Always check for allergies before applying any topical agents. Monitor closely for signs of infection. Neosporin is a popular antibiotic ointment that can cause a skin reaction that may be mistaken for infection and, therefore, might not be an ideal choice.

Shear-force lacerations tend to be "cleaner" wounds but can vary in depth and severity. After thoroughly cleaning the wound with BZK or freshwater, try to close the wound. If steri-strips are available, this is great!

If not, steri-strips can be made with duct tape. That's right—narrow strips of duct tape can close the wound. Squeeze the edges of the wound together and apply the strips from one side across to the other, taut enough to keep the wound edges together. Benzoin can be used to help with the adhesion if this is available. A scalp wound may require hair to be clipped in the surrounding area to allow closure or, if the hair is long enough, the hair can be tied across the wound to help with closure.

A puncture wound has a greater potential for infection and should be cleaned as well as possible. Closing a puncture wound is never the best idea due to the risk of infection, unless it is a very large puncture wound, which may benefit from being taped closed and allowing drainage. Cleanse well by irrigation, if possible, and apply an antibiotic ointment and a dressing.

Prevention. Awareness of the environment, care in handling sharp instruments, and staying alert are all obvious preventives for lacerations.

Bruises, Strains, Sprains, and Dislocations

Symptoms. Soft-tissue injuries include **contusions** (bruises), sprains, and strains. A **strain** is an injury to tendons and muscle fibers usually caused from overexertion such as lifting and pulling, from poor body mechanics, or from a poorly sized or secured backpack. The back and neck suffer the most from strains. A **sprain** occurs from stretching or tearing ligaments at the joints; varying degrees of tenderness, discoloration, swelling, and pain may be noted. Unfortunately, similar symptoms occur with a fracture, making field diagnosis difficult. The ankles and knees are the joints most often sprained. Pain with weight bearing can indicate a fracture and should be avoided. **Dislocation** is the displacement of a joint that will show an obvious deformity and pain. The more common joints to be displaced are the shoulders, knees, ankles, and fingers.

Treatment. All soft-tissue injuries are best treated with application of cold if possible to decrease swelling, bruising, pain, and disability. Out in the wilderness, cold is not always available, though. Water from a cold stream can help, snow is always useful, and, if available, use chemical cold packs. Never apply heat. If a limb is affected, elevate it above the heart if possible. Apply a compression dressing with an elastic bandage if available. When wrapping, start from farthest away from the head and wrap toward the head. Use a figure-eight pattern if the injury is to the ankle. Always check circulation below the affected area after applying a wrap to make sure the wrap is not too tight.

Gentle stretches and ibuprofen are helpful for **strains.** If a SAM (Structural Aluminum Malleable) splint is available, use this to stabilize.

Stabilize **sprains** with a SAM splint, or make a splint out of whatever is handy, such as a tent pole or a branch (see Figure 13-8). Be sure to remove hiking boots if the swelling becomes severe to prevent problems with circulation. Frequently check the circulation. Ibuprofen is the right medicine to take to help with inflammation but should not be used if the victim is allergic. Ibuprofen should be taken with food.

Dislocations can be alarming and more difficult to manage for the inexperienced. Relocation of a joint should be done as soon after the injury as possible, prior to the muscles going into spasm. Disruption of the circulation is always a concern and, therefore, should be checked about every fifteen minutes before and after relocation. There are very specific ways to relocate a dislocation. Attempting relocation by a layperson is very controversial but may be necessary due to compromise of circulation or just for evacuation. Relocating a joint will always require gentle countertraction and is very painful. The relocated limb should be supported with a sling or splint. Evacuate the victim as soon as possible.

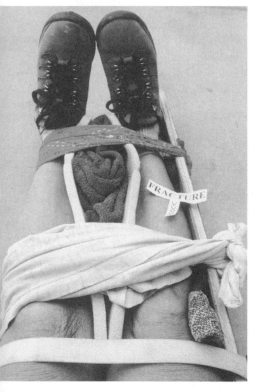

Figure 13-8. *Splinting with available materials* (Photo by Carol Murdock)

Fractures

Symptoms. Fractures (broken bones) occur as either closed (no break in the skin) or open (opening in the skin exists with or without a bone protruding). Open fractures are obvious with a protrusion (bone showing), but the fracture may not be so obvious if the bone is not showing. Always suspect a fracture if there is a deformity in a limb, rapid swelling and bruising with an injury, pain and tenderness over a specific spot (point tenderness), a grating or grinding (crepitus) sensation or sound with movement of the limb, motion where there isn't a joint, or the inability to use the limb. Fractures are often mistaken as sprains, but an injury with these symptoms should be considered a fracture until proven otherwise by an X-ray.

Treatment for fractures in the field is preventing movement with a splint. An open fracture that is protruding can benefit from a rinse with fresh disinfected water and a dressing

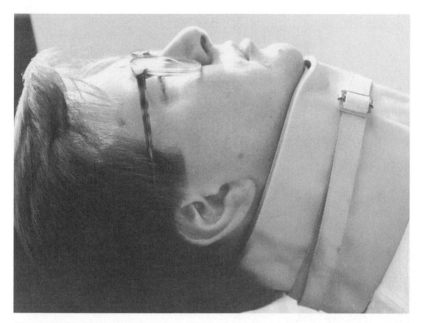

Figure 13-9. *Improvised cervical collar* (Photo by Carol Murdock)

before immobilizing. SAM splints are ideal, but other items in your gear can also be used, such as camera tripods, tent poles, trekking poles, or ice axes. For an improvised neck collar, clothing that is taped into a roll, then taped in place can work as well as a SAM splint (see Figure 13-9). Closed fractures can be more damaging to the soft tissue due to the shearing of tissue from the mobile bone, and if the fracture can be gently reduced (put back in place), this may prevent further tissue damage.

Bleeding

Symptoms. Open wounds and nosebleeds can bleed, and bruising may indicate internal bleeding.

Treatment. Most bleeding from wounds can be stopped using direct pressure. Wear gloves; apply gauze and continue to hold pressure until the bleeding has stopped. This may take as much as thirty minutes. Never remove the dressing, but apply more dressings on top of the existing dressing. If the bleeding doesn't appear to slow down, verify you are applying pressure directly over the wound. Every time you stop to check for bleeding, it restarts the clock for the time pressure must be held, so do not keep peeking every two minutes!

Often a person with a nosebleed will try to stop the bleeding by tilting his or her head back and pinching the cartilage of the nose. Well, pinching

the nose is correct, but it is best to lean with the head *forward* to prevent the dripping of blood down the throat, which will lead to aspiration or nausea and vomiting (see Figure 13-10). If bleeding continues for greater than ten minutes, insert a rolled-up piece of gauze or a woman's tampon in the nostril, which can help to stop the bleeding. Yes, women's tampons or sanitary napkins are great for stopping or absorbing bleeding.

Impalement

Symptoms. A sharp object piercing a part of the victim's body will likely cause pain and bleeding.

Treatment. Impalements should not be removed except in very rare circumstances. Leave the object in place, as removal can cause severe bleeding as well as tissue and nerve damage. Also try to ensure no movement of the object while it is in place. Apply a bulky dressing; this can be a towel, rolled-up clothing and tape, or an elastic wrap in place. If needed to control bleeding, be sure to apply pressure around the impaling object

Figure 13-10. *For nosebleeds, apply pressure to the soft cartilage at the bridge of the nose. Have the victim sit upright and lean the head slightly forward.* (Photo by Carol Murdock)

as best as you can; this will not be comfortable for the victim and he or she may resist. If the impalement is of the eye, support the same way but also cover both eyes to prevent movement. Get the victim to medical care as soon as possible.

MORE SERIOUS CONDITIONS

Again, prevention tips are not necessarily possible for these conditions and so are not always included in this section.

Shock

Symptoms. Severe burns, blood loss, heart failure, allergic reactions, infection, and spinal trauma are a few of the causes of a life-threatening condition known as shock. Despite the cause, the symptoms are all basically the same and will need extensive and immediate medical attention. Signs and symptoms include pale, cool, and sweaty skin; restlessness or anxiety; a fast, faint pulse; rapid and possibly irregular breathing; and potential combativeness. Recognize the symptoms and act quickly.

Treatment. Control bleeding, provide warmth, provide spinal support, splint fractures, and keep the victim lying down or in the recovery position (lay the victim on his or her side) unless this causes more difficulty in breathing. If the victim is diabetic, the cause of the symptoms, if not obvious, may be low blood sugar (hypoglycemia), and the victim could benefit from drinking sugary liquid (see "Diabetic Emergencies" below). Monitor the victim closely and continuously until help arrives. No matter the cause, evacuation *must* happen as immediately as possible.

Stroke

Symptoms. Strokes, also called cerebral vascular accidents (CVA), can be caused by lack of oxygen to an area (*ischemia*) or from bleeding. This happens when a blood clot blocks blood flow to a part of the brain or when a blood vessel in the brain ruptures. It is impossible to identify the type of stroke when out in the backcountry. Most important is to recognize the possible signs and evacuate the victim as soon as possible. CVA is a time-sensitive process and needs definitive treatment in less than six hours to help prevent permanent damage or death. Any or all of these symptoms can indicate a CVA is occurring: a change in mental status (drowsy, confused, lethargic, comatose), weakness or numbness to usually one side of the body or limbs, one-sided facial drooping, difficulty or inability to speak, dizziness or stumbling, and possibly the sudden onset of a severe headache.

Treatment. Keep the victim with his or her head inclined at about 30 degrees and *do not* give aspirin, which can exacerbate hemorrhage. Until you know for sure that the stroke is not the bleeding kind, you must avoid aspirin or ibuprofen. These victims *must* be evacuated immediately.

Prevention. Manage your high blood pressure.

Heart Attack

Symptoms. A heart attack, or acute myocardial infarction (AMI), is heart tissue injury caused by lack of blood and oxygen to a portion of the heart. The hallmark symptom is chest pain that is crushing, pressured, squeezing, or aching in the midchest. Other accompanying symptoms are nausea, sweating, shortness of breath, lightheadedness, weakness, and radiation of pain to the jaw and/or left shoulder and arm. Women tend to not have these "classic" symptoms but may just have some nausea or indigestion-like pain, with or without some of the other accompanying symptoms. If the victim is younger, do not fall into the trap of thinking that they cannot be having an AMI. Indigestion and upper abdominal pain can mimic an AMI but are considered a secondary cause until proven otherwise.

Treatment. Ideally, 325 mg of aspirin should be chewed by the victim as soon as possible to help with preventing a hard clot being formed in the heart. If the victim is a heart patient, he or she may also have some nitroglycerin tablets. If so, in addition to chewing the aspirin, one nitro tablet should be placed under the tongue every five minutes for a maximum of three times if the pain continues. Be prepared to possibly start CPR, as rhythm disturbances often occur with AMI. Evacuate! A heart attack can result in death.

Diabetic Emergencies

Diabetes is a chronic illness that entails a disruption of the balance of blood sugar (glucose) and insulin. Some diabetics manage their illness with insulin or other injections and others with oral anti-diabetic medication. Before venturing into the wilderness, all diabetics need to be well conditioned for the type of activities expected, and their illness should be stable for several months prior to the trip. They need to bring along not only enough medication for the expected time away but extra in case of emergency. If injectables are brought along, proper temperature control for the injectable medication must be maintained. A sugar source such as oral glucose paste, energy gel, a packet of sugar, or a small tube of cake frosting should be included in the personal first-aid kit for emergencies. A change in diet, poor monitoring and management of medications, or overexertion can cause one of two problems diabetics are at risk for: diabetic coma from too much sugar (hyperglycemia) or insulin shock from too much insulin or too little sugar (hypoglycemia).

Diabetes and high altitude do not always go together well. There is an association with high altitude and diabetic ketoacidosis (toxic levels of blood acids caused by fat, rather than glucose, being used for energy), which can lead to diabetic coma. The cause is not clear but may be induced by freezing temperatures, loss of appetite from hypoxia (oxygen deficiency), or increased incidence of altitude sickness. Diabetics need to be aware of this possibility and be prepared to closely monitor their blood sugar, food intake, and medications at altitude.

Symptoms of hyperglycemia. This condition is not very common in the backcountry, and most diabetics recognize the symptoms early. Common causes are from medication that has become unstable and ineffective from temperature extremes, dehydration, increased stress, infection, and too much food with too little insulin. Symptoms start slowly and can include dry mouth, frequent urination, abdominal pain, nausea and vomiting, blurred vision, fatigue, and at worst, coma. The skin may become red, warm, and dry. The breath may smell fruity, and the pulse may become very rapid and weak.

Treatment starts with hydration, as most often the victim is dehydrated. Adjusting with insulin might be tried by the victim, but if too much insulin is given, hypoglycemia can occur. Evacuate if the hyperglycemia is significant or continues to worsen.

Symptoms of hypoglycemia can happen rapidly and be mistaken for a CVA (stroke). Confusion, irritability, incoordination, tremors, weakness or numbness, headache, seizures, and insulin shock are late signs.

Treatment is giving glucose. If the victim's level of consciousness is sketchy, you can rub the glucose on their gums or put it under the tongue. Once the victim has an improved level of consciousness, give the person a small meal with some complex carbohydrates and protein to prevent recurrence. The victim must now be monitored for up to six hours to ensure no relapse of symptoms. These victims will not require evacuation unless they continue to have recurrence of their hypoglycemia or they do not completely clear the symptoms.

ALTITUDE ILLNESS

Altitude illness is a direct result of lower air pressure causing some degree of *hypoxia* (oxygen deficiency in the body's tissues), usually starting at approximately 8000 feet (2500 meters). A more rapid ascent to higher altitudes without acclimating (increasing the efficiency of oxygen delivery to the tissues) increases the susceptibility of experiencing some degree of altitude illness. Other factors that may contribute to susceptibility to altitude illness are altitude of residence, preexisting illness, poor hydration, level of activity, and genetics.

Human bodies easily adjust to the moderate hypoxia of altitude as long as they are given time to do so. Generally this takes approximately three to five days. Acclimation occurs by the body increasing the breathing rate and increasing urination; therefore, people going to higher altitudes should avoid alcohol or sleeping pills, which can promote or worsen the symptoms.

There are three syndromes associated with altitude illness: acute mountain sickness (AMS), high-altitude cerebral edema (HACE), and high-altitude pulmonary edema (HAPE).

The old adage of "climb high, sleep low" is the reminder used for climbers. Consider obtaining a prescription of acetazolamide (Diamox) to speed acclimation, especially if planning a rapid ascent. Normal dosing is 125 mg twice daily starting the day prior to ascent and continuing for twenty-four hours after completing ascent. The dosing can be increased to 250 mg two to three times daily for up to three days for mild to moderate AMS but could cause some tingling in the fingers, toes, and/or lips; increased urination; and taste changes. Do not take Diamox with a known serious allergy to sulfa. Diamox works by speeding up the respiratory rate by acidifying the blood, which increases the drive to breathe. Other drugs used for altitude are dexamethasone (Decadron, a steroid) and nifedipine, but these should be discussed with a medical provider to consider if these would be appropriate for the planned itinerary.

Most often victims with worsening symptoms of altitude illness will not recognize the symptoms themselves or will not speak up in fear of ruining the trip for the other trekkers. This is life-threatening judgment, and all group members need to understand the severity of ignoring the symptoms. The trip may be "ruined" but would be much worse trying to manage this type of medical emergency so remotely, especially if a trekking buddy dies. Once symptoms are recognized, it is best to immediately descend at least 2000 feet (600 meters) while monitoring the victim to see if symptoms are improving. Always have a rescue plan in place.

Acute Mountain Sickness (AMS)

Symptoms. Headache is the most prominent symptom of this most common form of altitude illness, and it may be accompanied by nausea, restlessness, fatigue, loss of appetite, and at times vomiting. Think "hangover" here. An early sign can be swelling of the face and hands. Headache is often the first sign, appearing within two to twelve hours of arrival at altitude, and it can generally resolve within twenty-four to seventy-two hours.

Treatment is to treat the symptoms: give the victim acetaminophen (Tylenol) or ibuprofen (Advil or Motrin) for the headache, or start Diamox or increase the dose of this to 250 mg two to three times daily. Have the victim rest and stop the ascent, hydrate, and, if available, graze on a bland carbohydrate meal. Never continue to ascend until these symptoms are resolved.

Prevention. Taking approximately three to five days to acclimate should help people avoid AMS; avoiding alcohol or sleeping pills also should help. Sometimes even these measures don't prevent AMS, however.

High-Altitude Cerebral Edema (HACE)

Symptoms. HACE is a severe progression of AMS and is most often associated with HAPE (see the next section). Drowsiness, confusion, lethargy, and loss of coordination (ataxia) develop in addition to preexisting AMS symptoms (see the preceding section). This loss of coordination will be increasingly obvious, with the victim staggering, having trouble with balance (using a wide stance), and, if you test the person, he or she will be unable to walk a straight line heel to toe, as if drunk.

Treatment. This condition requires immediate descent to a lower altitude, as death can occur in as little as twenty-four hours after ataxia develops.

Prevention. Same as for AMS (above).

High-Altitude Pulmonary Edema (HAPE)

Symptoms. The development of HAPE can be more deadly than HACE. Early signs are breathlessness with activity, which increases to breathlessness at rest, a cough, and weakness.

Treatment. Immediate application of oxygen and/or descent is imperative. Most of us do not have oxygen available, therefore descent to a lower altitude with as little effort from the victim as possible is an absolute necessity. Rescue descent should be planned prior to the expedition!

Prevention. Same as for AMS (above).

BE PREPARED

When preparing for that outward-bound adventure, don't forget to pack the common sense! We get so focused on the trip details of destination and gear that we often underestimate or ignore the "what-ifs." Consider your first-aid kit and skills as an integral piece of your gear. With good preparation, you can more confidently ensure less stress and chaos should something challenging occur on your trip. Happy trails!

Getting Lost and Dealing with It

Jeff Marchand and Donald B. Stouder

If everyone who ventured into the wilderness were prepared to do so, there would be less need for this chapter, but for many reasons—avoidable or unavoidable—people do get lost or injured in the outdoors. Thoughtful planning can often prevent these occurrences.

PREPARE IN ADVANCE

When you go into the wilderness, to some extent you leave behind the safety net of cell phone communication and the emergency response of fire departments and emergency medical technicians. To what extent varies depending on how far you are from a metropolitan area and how far into the wilderness cell phone coverage extends. This chapter discusses the use of cell phones and other devices, but for now let's assume you will not have cell phone service, as in many places in the backcountry, you will not.

No one plans to be lost or injured, but when it does happen, the outcome largely depends on the preparations that were made in advance. Thoughtful planning, even for day trips, greatly reduces the risk of an unfortunate, or even deadly, situation. Here are three basic things you should always do.

Leave Your Itinerary with a Contact Person

First, leave a detailed itinerary with someone you trust—your contact person. Agree on a time of return, allowing plenty of room for changes in your schedule, and then do your best to meet that intended itinerary.

Provide your contact person with a list of emergency contacts, including the phone number for the agency that has jurisdiction over the area you'll be visiting, and instruct your contact person when to call for help if you do not return by a certain time. If you get into a situation where you need help and can't get out, at least your contact person will be aware of your predicament and will know who to call to request a rescue—and help will come eventually.

Bring Navigation Tools and Know How to Use Them

Second, never go into an unfamiliar area without the basic tools of navigation: map and compass and the competence to use both effectively (even if you are a GPS wiz).

Bring the Ten Essentials

Third, carry the essential safety and survival items appropriate for your trip. Ask yourself, "What would I need to survive the worst conditions I could realistically encounter?" Always carry the Ten Essentials (see Chapter 5, "Gearing Up"). There is always the possibility of getting stuck out overnight if you or someone you're with becomes lost or injured or if it is not safe to continue.

BEING LOST AND DEALING WITH IT

If you become lost, admit it to yourself early and start dealing with it in a rational manner. Stop moving and think. If you stop before you become completely disoriented, you can usually find your way back to a known location. Don't wander about without a coherent plan. Remember the acronym **STOP:**

- Sit
- Think
- Observe
- Plan

Rejoining a Group

If you've gotten separated from your group and become disoriented, *stop* and listen for them. They may be signaling you. Call to them or, far better, use your whistle—you can blow a whistle much louder and for much longer than you can yell.

Make some intelligent movements toward where you think they went, or climb to a nearby high point for a better view, making sure you can find your way back to your last known location. Don't go far from the place where you became aware you were lost. When your companions realize you are missing, they will begin looking for you where they last saw you.

If you aren't successful in rejoining your group, then remember the cardinal rule: *Don't panic.*

If you've absorbed all the information contained in this book and are reasonably well equipped, then you know everything you need to do in order to survive. The most important thing you need now is the patience to sit down and think clearly and calmly about your choices.

Should you sit still, make yourself comfortable, and wait to be found? Or should you attempt to find your way out? Consider the factors.

Will the weather hold up? How long until sunset? How prepared are you for a bivouac? Do you have the proper navigational tools? If so, can you locate yourself on the map and navigate to a position of safety or possible rescue? Are you sure? What obstacles lie along the way? How long will it be before someone reports you as missing?

Staying Put and Awaiting Rescue

You may decide to stay put and let the searchers find you. If so, take care of yourself. Find shelter; conserve your strength; protect yourself as best you can from wind and rain, heat or cold, and burning sunlight.

Then make yourself as conspicuous as possible. If the sun is up, build a smoky fire, thinking very carefully about how you'll do this safely in wildfire-prone areas. To catch the attention of aerial searchers, lay out bright-colored clothing or camping gear on a hilltop or in a clearing. Re-arrange the natural features of the landscape (rocks, branches, etc.) into some unnatural geometric form, if that doesn't take too much energy.

Remember, *three of anything*—whistle blasts, gunshots, rock piles—is the universal signal for distress. Use a signal mirror if you have one. At night, build a safe fire both to keep warm and to attract attention. Above all, know that when you are missed, someone will be looking for you. Relax; all you have to do is survive until you are found.

Finding Your Own Way Back Out

If you are confident you can find your way back on your own, be reasonable about doing it. You don't want to find yourself hurrying across the desert in midday heat or stumbling in darkness over unknown terrain.

When you do successfully find your way back out, immediately communicate your return to your contact person and anyone else who may be out looking for you.

DEALING WITH A MISSING HIKER

Discovering that a friend, relative, or member of your party is missing is a terribly unnerving experience. But again, that's never an excuse to panic. You may be able to locate the missing person with whistles and a quick search of the immediate area, or you may need to contact the authorities to launch an organized search. Take into consideration who is missing and that person's experience, age, and health status. Also consider whether or not the person has the proper equipment and how long he or she has been missing. The appropriate time to initiate a search may depend on current or anticipated weather conditions and the time of day.

Determine Where the Person Was Last Seen

First, try to establish where the person was last seen ("point last seen," or PLS). It's very important that the area near the PLS remain undisturbed so that future searchers can examine it carefully for clues such as tracks and scents.

Try to Locate the Person

Before you leave the PLS, shout or whistle to see if the lost person responds. This should be followed by a brief search of the trails, being careful not to disturb footprints or other possible places a person could have gone in the area around the PLS. Those who are searching should stay in pairs and keep communicating with others as much as possible. Each searcher should be on the lookout for clues such as footprints or personal belongings. If there's no indication of success after about two hours, then it's time to call for outside help.

Summon Outside Help

To summon help to find a lost person (or to evacuate an injured person), you'll need to notify the local law-enforcement authority, be it the county sheriff, park ranger, or other authority. Fortunately for outdoor enthusiasts, most areas are served by search and rescue teams. Most teams are volunteers; some are part of the sheriff's or parks department, while others are independent groups. All operate under the authority of a local agency, usually the county sheriff or the National Park Service, and as a rule, the individual rescuers have received extensive training.

CALLING 9-1-1 WITH A CELL PHONE

When cell-phone coverage is available, the emergency telephone number 9-1-1 is the fastest way to reach the right agency to get help. Before making the call, organize all the information you need to provide, just as you would for sending someone out for help (see the next section).

More people are carrying cell phones into the wilderness for many reasons. In an emergency situation, a cell phone may aid in summoning help, although cell phone coverage is not always available in areas remote from cities. A prepared hiker will also have the Ten Essentials and navigation equipment and have well-rehearsed survival skills.

Batteries, cell signal, and texting. If you plan to rely on a cell phone, remember that cell phone battery life is limited, so consider turning the phone off until you need to use it, and carry extra batteries as well. Also, research service coverage in the areas you plan to hike. Remember, rugged terrain can block signals. If you have a poor signal, you may be able to improve it by moving to a different location. Try to find an open area free from obstructions, or move to higher ground. You have a better chance for a good signal on a ridge than you do at the bottom of a canyon. If you are able to see a populated area in the distance from a high point, you may have a better chance of having cell phone reception. In case of fluctuating coverage, text your at-home contact or a friend (not 9-1-1). A text signal can transmit more information than a conversation if there is only a moment of coverage.

Providing your location. When calling for help, dial 9-1-1. Any cellular service carrier must connect a 9-1-1 call to a call center regardless of whether the call is made by a customer of their service or not. Using 9-1-1 can provide the authorities the telephone number and approximate location of where the call is originating. Newer technology has incorporated GPS information into cell phones, which provides to emergency responders a more accurate location of the caller.

Sending Someone Out for Help

Self-reliance should always be your goal, but you need to know the best procedures to follow for contacting the proper authorities when there is an emergency that requires sending someone out for help.

Dividing the group. You must decide how to divide the group and your resources. When determining who should go for help and who should stay, consider, for both the group and the messengers, the following:

- leadership
- the skills of each person (such as navigation and first aid)
- physical ability
- equipment
- water supply
- how long it will take for rescuers to reach you

Organizing the information for emergency responders. If the distance to the nearest source of help is long, send at least two well-equipped people. They must carry detailed information about these concerns:
- what and where the problem is
- what equipment and experience the group has
- the name, age, gender, and condition of any injured person (for information on assessing injury, see Chapter 13, "Ouch! First Aid in the Backcountry")

Deciding on a rescue location. Messengers going for help should know whether the group intends to stay in place, relocate to another identifiable location, or move themselves toward the original destination, the start point, or a better point of rescue. Since contact between the members traveling for help and the remaining members may not be reliable via cell phones or other technology, it is important that members of the group are in agreement about where professional rescue assistance can find the remaining members of the group. Those going for help should mark their return trail so rescuers can quickly follow their trail back to find the group's location.

LETTING THE SEARCH AND RESCUE TEAM DO THEIR WORK

You can expect searchers to respond as quickly as possible once they know someone is missing, but it may take several hours or more for them to mobilize and get to your location. They will consider all the possibilities of how the person became missing and what the missing person might do.

When the search and rescue team arrives, let them take over. Allay your considerable anxiety with the knowledge that they know their business better than anyone else.

The search effort concentrates on the most likely areas first. They start with the PLS and try to determine the direction the lost person went. Using a variety of search tactics—possibly including trackers, search dogs, aircraft, and four-wheel-drive vehicles—the area where the missing person is believed to be is confined and systematically searched. Searchers are looking not only for the lost person but also for clues that the lost person may have left. A clue can be a track, a piece of discarded gear, or any sign that the lost person has been there. By finding and following clues, the searchers can find the lost person much faster than if they were looking only for the person.

Everyone should learn about their local search and rescue organizations and consider giving them their support. The National Association for Search and Rescue (see "Resources" in the appendix) is a good resource for information and training.

Using Personal Locating Devices

Rescuers are required to respond to every signal from a personal locating device as if it were a life-threatening event, so these devices are to be used only in a true emergency—a situation involving a chance of serious bodily harm or the potential of death, and only after you have exhausted all means to remedy the situation on your own. Do not rely on these devices for your safety instead of having and using common sense, and be mindful that any device can fail. Do not take more risk simply because you are carrying one. In fact, if you would not go into the wilderness without the device, you should rethink going at all.

However, these devices, when used correctly, do alert authorities that there is someone in distress and aid in getting responders to the location. They have been credited with saving lives.

Personal locator beacons (PLBs) are lightweight, pocket-sized units designed to be carried by individuals, and they operate much the same as emergency beacons used on ships and aircraft. The battery will last at least five years. They are somewhat costly, with prices ranging between $400 and $600, but they can be rented. The devices must be registered with the Federal Communications Commission.

When activated, the PLB signal is received by an international search and rescue satellite system, with worldwide coverage that can determine the location of the unit within a few miles and notify the local search and rescue authorities. Newer PLBs have integrated GPS technology to improve the location accuracy down to about 300 feet (100 meters). The units will transmit for a minimum of twenty-four hours.

Personal satellite tracking and messaging (SPOT) devices use the private Globalstar satellite system to send messages and provide GPS tracking. They are one-way communicators that will summon search and rescue, send short "I'm okay" messages to family and/or friends, and track your path for yourself or family members. Coverage, however, is not worldwide and may be limited to specific service areas. The cost of these units is approximately $99, and they require an annual service fee of about $100.

Use them responsibly. There is some concern that both PLB and personal satellite tracking and messaging devices may contribute to people going into the wilderness less prepared than they would without the device. As a result, people may take more risk or expect to be rescued in circumstances that are merely uncomfortable or inconvenient but not life threatening. It is important to know that these devices are not a replacement for being properly prepared with the skills and equipment necessary for the wilderness environment. Even in true emergencies, rescuers may not be able to reach a hiker quickly, and survival skills may be needed during the period of time it takes to be located.

PAYING FOR THE COST OF SEARCH AND RESCUE

There has been some debate over whether or not people calling for rescue, specifically those seen as being negligent and getting themselves into situations that a reasonable person would have avoided, should be charged for their own rescue costs. Perhaps if people knew it is mostly vounteers who foot the bill for their rescue, they would be more responsible for their own safety.

Search and rescue operations are conducted primarily by volunteers, who usually pay for their own equipment, provide their own transportation, volunteer their time, and are only partly paid by government agencies. The debate is fueled when a single rescue incident results in burdensome costs or occurs in a jurisdiction that doesn't have the money to cover the expense.

An option often discussed to balance the costs between taxpayers and the person needing rescue is to charge all wilderness visitors a small use fee to be put toward a budget for rescues. The counter proposal is that individuals needing a rescue should pay the cost of that rescue, so that the general public can enjoy the wilderness without being charged a use fee to pay for someone else's rescue. The counter argument is that charging people for the cost of their own rescue would discourage frivolous calls for help; when a person needing rescue considers the cost of a helicopter ride, the distinction between mere discomfort or inconvenience and a true emergency involving the risk of severe bodily harm or potential death becomes surprisingly clear.

The debate will continue, but it would be more easily resolved if all of us would act responsibly and be prepared when we go into the wilderness, so that we would call for help only after all our other options have been exhausted.

Most people who venture into the wilderness enjoy an outing without incident and return home safely. Reading this book is a great step toward protecting yourself, respecting the environment, and preserving it for those who follow.

As John Muir said, "The mountains are calling, and I must go."

Appendix: Resources

CHAPTER 2
Reading

Hampton, Bruce, and David Cole. *Soft Paths: How to Enjoy the Wilderness without Harming It.* 3rd ed. Mechanicsburg, PA: Stackpole Books, 2003.

Lamb, Jennifer, Glen Goodrich, Susan Chadwick-Brane, and Chad Henderson. *Wilderness Ethics by NOLS.* Mechanicsburg, PA: Stackpole Books, 2006.

Leave No Trace, Center for Outdoor Ethics. www.lnt.org.

McGivney, Annette. *Leave No Trace: A Guide to the New Wilderness Etiquette.* 2nd ed. Seattle: Mountaineers Books, 2003.

Muir, John. *John of the Mountains: The Unpublished Journals of John Muir.* Edited by Linnie Marsh Wolfe. Madison: University of Wisconsin Press, 1938.

———. *My First Summer in the Sierra.* Boston: Houghton Mifflin, 1911.

Wark, Jim, and Roderick Nash. *Leave No Trace: The Vanishing North American Wilderness.* New York: Universe, 2011.

CHAPTER 3
Resources

CrossFit: www.crossfitnashua.com/what-is-crossfit.

Mayo Clinic: www.mayoclinic.com.

University of California San Francisco Medical Center: www.ucsfhealth.org.

Web MD: www.webmd.com.

Women's Health: www.womenshealth.gov.

CHAPTER 4
Reading

Berger, Karen. *Hiking and Backpacking: A Trailside Guide.* New York: W. W. Norton, 2003. Includes tips on how to walk, what to wear, what to carry, food, no-trace camping, backcountry safety and rescue, and navigation.

Curtis, Rick. *The Backpacker's Field Manual*. Rev. ed. New York: Three Rivers Press, 2005. A good overall guide for trip planning, equipment, cooking, nutrition, first aid, navigation, wilderness travel, safety, and weather observation.

Eng, Ronald C., ed. *Mountaineering: The Freedom of the Hills*. 8th ed. Seattle: Mountaineers Books, 2010. The 50th-anniversary edition of this classic guide for mountaineers; clothing, equipment, food, navigation, and wilderness travel are only the first chapter—there's more.

Jacobson, Cliff. *Camping Secrets*. 4th ed. Guilford, CT: FalconGuides, 2013. In this 25th-anniversary edition "lexicon of camping tips only the experts know," topics are organized alphabetically, from Anchor to Yard Goods.

Logue, Victoria. *Hiking and Backpacking: Essential Skills, Equipment, and Safety*. 2nd ed. Birmingham, AL: Menasha Ridge Press, 2004.

Resources

Bureau of Land Management: www.blm.gov/nhp.
National Park Service: www.nps.gov.
US Forest Service: www.fs.fed.us.

CHAPTER 5
Reading

To keep current on equipment and manufacturers, read equipment articles and reviews in magazines such as *Backpacker Magazine* or *Outside*. Back issues may be available at your local library or online, and hiking clubs may have also publications with equipment articles. Below are some books to consider as well:

Clelland, Mike. *Ultralight Backpackin' Tips*. Guilford, CT: Globe Pequot Press, 2011.

Jardine, Ray. *Beyond Backpacking*. 3rd ed. La Pine, OR: Adventure Lore Press, 1999.

———. *Trail Life: Ray Jardine's Lightweight Backpacking*. La Pine, OR: Adventure Lore Press, 2009.

Jordan, Ryan, et al. *Lightweight Backpacking 101*. 3rd ed. Bozeman, MT: Beartooth Mountain Press, 2001.

Jordan, Ryan, ed. *Lightweight Backpacking and Camping*. Bozeman, MT: Beartooth Mountain Press, 2006.

Ladigin, Don, and Mike Clelland. *Lighten Up! A Complete Guide for Light and Ultralight Backpacking*. Guilford, CT: Globe Pequot Press, 2005.

Resources

To buy equipment locally, check the Internet for backpacking, camping, and sports outfitting stores and search for articles, reviews, and suppliers. Here are some sources for lightweight backpacking gear:

Adventures in Stoving: www.adventuresinstoving.blogspot.com.

Backpacking: www.backpacking.net.

Backpacking Light: www.backpackinglight.com.

Gossamer Gear: www.gossamergear.com.

Hike Light: www.hikelight.com.

Hike Lighter (ultralight hiking blog): www.hikelighter.com.

Lightweight Backpacking 101: www.lightweightbackpacking101.com.

Minimus (products in very small quantities): www.minimus.biz.

Mountain Laurel Designs: www.mountainlaureldesigns.com.

Ray Jardine: www.rayjardine.com.

Six Moon Designs: www.sixmoondesigns.com.

Tarp Tent: www.tarptent.com.

Thru-Hiker: www.thru-hiker.com.

Ultralight Adventure Equipment: www.ula-equipment.com.

Zen Stoves (home of the alcohol stoves): www.zenstoves.net.

Z Packs: www.zpacks.com.

CHAPTER 6

Reading

Applegate, Elizabeth. *Encyclopedia of Sports and Fitness Nutrition.* Roseville, CA: Prima Publishing, 2002. Liz Applegate's articles are regularly featured in *Runner's World* magazine; this comprehensive work is an overview on the nutritional needs of athletes and people of all ages.

Clelland, Mike. *Ultralight Backpackin' Tips.* Guilford, CT: Globe Pequot Press, 2011. Information on calculating calorie estimates for meal weights, cooking with cozies, and ultralight meal philosophies from a vegetarian author.

Coleman, Ellen. *Eating for Endurance.* Boulder, CO: Bull Publishing, 2000. A nutrition guide for endurance athletes with good information on your body's use of glycogen and fat, protein in the diet, hydration, and eating for performance.

Ladigin, Don. *Lighten Up! A Complete Handbook for Light and Ultralight Backpacking.* Guilford, CT: Globe Pequot Press, 2005. Information on how to choose lightweight kitchen equipment, boil-in-bag cooking, and steam baking.

Reinfeld, Mark, Bo Rinaldi, and Jennifer Murray. *The Complete Idiot's Guide to Eating Raw*. New York: Penguin Group, 2008. Very good recommendations for plant-based nutrition.

Skurka, Andrew. *The Ultimate Hiker's Gear Guide, Tools and Techniques to Hit the Trail*. Washington, DC: National Geographic, 2012. Good tips on foods for long-distance hiking.

Townsend, Chris. *The Advanced Backpacker*. Camden, MN: Ragged Mountain Press, 2001. Advice for long-distance trips, preparation and planning, food, and resupply methods.

Underkoffler, Renee Loux. *Living Cuisine: The Art and Spirit of Raw Foods*. New York: Penguin Group, 2003. Excellent reference for raw foods and vegetarian nutrition.

Cookbooks

Black, Teresa "Dicentra." *One Pan Wonders: Backcountry Cooking at Its Finest*. Asheville, NC: Black Mountain Publications, 2008.

Conners, Tim, and Christine Conners. *Lip Smackin' Backpackin'*. Helena, MT: Falcon Publishing, 2000.

————. *The Scout's Outdoor Cookbook*. Guilford, CT: Globe Pequot Press, 2008.

Herod, Lori. *Foil Cookery: Cooking without Pots and Pans*. Arcata, CA: Paradise Cay Publications, 2007.

Kirkconnell, Sarah Svien. *Freezer Bag Cooking: Trail Food Made Simple*. Maple Valley, WA: Bay Street Publishing, 2005.

Latimer, Carole. *Wilderness Cuisine*. Berkeley, CA: Wilderness Press, 1991.

March, Laurie Ann. *A Fork in the Trail: Mouthwatering Meals and Tempting Treats for the Backcountry*. Berkeley, CA: Wilderness Press, 2008.

Miller, Dorcas S. *More Backcountry Cooking: Moveable Feasts from the Experts*. Seattle: Mountaineers Books, 2002.

Pearson, Claudia. *NOLS Cookery*. Mechanicsburg, PA: Stackpole Books, 2004.

Prater, Yvonne, and Ruth Dyar Mendenhall. *Beyond Gorp: Favorite Foods from Outdoor Experts*. Seattle: Mountaineers Books, 2005.

Thomas, Dian. *Recipes for Roughing It Easy: Great Outdoor Recipes for the Backwoods and Backyard*. Holladay, UT: Dian Thomas Publishing, 2001.

Yaffe, Linda Frederick. *Backpack Gourmet*. Mechanicsburg, PA: Stackpole Books, 2002.

Resources

Anti Gravity Gear: www.antigravitygear.com.

Brasslight Backpacking Stove: www.brasslite.com/potcozy.html.

CHAPTER 7
Reading

Burns, Bob, and Mike Burns. *Wilderness Navigation: Finding Your Way Using Map, Compass, Altimeter, and GPS.* 2nd ed. Seattle: Mountaineers Books, 2004.

Helms, Russell. *GPS Outdoors: A Practical Guide for Outdoor Enthusiasts.* Birmingham, AL: Menasha Ridge Press, 2006.

Hinch, Stephen. *Outdoor Navigation with GPS.* 3rd ed. Birmingham, AL: Wilderness Press, 2010.

Kjellstrom, Bjorn. *Be Expert with Map and Compass.* 3rd ed. Hoboken, NJ: John Wiley & Sons, 2009.

Letham, Lawrence. *GPS Made Easy: Using Global Positioning Systems in the Outdoors.* 5th ed. Seattle: Mountaineers Books, 2008.

Randall, Glenn. *Outward Bound Map and Compass Handbook.* 3rd ed. Guilford, CT: Globe Pequot Press, 2012.

Resources
US Geological Survey topographic maps and many other maps useful for hikers can be purchased at outdoor equipment stores, map stores, on the Internet, or through the USGS. To purchase paper maps or download free maps from the USGS, visit: http://store.usgs.gov.

Google Maps: https://maps.google.com.

Magnetic declination calculator (point-and-click): www.magnetic-declination.com.

National Geophysical Data Center's declination calculators: www.ngdc.noaa.gov/geomag-web/#declination.

CHAPTER 8
Reading

Bastone, Kelly. "Killer Trips: Weather." *Backpacker Magazine,* October 2012. www.backpacker.com/weather-killer-trips-destinations/destinations/16888.

Densmore, Lisa. *Backpacker Magazine's Predicting Weather: Forecasting, Planning, and Preparing.* Backpacker Magazine Series. Guilford, CT: FalconGuides, 2010. Excellent and small enough to be carried on a trek.

McCafferty. Keith. "How to Make Your Own Weather Forecast." *Field and Stream Magazine,* March 2004. www.fieldandstream.com/articles/fishing/fly-fishing/when-fish/2004/03/how-make-your-own-weather-forecast.

National Oceanic and Atmospheric Administration. *Weather Spotter's Field Guide.* US Department of Commerce, National Weather Service, June 2011. www.nws.noaa.gov/om/brochures/SGJune6-11.pdf.

Shillington, Ben, and Rebecca Sandiford. *Winter Backpacking: Your Guide to Safe and Warm Winter Camping and Day Trips.* Beachburg, ON: Heliconia Press, 2009.

Resources

Current weather reports for cities and zip codes: www.weather.com.

Map showing current and recent positions of weather fronts across North America: www.weather.unisys.com/index.php

National Oceanic and Atmospheric Administration's cloud identification chart: www.nws.noaa.gov/os/brochures/cloudchart.pdf.

National Oceanic and Atmospheric Administration on lightning weather phenomena, information, safety tips, and photographs: www.lightningsafety.noaa.gov.

National Weather Service: www.nws.noaa.gov. List of phone numbers to call to receive a weather forecast via phone: www.weather.gov/pa/recordedforecasts.php.

Naval Research Laboratory's weather satellite maps: www.nrlmry.navy.mil/sat_products.html. Check those in the Eastern Pacific—EPAC—and estimate how many days before storms arrive; they show up as big white "commas" on the globe.

Sierra Nevada weather and forecast: www.sierrabackpacker.com/weather.htm.

Weather Bug (freeware computer software): www.weatherbug.com/aff/default.asp?zcode=z6162.

The Weather Prediction (more than 300 different forecasting hints and articles about weather): www.theweatherprediction.com/habyhints/index.html.

Weather Underground (different types of weather maps): www.wunderground.com.

CHAPTER 9

Reading

Brainerd, John W. *The Nature Observer's Handbook: Learning to Appreciate Our Natural World.* Guilford, CT: Globe Pequot Press, 1986.

Eng, Ronald C., ed. *Mountaineering: The Freedom of the Hills.* 8th ed. Seattle: Mountaineers Books, 2010.

Fletcher, Colin, and Chip Rawlins. *The Complete Walker IV.* New York: Alfred A. Knopf, 2002.

Meyer, Kathleen. *How to Shit in the Woods: An Environmentally Sound Approach to a Lost Art.* Berkeley: Ten Speed Press, 2011. A lighthearted but serious account of how to take care of toilet needs while enjoying the outdoors.

Resources
American Mountain Guides Association (offers training on glacier travel): http://amga.com/

CHAPTER 10
Reading

Herrero, Stephen. *Bear Attacks: Their Causes and Avoidance.* New York: Lyons Press, 2002. A good blend of anecdotal and research information; highly recommended for those planning backcountry trips in the grizzly territories of the United States and Canada.
Smith, Dave. *Backcountry Bear Basics: The Definitive Guide to Avoiding Unpleasant Encounters.* 2nd ed. Seattle: Mountaineers Books, 2006.

Resources
Backpacker Magazine's food-hanging methods: www.backpackermagazine.com/skills

CHAPTER 11
Reading

Abbey, Edward. *Desert Solitaire: A Season in the Wilderness.* New York: Touchstone, 1990.
Hogue, Lawrence. *All the Wild and Lonely Places: Journeys in a Desert Landscape.* Washington, DC: Island Press, 2000.
Larson, Peggy Pickering. *The Deserts of the Southwest: A Sierra Club Naturalist's Guide.* 2nd ed. San Francisco: Sierra Club Books, 2000.
Schad, Jerry. *California Deserts.* Helena, MT: Falcon Publishing, 1997.
Shelton, Richard. *Going Back to Bisbee.* Tucson: University of Arizona Press, 1992.
Zwinger, Ann. *The Mysterious Lands: A Naturalist Explores the Four Great Deserts of the Southwest.* Tucson: University of Arizona Press, 1996.

CHAPTER 12
Reading

Daffern, Tony. *Backcountry Avalanche Safety: Skiers, Climbers, Boarders, and Snowshoers.* 3rd ed. Surrey, BC: Rocky Mountain Books, 2009.
Eng, Ronald C. *Mountaineering: The Freedom of the Hills,* 8th ed. Seattle: Mountaineers Books, 2010. Includes extensive coverage of snow and glacier travel; a classic in its field.

Ferguson, Sue, and Edward R. LaChapelle. *The ABCs of Avalanche Safety.* 3rd ed. Seattle: Mountaineers Books, 2003. The classic pocket guide to avoiding avalanches—updated with the latest in technology and technique.

Giesbrecht, Gordon, and James Wilkerson. *Hypothermia, Frostbite, and Other Cold Injuries: Prevention, Survival, Rescue, and Treatment.* 2nd ed: Seattle: Mountaineers Books, 2006.

Gorman, Stephen. *The Winter Camping Handbook.* Woodstock, VT: Countryman Press, 2007.

Hindman, Steve. *Cross-Country Skiing: Building Skills for Fun and Fitness.* Seattle: Mountaineers Books, 2005.

McManners, Hugh. *The Complete Wilderness Training Guide.* London: Dorling Kindersley, 2007.

O'Bannon, Allen, and Mike Clelland. *Allen and Mike's Really Cool Backcountry Ski Book.* Guilford, CT: FalconGuides, 2007.

Parker, Paul. *Free-Heel Skiing: Telemark and Parallel Techniques.* 3rd ed. Seattle: Mountaineers Books, 2001.

Prater, Gene. *Snowshoeing: From Novice to Master.* 5th ed. Seattle: Mountaineers Books, 2002. Includes a well-illustrated section on snow camping.

Randall, Glenn. *The Outward Bound Staying Warm in the Outdoors Handbook.* New York: Lyons Press, 2000. No other book addresses the issue of avoiding cold so succinctly and completely.

Tilton, Buck, and John Gookin. *NOLS Winter Camping.* Mechanicsburg, PA: Stackpole Books, 2005.

Volken, Martin, Scott Schell, and Margaret Wheeler. *Backcountry Skiing: Skills for Ski Touring and Ski Mountaineering.* Seattle: Mountaineers Books, 2007.

Resources

American Avalanche Association (lots of information on avalanche education, avalanche centers, avalanche reports and professions): www.avalanche.org.

American Mountain Guides Association: www.amga.com. For more than thirty years, the AMGA has supported the guiding community through excellence in education, standards, and certification to enhance the quality of services provided to the public, while serving as a resource for accessing and protecting the natural environment.

Primitive Ways (igloo-building information): www.primitiveways.com/igloo.html.

CHAPTER 13
Reading

Auerbach, Paul S., Howard J. Donner, and Eric A. Weiss. *Field Guide to Wilderness Medicine.* 3rd ed. Philadelphia: Mosby, 2008.

Auerbach, Paul S., David Della-Guistina, and Richard Ingebretsen. *Advanced Wilderness Life Support.* 7th ed. Salt Lake City, UT: AdventureMed–Wilderness Medicine Education, 2011. Student manual.

Centers for Disease Control and Prevention. *The Yellow Book 2012, CDC Health Information for International Travel.* New York: Oxford University Press, 2012.

Jong, Elaine, and Christofer Sanford. *The Travel and Tropical Medicine Manual.* 4th ed. Philadelphia: Saunders, 2008.

Markeson, David, Jeffrey D. Ferguson, et al. "Part 17: First Aid: 2010 American Heart Association and American Red Cross for First Aid." *American Heart Association Journals.* www.circ.ahajournals.org.

Tilton, Buck. *First Aid: A Complete Illustrated Guide.* Guilford, CT: Globe Pequot Press, 2010.

Weiss, Eric A. *Wilderness and Travel Medicine: A Comprehensive Guide.* 4th ed. Seattle: Mountaineers Books, 2012.

Resources

West Nile Virus Fact Sheet. Centers for Disease Control and Prevention: www.cdc.gov.

CHAPTER 14
Reading

Cooper, Donald C., Patrick "Rick" LaValla, and Robert "Skip" Stoffel. *Search and Rescue Fundamentals.* 3rd ed. Olympia, WA: Emergency Response Institute, 1996. Basic skills and knowledge to perform wilderness inland search and rescue.

National Association of Search and Rescue. *Fundamentals of Search and Rescue.* Centerville, VA: Jones and Barlett Learning, 2005.

Setnicka, Tim J. *Wilderness Search and Rescue.* Boston: AMC Books, 1980. The bible of search and rescue techniques.

Shimanski, Charley. *General Backcountry Safety: A Resource for All Backcountry Users.* San Diego: Mountain Rescue Association, 2008. www.mra.org/images/stories/training/SARforleaders.pdf

Resources

Federal Communications Commission's "Wireless 911 Service Consumer Fact Sheet": http://transition.fcc.gov/cgb/consumerfacts/wireless911srvc.pdf.

Mountain Rescue Association (an organization of teams dedicated to saving lives through rescue and mountain safety education): www.mra.org/images/stories/training/backcountrysafety.pdf.

National Association for Search and Rescue (provides training, certification, and advocacy on behalf of search and rescue): www.nasar.org.

National Oceanic and Atmospheric Administration's search and rescue satellite-aided tracking: www.sarsat.noaa.gov/emerbcns.html.

Index

Note: Page numbers in *italic* refer to figures and tables.

About the Contributors

Kristi Anderson

Kristi had no camping or backpacking experience before taking the Wilderness Basics Course (WBC) in 1996 and quickly became hooked. She has participated with the class ever since, as a leader and as staff, and has made good on the techniques she learned in class by going on fabulous trips to the Grand Canyon, Yosemite, and the Rocky Mountains. Her favorite destination is Zion National Park in Utah.

Bill Edwards

A member of the San Diego Chapter of the Sierra Club for the past thirty-five years, Bill has taught WBC courses for thirty years, with an emphasis on land navigation outings. He has backpacked throughout much of the Southwest and is an unapologetic lover of the desert environment. Bill is also a naturalist trail interpreter for the Canyoneers San Diego Natural History Museum and for Mission Trails Regional Park.

Robert L. Feuge

From his earliest days, Bob has explored the terrain of the Southwest. When career moves took him to California, he became enamored with the Sierras, particularly Yosemite National Park. In 1986 Bob took up backpacking in order to explore deeper into the Sierras. At the same time, he avidly read the writings of John Muir. In 1989 he joined the Sierra Club and took the Basic Mountaineering Course (now the WBC). As a result, Bob became even more hooked on exploring the wilderness. In 1991 he joined the staff of the WBC and served four years as snow camp coordinator. Subsequently, he served as vice chairman and then chairman in 1997–98. In 1999 he and his wife moved to Sedona, Arizona, where he lives today, avidly exploring the red rock country.

Skip Forsht

Skip Forsht began hiking and backpacking as a Boy Scout in Rhode Island. After moving to California in his twenties and discovering the Sierra Nevada and Anza-Borrego Desert State Park, he knew he was in the right place. He has been a Sierra Club leader and assisted with the WBC since 1996, helping to train new leaders. He has backpacked the California portion of the Pacific Crest Trail and has his sights set on Oregon and Washington now. Skip provided valuable review of all the chapters for the third and fourth editions of this book.

Mike Fry

Mike started backpacking with the Boy Scouts of America nearly sixty years ago. It didn't work out. Many years later, in 1968 he joined the Sierra Club and took the Basic Mountaineering Course in 1970, and his life was changed forever. He became a chapter outings leader in 1972. He helped form the cross-country ski section in 1975 and served as chair for thirty-eight years. He has built and rebuilt 6 miles of hiking trail on Mount Woodson for the last twenty-two years.

David M. Gottfredson

Formally trained in chemical engineering, David has been hiking and camping since he was a child growing up in the foothills of southern California. Introduced to hiking in the desert through what was then the Sierra Club San Diego Chapter's Basic Mountaineering Course in 1986, he went on to serve as an instructor and treasurer of the course for the next sixteen years. He is an avid hiker who splits his time between the desert and the mountains and particularly enjoys hiking in the Southwest, especially in Utah and Arizona.

Alfred F. Hofstatter

As a Boy Scout, Alfred embraced the experience of camping and hiking and has continued to pursue his outdoor adventures to this day. He introduced his passion to his sons and grandchildren and now goes camping with them in the Sierras and Alaska. He has been on the staff of the WBC since 1999 and was instrumental in introducing Leave No Trace into the curriculum. As a chapter outings leader, he leads training outings for the WBC. Alfred also enjoys gardening, traveling, and teaching land navigation.

Pauline Jimenez

Pauline discovered backpacking in 1976 through the Basic Mountaineering Course offered by the San Diego Chapter of the Sierra Club. She became a chapter outings leader in 1993 and later an instructor for the course. She enjoys camping and backpacking in Anza-Borrego Desert State Park, leading longer summer trips in the Sierra Nevada, and trail-testing new recipes. Pauline also leads nature outings on behalf of the San Diego Natural History Museum and is a member of the Desert Protective Council. Her trail avocations include ethnobotany, "naked eye" astronomy, and harmonica concerts under the stars.

Nancy Jungling

Nancy is a physical therapist and member of the Sierra Club. She is a graduate of the WBC and has served as a chapter outings leader and medical coordinator for the San Diego Chapter. She has enjoyed hiking, camping, and backpacking in Utah's Zion National Park, California's Anza-Borrego Desert State Park and Yosemite National Park, and Arizona's Catalina State Park. Nancy enjoys the meditative qualities of nature. She loves the smell of rain and the presence of deer on the trail, and she thanks her husband for carrying the bear canister and the tent and the stove so that she is free to track the marmots!

Jeff Marchand

Jeff is an avid hiker, biker, skier, and sea kayaker who grew up in the Pacific Northwest. His interests in outdoor education and search and rescue began in the late '70s. He was an active member of the San Diego Mountain Rescue Team for seventeen years. He has been involved with the North County Group of the San Diego Chapter of the Sierra Club since 1991 and was chairman of their Wilderness Basics Course for thirteen years.

Jerry Schad

Jerry held bachelor's and master's degrees in astronomy and taught astronomy and physical science at San Diego Mesa College. His interests ranged from astronomy and teaching to photography and writing. Jerry was the author of fifteen books, including a college-level textbook for introductory physical science courses and the top-selling Afoot & Afield series of hiking guidebooks that cover nearly all of southern California. In the last year of his life, Jerry enjoyed spending time with his wife, Peg Reiter, as they walked, hiked, and traveled. Jerry passed away at age sixty-one from kidney cancer.

Marty Stevens

Ever since his father took him as a young boy on canoe trips in the Boundary Waters Canoe Area Wilderness of Minnesota, Marty has been an outdoor enthusiast. He is an avid hiker, backpacker, and cross-country skier who spends much of his free time in the High Sierra, the backcountry of San Diego County, or the snowy slopes of California. He has rafted the rivers of the Northwest and hiked New Zealand, the big island of Hawaii, and 846 miles of the Pacific Crest Trail.

Bob Stinton

A native of San Diego, Bob has been exploring the Southwest and Sierras since his early years on family and scouting trips. After completing the San Diego Chapter of the Sierra Club's Basic Mountaineering Course (now the WBC) in 1972, he became a chapter outings leader and has been active in the program since. Bob enjoys traveling off-trail, cross-country routes on foot, skis, or snowshoes, exploring and enjoying the less-traveled places.

Earl Towson

A retired aerospace engineer with a lifelong love of astronomy and science who enjoys nature, Earl teaches classes for the Sierra Club's Nature Knowledge Workshop in Astronomy, Geology, Soils, and Weather. He lectures at San Diego State University on astrobiology for the Jet Propulsion Laboratory and for the Boy Scouts of America's National Camp School (NCS). At NCS he teaches forestry, birding, mammals, reptiles, botany, environmental science, and more. He has done extensive backpacking in the Sierras and Rockies.

Eugene A. Troxell

Eugene is a retired philosophy professor from San Diego State University (SDSU). After receiving his doctorate in philosophy from the University of Chicago in 1966, he taught continuously at SDSU until he retired in 2000. He is coauthor or the book *Making Sense of Things*. His philosophic specialties include the later philosophy of Ludwig Wittgenstein and ethics, particularly environmental ethics. In his younger days, he did a great deal of camping and hiking. After retiring he has worked with the Institute on Religion in an Age of Science on developing pantheism into a viable religious naturalism.

Glen Van Peski

Glen is the founder and chairman of Gossamer Gear, a leading cottage manufacturer of lightweight backpacking gear, and also serves as city engineer for the city of Carlsbad. Glen is a regular, if slow, runner of marathons and half-marathons and an avid backpacker. He is an internationally sought-after speaker and author on ultralight backpacking equipment and techniques. Glen is an instructor and guide with Wilderness Outings and other outdoor education organizations.

Diane Purkey Wilson

Diane's childhood camping trips with her grandparents led to the Sierra Club's Basic Mountaineering Course and a lifelong passion for hiking, backpacking, and land navigation, which she now teaches for the WBC in San Diego. She is also a leader trainer for the San Diego Chapter of the Sierra Club. Diane provided valuable review of all the chapters for the fourth edition of this book.

Laura A. Wolfgang

Laura served in the US Navy for twenty years as a nurse, in her last years serving as a nurse practitioner. She has experience in aeromedical evacuations, trauma training, intensive care, travel medicine, and infectious diseases. She has been certified in Advanced Wilderness Life Support. She loves adventure and the outdoors and is quite active with hiking, camping, surfing, and cycling.

Ted Young

A native Southern Californian, Ted has long enjoyed visiting California's deserts in the winter and the mountains in summer. His favorite kind of summer vacation is backpacking to a base camp near timberline in the Sierra Nevada and then spending the days hiking cross-country—ideal circumstances for refining wilderness navigation skills.

Other Contributors

The following people provided photographs or content for previous editions of this volume: Priscilla Anderson, Scott Anderson, Hal Brody, Nelson Copp, Keith Gordon, Jan Hawkins, Jim Matlock, Mark Mauricio, Carolyn Moser, Dave Moser, Donald B. Stouder, Dave Ussell, and Olive Wenzel.

MOUNTAINEERS BOOKS is a leading publisher of mountaineering literature and guides—including our flagship title, *Mountaineering: The Freedom of the Hills*—as well as adventure narratives, natural history, and general outdoor recreation. Through our two imprints, Skipstone and Braided River, we also publish titles on sustainability and conservation. We are committed to supporting the environmental and educational goals of our organization by providing expert information on human-powered adventure, sustainable practices at home and on the trail, and preservation of wilderness.

The Mountaineers, founded in 1906, is a 501(c)(3) nonprofit outdoor activity and conservation organization whose mission is "to explore, study, preserve, and enjoy the natural beauty of the outdoors." One of the largest such organizations in the United States, it sponsors classes and year-round outdoor activities throughout the Pacific Northwest, including climbing, hiking, backcountry skiing, snowshoeing, bicycling, camping, paddling, and more. The Mountaineers also supports its mission through its publishing division, Mountaineers Books, and promotes environmental education and citizen engagement. For more information, visit The Mountaineers Program Center, 7700 Sand Point Way NE, Seattle, WA 98115-3996; phone 206-521-6001; www.mountaineers.org; or email info@mountaineers.org.

Our publications are made possible through the generosity of donors and through sales of more than 500 titles on outdoor recreation, sustainable lifestyle, and conservation. To donate, purchase books, or learn more, visit us online:

MOUNTAINEERS BOOKS

1001 SW Klickitat Way, Suite 201 • Seattle, WA 98134
800-553-4453 • mbooks@mountaineersbooks.org
www.mountaineersbooks.org

Leave No Trace strives to educate visitors about the nature of their recreational impacts and offers techniques to prevent and minimize such impacts. Leave No Trace is best understood as an educational and ethical program, not as a set of rules and regulations.
For more information, visit www.lnt.org or call 800-332-4100.

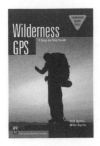